Above All, We Are Jews

Above All, We Are Jews

A BIOGRAPHY OF
Rabbi Alexander Schindler

MICHAEL A. MEYER

Foreword by Jonathan D. Sarna
Afterword by Rabbi Rick Jacobs

REFORM JUDAISM PUBLISHING, A DIVISION OF CCAR PRESS
CENTRAL CONFERENCE OF AMERICAN RABBIS
5785 · NEW YORK · 2025

Copyright © 2025 by the Central Conference of American Rabbis. All rights reserved. No portion of this book may be copied in any form for any purpose without the written permission of the Central Conference of American Rabbis.

Published by Reform Judaism Publishing, a division of CCAR Press
Central Conference of American Rabbis
355 Lexington Avenue, New York, NY 10017
(212) 972-3636 | info@ccarpress.org | www.ccarpress.org

Cover photo: Courtesy of the Union for Reform Judaism

LIBRARY OF CONGRESS CATALOGING-IN-PUBLICATION DATA

Names: Meyer, Michael A., author. | Sarna, Jonathan D., writer of foreword. | Jacobs, Rick, writer of afterword.
Title: Above all, we are Jews : a biography of Rabbi Alexander Schindler / Michael A. Meyer ; Jonathan D. Sarna, Rabbi Rick Jacobs.
Description: First edition. | New York : Central Conference of American Rabbis (CCAR), 2025. | Includes bibliographical references and index. | Summary: "Rabbi Alexander Schindler (1925–2000) was an extraordinarily influential leader in the history of Reform Judaism. From 1973 to 1996, he served as president of the Union of American Hebrew Congregations (today's Union for Reform Judaism), where his charisma and vision raised the Reform Movement to unprecedented influence"—Provided by publisher.
Identifiers: LCCN 2024045837 (print) | LCCN 2024045838 (ebook) | ISBN 9780881236583 (paperback) | ISBN 9780881236590 (ebook)
Subjects: LCSH: Schindler, Alexander M. | Reform Judaism—United States—History—20th century. | Rabbis—United States—Biography.
Classification: LCC BM755.S252 M49 2025 (print) | LCC BM755.S252 (ebook) | DDC 296.092 [B]—dc23/eng/20241011
LC record available at https://lccn.loc.gov/2024045837
LC ebook record available at https://lccn.loc.gov/2024045838
LC ebook record available at https://lccn.loc.gov/2024045838

Book design by Scott-Martin Kosofsky
at The Philidor Company, www.philidor.com

Printed in the United States of America
10 9 8 7 6 5 4 3 2 1

> "The righteous require no monuments;
> their words are their memorials."
> —Rabban Shimon ben Gamliel

In memory of Alex, *zecher tzadik l'vrachah*,
who changed our world and the world
through his words, passion, and vision.

With love,
His beloved spouse and best friend of forty-four years, Rhea

His adoring children and children-in-law,
Elisa and Larry, Debby and Bob,
Josh and Hadley, Judy and Chip, Jonathan and Heather

His proud grandchildren and grandchildren-in-law,
Jonah and Arielle, Naomi and Calvin, Micah and Kiara, Hannah,
Maximilian and Barbara, Stella, Bibiana, Moses, Maxwell,
Alec, Alexander, and Ella

> "Of all the possessions, a friend is the most precious."
> —Herodotus

In loving memory of Alex, *z"l*,
whose friendship we cherished and felt blessed to know.

Leslee, David, Emily, Lily, and Leo Rogath

Contents

Foreword *Jonathan D. Sarna*	ix
Preface	xiii
1. Origins and Youth	1
2. Ascending the Ladder	19
3. Becoming the Voice of Reform Judaism	39
4. Spokesman for American Jewry	61
5. Reaching Out	99
6. Issues and Actions	119
7. Reaching In	161
8. The Private Life	181
Afterword *Rabbi Rick Jacobs*	189
Notes	193
Index	241
About the Author	254

Foreword

Jonathan D. Sarna

"There were giants in the earth in those days."

WITH THAT QUOTATION from the King James translation of the Book of Genesis (6:4), Rabbi Alexander Moshe Schindler, the subject of this luminous biography by the preeminent Jewish historian Michael A. Meyer, began one of his most self-revealing and least-remembered compositions: his introduction to Marc Lee Raphael's *Abba Hillel Silver: A Profile in American Judaism*.[1]

The "giant" whom Rabbi Schindler depicted in his seventeen-page introduction was, like himself, an eminent Zionist and communal leader as well as a devoted Reform rabbi—in Silver's case, in Cleveland. Schindler described him, along with the New York Zionist leader and Reform rabbi Stephen S. Wise, as "the last of a species of inspired leaders who with tremendously persuasive eloquence and moral intensity tried to influence the American Establishment."[2]

Yet in writing about Silver's legacy, it is clear that Schindler, then in his sixties and a survivor of two heart attacks, had in mind his own legacy as well. Why, he wondered, had Silver been so forgotten after his death? Why, "despite the man's powerful personality, despite his famous oratorical talent, his wide-ranging intellect, and his much-vaunted political skills,"[3] did more than twenty-five years elapse before any biography of him appeared? Could it be that his success "at organizing the American Jewish community and mobilizing its latent political power" made his own role in the Jewish world "obsolete"?[4]

Schindler understood that Silver had operated in an entirely different national context than he himself did. "Jewish leadership," he explained "was helplessly isolated" in those days, and Jews faced formidable domestic foes.[5] What impressed him, though, was how much the Lithuanian-born Silver nevertheless accomplished. His introduction to Raphael's biography claimed Silver (a fellow East European) as a spiritual ancestor, attributing to him ideas and achievements that, as Meyer shows, Schindler as a leader himself sought to advance:

- Silver "indelibly impressed his Zionist faith upon the movement as a whole."[6]
- He helped move Reform "away from its rather cold intellectualism and reserved style of worship."[7]
- He paved the way for "its eventual institutional transplantation from Cincinnati to New York, the teeming center of American Jewish life."[8]
- He "did not reject the messianic universalism or missionary purpose of Reform Judaism, he only refused to see either as a substitute for Jewish nationalism."[9]
- He promoted "the sense of classic harmony in Jewish life…the total program of Jewish life and destiny—the religious and moral values, the universal concepts, the mandate of mission, as well as *the Jewish people itself*, and all its national aspirations."[10]
- He "spoke within the Zionist movement (and beyond) as a rabbi: as a teacher and preacher deeply committed to…the synagogue in general as the central institution of Jewish life."[11]
- He "defended the modern rabbinate and synagogue against the intellectuals who sought to supplant religious institutions with secular alternatives."[12]
- He "possessed a panoramic, inclusive vision of Judaism and the Jewish people that was unique among his more nearsighted contemporaries."[13]

Schindler even plucked from Silver's writings a paragraph, dating to 1948, that summarized many of his own most deeply cherished commitments:

> There are no substitutes in Jewish life for religion. Neither philanthropy, nor culture, nor nationalism is adequate for the stress and challenge of our lives. All these interests can and must find their rightful place within the general pattern of Judaism. But the pattern must be of Judaism, the Judaism of the priest, the prophet, the saint, the mystic, and the rabbi; the Judaism which speaks of God, and the worship of God, and the commandments of God, and quest for God.[14]

By the time Schindler was done writing about Silver, it was clear that he had been one of his most important rabbinic role models. Indeed, he refers in a footnote to a personal conversation with Silver (who died in 1963, when Schindler, at thirty-eight, was just a decade into his own rabbinate) concerning public speaking and sermon writing. "The true undergirding of his power as an orator," an impressed Schindler recalled, "were arduous effort, concentration, scholarship and rehearsal."[15] As Meyer shows here, Schindler learned that lesson well. Arduous effort—long hours of hard focused work at his desk—characterized Schindler right up to his final, fatal heart attack.

Rabbi Schindler's feisty mother, Sali, who lived into her early nineties, worried about her son. She asked me, when I met her in Worcester where she lived in old age, to write to her "dear Alex" to beg him not to work so hard. "He toils day and night," she fretted, and then she added brightly, "but he never forgets to phone me, no matter where he is!"

Schindler, who called his mother so regularly, was a great deal warmer and more beloved than his role model ever was. He diplomatically characterized Silver as "revered more than loved—a leader aloof from the people."[16] Schindler greatly improved upon Silver in this regard; he was very much a people person. He loved all Jews and won respect across the spectrum of American Jewish life—exemplified by his late-in-life leadership roles in trans-denominational Jewish organizations such as the Joint Distribution Committee, the Memorial Foundation for Jewish Culture, and the World Jewish Congress. There he interacted effortlessly, and sometimes in pungent Yiddish, with Jews far removed from his own Reform moorings, disarming them with jokes and stories drawn from his East European background and eventful life. Akin to the Hasidic master, Rabbi Avraham Yehoshua Heshel of Apt (Opatów), he was known—even by many of those who strongly disagreed with him on religious matters—as an *ohev Yisrael*, a lover of the Jewish people in its totality.

Why, in spite of all this, did he fall into the very same neglect that Silver experienced—a quarter of a century elapsing before this first-of-its-kind biography? One suspects that changes in American Jewish life, particularly divisions over Israel and widespread religious polarization, rendered his outlook, in the eyes of contemporaries, no less "obsolete" than some had found Silver after his passing. Tellingly, no Reform rabbi ever again headed the Conference of Presidents of Major American Jewish Organizations. Nor has any European-born rabbi since his death ascended to a top leadership position within the Reform Movement; the generation of Holocaust-era rabbis has passed from the scene. In recent years, even Schindler's signature innovations—outreach and patrilineal descent—have drawn new criticism, especially as Reform Judaism's numbers and coffers have contracted.

Nevertheless, as Michael A. Meyer's pioneering biography properly proclaims, "since his time there has been no one in Reform Judaism who reached his level of influence—and few in American Jewish life more broadly" (page xv). *The New York Times*, in a glowing obituary on November 16, 2000, likewise understood that an era ended with his passing: "Rabbi Schindler played two major roles in American Jewish life, one religious, the other secular; either would have made him one of the most influential American Jewish leaders of the latter half of the 20th century."[17]

Looking back a quarter of a century later, and after reading this eye-opening biography, the very same Biblical passage that Schindler quoted with reference to Abba Hillel Silver seems to me rightly to apply to him: "There were giants in the earth in those days."

> Dr. Jonathan D. Sarna is University Professor and the Joseph H. & Belle R. Braun Professor of American Jewish History at Brandeis University. He also is the past president of the Association for Jewish Studies and Chief Historian of the National Museum of American Jewish History in Philadelphia. Author or editor of more than thirty books on American Jewish history and life, his *American Judaism: A History*, recently published in a second edition, won six awards including the 2004 Everett Jewish Book of the Year Award from the Jewish Book Council. Sarna is a fellow both of the American Academy of Arts and Sciences and of the American Academy of Jewish Research, and he holds four honorary degrees. His most recent books are *Coming to Terms with America*, a volume of essays; and *Yearning to Breathe Free: Jews in Gilded Age America*, coedited with Adam Mendelsohn.

Preface

Rabbi Alexander Moshe Schindler (1925–2000) was a central figure within American Judaism whose significance has yet to be fully understood. His successor as president of the Union of American Hebrew Congregations (UAHC, now called Union for Reform Judaism, or URJ), Rabbi Eric Yoffie, believes he was the "last great national leader of American Jewry."[1] His good friend for many years but frequent political adversary, Henry Kissinger, called him "a preeminent figure of conscience and leadership, not only within the American Jewish community, but for all concerned with human issues around the globe."[2]

It was Alexander Schindler who brought Reform Judaism to the height of its influence. Within a favorable American environment, his charisma and vision allowed it to grow to its maximum size and energy. Whereas other well-known Reform Jews of the twentieth century, such as Rabbis Stephen Wise and Abba Hillel Silver, gained their fame on account of their Zionist advocacy, Schindler's reputation rests in large measure upon his activism within the congregational union of Reform Judaism.

With passion and effect, he brought into existence an institutional structure that reached out to Jews on the periphery of Jewish life and welcomed them into the religious community. Unafraid of lively debate—indeed nourishing it—he recognized that the unprecedented increase in interfaith marriages demanded acceptance of the intermarried rather than rejection if Jewish life within an enticing American society were to flourish. Although more traditional Jews objected vociferously, he advocated acceptance of patrilineal descent as a marker of Jewishness so that children whose fathers alone were Jewish would not be lost to the faith. Though with less success, he likewise sought to strengthen the Jewish community with an influx of non-Jews coming from outside its sphere, who would be drawn to its faith and customs.

Schindler was a highly controversial figure not only with regard to the institutional changes he advocated within Reform Judaism but also with regard to his independent stand in relation to the policies of Israel. He was the first Reform leader to also be a principal leader of American Jewry as a whole. Elected as a Reform rabbi to chair the Conference of Presidents of Major American Jewish Organizations in 1976, he was widely respected across the religious spectrum. When, during Schindler's term as chair, Menachem Begin was elected prime minister of Israel, Schindler was able—against all expectations—to bridge the gap between a liberal American Jewry and a prime minister whose views on the State of Israel lay far to the right. Schindler's own opinions on Israel combined a deeply felt Zionism with a willingness to discard a tradition that American Jews should always blindly accept current Israeli policies. He saw the Diaspora as having an ineluctable responsibility to share in shaping the Israeli future.

He was a talented and effective speaker, listened to by his rabbinical colleagues, by the Reform laity, and by government officials in the United States and Israel. By conviction and practice a Reform Jew and critical of Orthodox rigidity, he nonetheless regarded other forms of Judaism with due respect. He defined himself and wanted to be remembered as an *ohev Yisrael*, a lover of the Jewish people in its totality.

Unafraid of espousing causes unpopular among many American Jews and non-Jews, Schindler spoke out for LGBTQ rights, full racial equality, and a clear separation of church and state. He had close connections with a range of key civil rights leaders, including Jesse Jackson, Andrew Young, Roy Wilkins, and Bayard Rustin. Never cowed into suppressing his opinions, he dealt forcefully with American presidents and legislators.

In a Reform Movement that had drawn its inspiration largely from antecedents in Central Europe, Schindler—though born in Germany—introduced novelty by drawing religious inspiration largely from Eastern European Jewry, especially Hasidism. Despite his stress on inclusiveness, he saw the need to draw boundaries; for example, he held that a congregation that excluded belief in God had its role within the Jewish people, but it had placed itself outside the bounds of a Reform Judaism that was anchored in religious tradition.

Although English was not his native tongue, Schindler was able to present his views—often in a poetic or dramatic vein—with an effect that was judged to be almost without parallel. At UAHC biennial assemblies, his speeches were consistently the highlight of the program. His listeners invariably felt that they had not come in vain. Since his time there has been no one in Reform Judaism who reached his level of influence—and few in American Jewish life more broadly.

Yet, despite these markers of significance, to this day there is no published Schindler biography.[3] I have been drawn to that task both to fill a significant gap in American Jewish history and also because, having had some personal contact with Alexander Schindler beginning with a summer camp in Wisconsin where he served as dean, I came to admire the man and his achievements. That is not to say, however, that I conceive of this biography as a tribute. I have given voice not only to Schindler's admirers but also to those who were critical of him or his policies. Here and there I have also included my own critical remarks. Like all significant figures, Schindler had professional and personal shortcomings. Despite my respect for him as a person and a leader, I have sought to achieve a balanced account.

This biography is based principally upon the extensive Schindler papers housed in the Jacob Rader Marcus Center of the American Jewish Archives in Cincinnati,[4] supplemented by other archives, interviews, and correspondence with individuals who knew Schindler either as members of his family or as professional associates.[5] In order to present this biography with greater coherence, I have gathered most of Schindler's personal life into a final chapter. It is my hope that these pages will enable future generations to better judge and appreciate Rabbi Schindler's place in Jewish history.

ACKNOWLEDGMENTS

In contemplating the writing of this volume, I realized that, unlike most subjects that I have dealt with in the more distant past, this one required drawing upon the memories of key individuals who knew Rabbi Alexander Schindler either personally, professionally, or both. I am therefore grateful to all those who agreed to in-person or virtual interviews or who answered questions in writing. I began my research by driving into the Berkshires to interview the still very alert Rhea Schindler, who had shared so much of Alex's life, its joys and sorrows. While there,

I was able to speak with his oldest child, Elisa Schindler Frankel, who supplemented what her mother was able to tell me. My first interview of a professional associate was with Rabbi David Saperstein, who had enjoyed a close relationship with Alexander Schindler over many years while leading the Reform Movement's Religious Action Center. David not only enthusiastically agreed to an interview but also took time to meticulously read the manuscript, calling attention to problems of style and content. Not long thereafter, I traveled to Westfield, New Jersey, for a long interview with Rabbi Eric Yoffie, Alexander Schindler's successor as president of the Union of American Hebrew Congregations. Eric likewise helpfully read the manuscript and made an important suggestion that strengthened my evaluation of his predecessor. Two other in-person interviews contributed to the manuscript. One was conducted with Rabbi Ira Youdovin, who had worked with Schindler as executive director of the Association of Reform Zionists of America, and Evely Laser Shlensky, a former chair of the Union's Commission on Social Action; and the other was with Alan Goldman, who chaired the Union's Board of Governors during Schindler's later years.

A special word of thanks is due to Rabbi Judith Schindler. She not only granted me an extensive interview in her home in Charlotte, North Carolina, but also read a draft of the final chapter on her father's personal life and answered many questions by email. Judy devoted herself to the project and, while understandably a great admirer of her father, fully shared my view that a proper biography required balanced, scholarly treatment.

I also wish to thank those individuals whom I was not able to interview in person, but who kindly submitted to a virtual interview. They include Lydia Kukoff, the author of *Choosing Judaism* and the long-term director of the Union's Outreach Program, and Rabbi Lennard Thal, for a time director of the UAHC Pacific Regional Council. Much appreciated written recollections came to me from Lawrence Bush, who had assisted with Alexander Schindler's speeches; Rabbi Clifford Kulwin, who knew Schindler during his service as director of international development for the World Union for Progressive Judaism; and Rabbi Robert Orkand, who was the Schindler family's rabbi at Temple Israel in Westport, Connecticut. Among the other correspondents to whom I am grateful for assisting in various ways are Professor Michael Brenner, Rabbi William Cutter, Dr. Jordan Finkin, Rabbi Joan Friedman, Caroline Greene, Rabbi Samuel Joseph, Rabbi Mark Kaiserman, Miriam Oles, Joshua Schindler, Keli Schmid, Russell Silverman, and Professor Jack Wertheimer.

This book could not have been undertaken without the assistance of the dedicated staffs at the Jacob Rader Marcus Center of the American Jewish Archives and the Klau Library, both on the campus of the Hebrew Union College–Jewish Institute of Religion in Cincinnati. Among the Klau librarians I am especially grateful to Abigail Bacon, Lisa Ben-Hur, and Hara Jun; at the Archives I owe particular thanks to its associate director, Dr. Dana Herman, and its managing archivist, Joe Weber. I am also grateful for the assistance I received from other libraries and archives in Germany, the United States, and Israel.

A special word of thanks is owed my long-time friend Professor Jonathan Sarna for writing a scholarly and interesting foreword that makes an independent, valuable contribution to the volume. I am likewise grateful to Rabbi Rick Jacobs, the current president of the Union for Reform Judaism, for his memories of Schindler and for placing the volume within the history of American Reform Judaism.

In the summer of 2023, I was able to present a portion of chapter 4, dealing with the relationship between Rabbi Schindler and Menachem Begin, at a seminar held to mark the retirement of Professor Shmuel Feiner at Bar Ilan University. I am grateful for the invitation and the hospitality I enjoyed there.

I wish, as well, to express my thanks to the entire diligent and competent staff at the CCAR Press. Among those with whom I was fortunate to have concentrated personal contact during the publication process, I would single out its director Rafael Chaiken, who explained the procedures of the press during a visit of mine to New York. He has been committed to the volume from the start and sought to make it a central achievement of the press. It has been an immense pleasure to work with my editor, Rabbi Anne Villarreal-Belford. She not only commented perceptively on content and immeasurably improved the text's syntax; she also heightened my own devotion to the subject with her enthusiasm for it. Other members of the staff who in their various capacities had a share in publication of the volume include CCAR Chief Executive Rabbi Hara Person, Assistant

Editor Chiara Ricisak, copyeditor Michelle Kwitkin, designer Scott-Martin Kosofsky, proofreader Debra Hirsch Corman, Press Operations Manager Debbie Smilow, and Press Marketing and Sales Manager Raquel Fairweather-Gallie. I am appreciative of all their contributions.

Finally, I owe boundless gratitude to Margie—the rabbi—my wife of well over sixty years, who carefully read and helpfully criticized the manuscript as she has done for all of my previous writings. Her love and encouragement have always sustained me.

CHAPTER I
Origins and Youth

As a tree is nourished abundantly from its roots when it is planted by a flowing stream, so are humans fed by the roots from which they sprang. Alexander Moshe Schindler's roots sustained him throughout his career and they provide an important background for his life. Though born in Germany, he was a son of East European Jews, scion of famous Hasidim. Notable among them, according to family tradition, was Rabbi Moshe Sofer of Pshevorsk (1720?–1806), a leading figure in the second generation of Hasidism. He was widely known for his homiletical and ethical work, *Or P'nei Moshe*, as a trusted scribe for *t'fillin* and mezuzot, and as a man of supreme holiness. A closer connection to Hasidism came from his paternal grandfather Abraham Schindler (1872–1943), who had been a follower of the Belzer Rebbe. A devoted Hasid, Abraham lived with his wife Nechama (Necha, 1869–1940) in Tyczyn, a small but vibrant Yiddish-speaking Jewish community in Polish Galicia, at that time a part of the Austro-Hungarian Empire. Throughout his life, Alexander remained proud of his small-town East European ancestry. Even though he was born and spent his first years in a major German metropolis, he never thought of himself as a German Jew, preferring to identify himself as a "Galizianer."[1]

In 1903 Abraham Schindler and his wife moved to Munich, with its larger and more diverse Jewish community, apparently for the economic opportunities that the city offered. Although there is no record of it, one may assume that perhaps Polish antisemitism also played a role in their decision. If so, then ironically he chose a city that two decades later would become the favored nucleus of the Nazi party and, in 1923, the site of the infamous Beer Hall Putsch, Hitler's first attempt at gaining political power.

Abraham, more commonly known as Reb Avrom Yitzchak, was able to open a grocery store in 1907 that featured kosher food and was under rabbinical supervision. It was frequented not only by fellow East European immigrants, but also by Munich's generally less observant German Jews (known as "yekkes"). The grocery prospered, especially in advance of Jewish holidays. When not working there, the bearded Avrom, his head properly covered, was regularly found in a small synagogue—a Hasidic *shtiebl* that bore the name Machzikei Hadas (champions of the faith)—where he was given the role of *chazan* (cantor). The men who participated in the prayers were followers of the Belzer Hasidic tradition, which militantly rejected the peremptory initiative of a largely secular Zionism out of devotion to an all-embracing divine providence. Whenever the current Belzer rebbe sent emissaries westward to raise funds from the relatively wealthier East European Jews in Munich, they would lodge at the Schindler home.[2] Avrom's wife, Necha, could say and sing the prayers fervently in Hebrew, but, typical of Orthodox Jewish women, had not learned the language sufficiently to know their exact meaning. These grandparents of Alexander Schindler remained in Germany until it was too late for escape. Necha died in 1940. Later, on August 13, 1942, Avrom was deported to the ghetto of Theresienstadt where he perished the next May.

Avrom and Necha had four sons and three daughters. Like his grandparents, all three of the daughters, Alexander's aunts, were murdered during the Holocaust. One of their younger sons died fighting for Austria in World War I; another, Ruben, was able to migrate to Palestine with his family in 1939, where he became a member of the dominantly German Jewish Kibbutz Shavei Zion. The youngest son, also named Alexander, became the father of Rabbi Pesach Schindler, who migrated from the United States to Israel, where he became head of the Conservative Yeshiva in Jerusalem and a well-known teacher of Talmud. Later in life, Alexander Moshe would have some contact with his broader family. Yet, he estimated that between twenty and twenty-five members of his extended family had perished. Their fate could not but deepen Alexander's determination to work at restoring the decimated Jewish people.

The eldest son, our Alexander's father (1892–1957), was called Lazar (or Leser) in German, but became better known by his Hebrew name, Eliezer. He was eleven years old in 1903 when the family left Tyczyn and settled permanently in Munich.[3] After a brief first marriage,[4] Eliezer married the seven years younger Sali Hoyda (1899–1992),[5] whom Eliezer had tutored in Hebrew and Judaica. They fell in love over the course of their lessons, to the displeasure of her father, who had hoped that his daughter would find a more established groom. They decided to elope, and in 1923 they were married in the lovely Austrian town of Innsbruck, directly south of Munich.[6]

Sali was an initiative-taking, feisty woman whom her son described as "an assertive and aggressive" mother and as "the strong person in the family."[7] Beginning in 1931, she ran "A & S Schindler" with her brother-in-law Alexander, which was a successful catalogue mail-order house that sold a wide variety of products "including crucifixes for local monasteries."[8] Not only had she taken business courses, she was also a pianist, who may therefore have nurtured Alexander's lifelong love of music. Sali's business skills gave the household a solidly middle-class character, enabling the employment of maids and tutors who, with the parents engaged in their work, played a large role in raising Alex and his older sister Eva. When, years later at the age of seventy, Sali was aboard a Swissair plane hijacked to the Jordanian desert by the Palestine Liberation Front, this self-assertive lady responded to a guerrilla's question, proudly and loudly declaring, "I am a Jew and an American."[9] After a long widowhood, she passed away in 1992. It was from his mother, Alexander claimed, that he had inherited his organizational skills.

Judging from the attention Alexander gave him in his speeches and writings, it was his father who exercised the greater influence on his life. Eliezer was more permissive than his forceful wife, with whom he sometimes privately clashed. It was he who brought young Alex and his sister to school in the morning and provided them with a treat when he took them home in the afternoon. Unlike his wife, Eliezer was not interested in commerce, though he did establish a small antiques business. Rather, he was drawn to the life of the spirit and to Jewish traditions in particular. His German was sufficiently fluent in 1919 for him to deliver a paid lecture titled "Was ist Judentum?" (What is Judaism?) to a non-Jewish audience gathered in a small Munich beer hall. But he always saw himself as an East European rather than a German Jew. Over the years he conducted an extensive correspondence on spiritual matters with Nathan Birnbaum, a one-time prominent Zionist who then turned anti-Zionist and Orthodox Jew. Eliezer adopted the motto of Birnbaum's Oylim (Spiritual Ascenders) Society: "Knowledge, compassion, and divine splendor." These three

The Yiddish poet Eliezer Schindler, Alexander Schindler's father, in Munich. *Courtesy of the Schindler family.*

values were engraved in Hebrew[10] on Eliezer's bookplate, and they were also inscribed on the bookplates of both his son Alexander and his granddaughter, Rabbi Judith Schindler. In describing his father, Alexander frequently used a characterization that he wanted to believe also described himself as a Jew: His father's essence, Alexander maintained, was being an *ohev Yisrael*, a lover of the people of Israel.

Central to Eliezer's life was the Yiddish language, in which he wrote and published his poetry and songs. He was also known for his translations and adaptations of popular folktales from various languages. His oeuvre appeared simultaneously in both secular and religious Yiddish venues.[11] Early on, he became attached to the Bais Yaakov movement that provided an Orthodox Jewish education for Jewish girls who, in general, learned only practical skills and frequently chose to converse in Polish. He believed that Jewish daughters who do not speak Yiddish created a barrier between themselves and the Jewish people. Eliezer wrote the first Bais Yaakov textbook for study of the Yiddish language and composed its first Yiddish anthem, which concluded piously: "We swear to protect the Torah, to serve our holy God." There is testimony to the effect that Schindler's songs were sung in the death camps, where they brought a measure of consolation and emotional support.[12] Steeped in the milieu of Yiddish literature and more broadly in the culture of the East European world, Eliezer did not feel at home in the America to which he was later able to escape. He brought with him across the Atlantic some fourteen collections of world folklore, perhaps as material for translation into Yiddish. But to an interviewer who asked him why he did not continue to write Yiddish poetry and songs in the United States, he supposedly replied sorrowfully: "I cannot do it anymore. My Bais Yaakov children are gone. I have nobody to write for. I cannot accept today's youth. I cannot make peace with the new world."[13] Yet, in 1950, he did publish in New York a volume of his rhymed lyrical poems, titled *Yiddish un hasidish* (Yiddish and Hasidic). Many of them are set to music, most are religious, some specifically for children, and still others admiring of nature or nostalgically recalling life back in Tyczyn. Even today, within the limited Yiddish revival, some of his songs are still performed.

Though living in Munich, Eliezer remained an Austrian citizen and was drafted into its army during World War I. Wounded and later captured by the Russians and interned for a time in Siberia, he managed to make his way back to Germany. The route took him to a settlement of Sabbotniks, a small Judaizing Christian sect, settled in the Russian steppes. For a time he remained among them, becoming their instructor in Judaism before returning to Munich in 1919. It was Eliezer's belief that these sectarians, as well as others on the Jewish periphery, should be brought fully into the Jewish faith. His son claimed that Eliezer "always believed that Judaism really is a missionary religion."[14] It was a notion Alexander Schindler would later popularize, calling it "outreach" to distanced Jews and non-Jews alike.

Long after Eliezer's death in 1957, his son chose to recall his father during the Yom Kippur memorial service at Brooklyn's Union Temple, where he regularly spoke at the High Holy Days. He said:

> My father died better than thirty years ago. Yet to this day I think of him on almost a daily basis. Many of my ideas are stimulated by his specific thoughts and by his manner of thought—the ethical assumptions and creative processes that informed his intellectual life. Often I make my decisions by the measure of what my father would have wanted me to do. And whenever I think of him, the sense of his continued presence is stronger than the knowledge of his death.[15]

That paternal influence was especially strong and constant in Schindler's conception of an assertive Judaism. Late in his career he wrote that "all my life my father reminded me that people who have no mission are suspected of having no message, of possessing nothing that is sufficiently worthy to share with others."[16] It was his father, he recalled, who first told him of Albert Einstein's statement: "I am sorry I was born a Jew, for it keeps me from choosing to be a Jew."[17]

For four years the young Alex Schindler attended the local Orthodox Jewish day school in Munich. From the age of ten, he continued his education at the non-Jewish Neues Realgymnasium school, where Albert Einstein had earlier been a student, while his Jewish education fell to overly qualified private Jewish tutors. Although Jewish teachers and students were gradually eliminated from general education in Nazi Germany, Alex's attendance was allowed since his parents held Polish passports, and Nazi legislation often privileged Jews with non-German documents. The school experience was fraught with unpleasantness: Alex was the only Jewish pupil. He later recalled that when the students prayed in the name of Jesus Christ "whom the Jews murdered," the whole class turned to look at him.[18] He noted that although he suffered no physical abuse, he was affected by deep emotional deprivation; no one in school befriended him. Not surprisingly, he became a shy child, turned in upon himself.

To forge a link with the broader Munich Jewish community, Alex's father took him not only to the Orthodox synagogue but also to the Liberal temple, where his mother was more at ease and where he was on good terms with its rabbi Leo Baerwald.[19] The home in which Alex grew up celebrated Jewish holidays, but it was not fully kosher—at least until his more observant sister Eva, who would later become an active Orthodox feminist, insisted upon two sets of dishes.

With Hitler's rise to power and the speedy arrest of leading Jewish politicians and intellectuals, Eliezer feared that he—having read *Mein*

Eva and Alex as children in Munich.
Courtesy of the Schindler family.

Kampf and openly warned against Hitler—might also be arrested and sent to the newly established Dachau concentration camp not far from Munich. In fact, within weeks of Hitler's rise to power, men of Hitler's SA (*Sturmabteilung*) came looking for Eliezer. In early March 1933, he was forewarned of his impending arrest and hid in a hospital; the following day, he escaped across the German border. He made his way to Zurich, where he lived without his wife or children for the next five years; he only saw them on vacation rendezvous, especially during summers. Their financial condition was sufficient to allow these regular meetings to take place at lovely resorts somewhere in Europe outside of Germany. Sali, who was not under threat, chose to remain in Munich in order to preserve the income from her still prospering business and to smuggle funds to her husband in Switzerland.[20]

It was not until the spring of 1938, shortly before Hitler personally ordered the destruction of the main synagogue of Munich, that Sali made the decision to sell A & S Schindler to non-Jews and leave Germany behind. She first sent twelve-year-old Alexander, born in October 1925, and his one-year-older sister, Eva, to Switzerland to join their father there. Fearing that some financial questions might lead to her arrest at the border, her departure for Zurich required a circuitous route. Shrewdly, she had surreptitiously kept two sets of books—one for herself and one for her Nazi-sympathizing employees or Nazi examiners of her accounts. Her daughter recalled that a caricature of her mother had appeared in the viciously antisemitic Nazi newspaper *Der Stürmer*.[21] First, Sali crossed the border to Poland, where she obtained help to continue on to Hungary dressed as a nun attending a eucharist congress in Budapest; from there, she traveled via Italy to a reunion with her husband and children in Zurich. Fortunately, they were among the relatively few who were able to obtain visas for America. A first cousin of Alex's grandfather lived in Brooklyn and was willing to swear out an affidavit that the Schindler family would not be a burden to the American economy. Thus, shortly after the family's reunion in Switzerland, Eliezer, Sali, Eva, and Alexander were able to depart for America via France, settling comfortably into the luxurious steamship *Normandie* that departed from Le Havre on July 27, 1938. They arrived in New York only five days later on August 1, just three months before the November Pogrom popularly known as Kristallnacht. Many years later, in 1993, Schindler recalled his first view of the Statue of Liberty from the deck of the steamship. His father had taken him by the hand to point it out. Although by then he had become a severe critic of much that went on in American public life, Schindler told young people gathered at a convention of the National Federation of Temple Youth, "America became my home, and I will always bless it, as should we all."[22]

The Schindler family first settled in the Washington Heights section of New York City. Alexander knew little English, and having read in German Karl May's popular adventure novels of the Wild West, he may have brought along a rather distorted but nonetheless exciting notion of his new home. He was now twelve years old, continuing his Jewish education and preparing for his bar mitzvah, which would take place a few weeks after the family's arrival in America, probably at the Jewish Center Synagogue in upper Manhattan served by the prominent modern Orthodox rabbi Leo Jung. His Torah portion was *B'reishit*, the first in Genesis, and thus fitting for an immigrant in a new land. Occasionally, his father took him to hear the Liberal rabbi and spell-binding orator Stephen Wise at Carnegie Hall. Encouraged by his mother, Alexander—still dressed in European knickers—was able to attend two prestigious public high schools, Stuyvesant and Townsend Harris. However, he was not a diligent student, frequently skipping class in order to attend movies and snatching truancy notices out of the family's mailbox before they reached his parents. He claimed it was the films that he watched—he especially loved *Casablanca*—that played a large role in improving his English. Despite this casual approach to his studies, Alexander was able to get a high enough score on the Regents Examination for him to enter City College in 1940 or 1941, at the early age of fifteen or sixteen, in order to study mechanical engineering. That proved to be a big mistake: He was not ready for college and he did not do well; in fact, he dropped out.

Shortly thereafter, in 1941, the family moved from New York to a farm that they had purchased in Lakewood, New Jersey. Eliezer's poetic soul had long entertained a romantic notion of life in nature. There they raised chickens and Sali established and ran a kosher bed and breakfast. The synagogue to which they belonged was Orthodox. For two years, until the age of eighteen, Alexander worked as a farmhand on the Lakewood farm. It was an isolating life that he did not particularly enjoy. Perhaps it even came as a relief when, having reached the age of eighteen, he was drafted into the American army.

Alexander Schindler's draft registration card, dated October 4, 1943, records him as being a resident of Lakewood, New Jersey, of medium height at five foot nine, and weighing 185 pounds. The card contains a striking feature: Alexander Moshe Schindler appears here as Alexander Monroe Schindler. Was this simply an error or a deliberate choice? Did the registrar make a suggestion to change his name, or did Alexander wish to shield his Jewishness upon entering the army? The answer is unknown. However, it is well known that Jews serving in the American army, like Black Americans, suffered discrimination. When later asked to state on a questionnaire whether he had ever suffered acts of anti-Jewish prejudice in America, he responded, "Here and there in the United States especially when I served in the army (not as a chaplain)."[23]

Alexander Schindler's parents, Sali and Eliezer, on the farm in Lakewood, New Jersey, ca. 1941. *Courtesy of the Schindler family.*

Corporal Alexander Schindler. *Courtesy of American Jewish Archives, Cincinnati, Ohio.*

Alexander was drafted on March 24, 1944. His military career began at Fort Dix, New Jersey, not far from the family farm. Then came basic artillery training at Fort Bragg in North Carolina. It was apparently at this point that an exciting opportunity presented itself. On vacations in Europe the young Schindler had learned how to ski. Having completed basic training, he now volunteered for what must have seemed an adventurous way of completing his army service by successfully submitting his name to join the highly regarded Ski Troops of the Tenth Mountain Division. Once accepted, he was shipped to Camp Hale in Colorado for specialized training and finally, for a longer period, to Camp Swift near Austin, Texas. He was to serve in the 604th Field Artillery Battalion, consisting of about fourteen thousand men. Their deployment from the East Coast came in December 1944. For security reasons, the men did not know where they were going when they set sail from Hampton Roads, Virginia, on January 6, 1945. Their destination, it turned out, was Naples in southern Italy. Schindler was to participate in the division's dangerous task of driving Nazi forces out of the hill country and fighting its way through the Po Valley, up the Apennines into the Alps, northward toward

Milan. What followed were four months of almost continuous combat. One record shows Alexander listed as missing. In fact, he lay severely wounded in an evacuation hospital after being blown out of a jeep by an artillery gun, one among the high number of casualties suffered by the division during its Spring Offensive.[24] While recuperating, his rank was raised to that of corporal. Despite his wounds he was eventually able to rejoin his unit soon after he recovered. During the crucial battle of Mount Belvedere, he was given an especially significant task: to act as a forward observer, determining the location of enemy emplacements so that the artillery could more accurately hit its targets and the infantry more safely move forward. It seems that for his mission he did not actually ski, but instead walked or rode. He was wounded again, this time accidentally strafed by American planes. He later recalled in regard to either his first or second wound, "My manhood was almost taken away."[25] The wounds earned him a Purple Heart, and his bravery was rewarded by a Bronze Star.

Having gained a hard-fought victory, the men of the Tenth Mountain Division were hailed by the local Italian population as conquering heroes; civilians threw flowers and handed out eggs, loaves of bread, and bottles of wine. But for Alexander Schindler, the war experience was a memory more of agony than of glory. He rejected outright the account in a textbook for children that referred to the Allied armies' glorious breakthrough to the Po Valley and the painless conquest of Milan. Speaking to Jewish war veterans a few years after the war, he recalled:

> I happened to be among those who broke through to the Po Valley. I recall no glory, only wiping my dirty face with a blood-stained shirttail. I was a part of that painless conquest of Milano. But all I remember is the picture of a soldier carrying the naked bleeding corpse of a four-year-old child and a man just back from work searching despairingly for his wife and children buried under the ruins of his home.[26]

He concluded that only those who have crawled on their stomachs in foxholes, hidden from the flak coming at them—those who had known war up close—were the only ones who could fully appreciate peace. Although Schindler was never a pacifist, he later became a vocal opponent of the nuclear arms race and a severe critic of America's role as "the world's leading arms merchant" and as the foremost proponent of a "nuclear balance of power."[27]

When the fighting in Italy had ceased, Schindler was able to convince his captain to lend him a jeep so that he could drive into Germany in a search for possible survivors from his family. Not surprisingly, he found no relatives alive in Munich. The significance of the foray, as it turned out, lay rather in his driving from Munich northward to Dachau. The concentration camp there had been liberated by American forces in April 1945. Although there were no longer men held as prisoners, he saw some of the former inmates trying to recover their strength. The contact with the camp left an indelible impression. He believed that the shocking and dispiriting experience of the living dead changed the direction of his life.[28] Only once very briefly did he again visit Germany. He avoided use of the German language and did not later associate himself with organizations, such as the Leo Baeck Institute, dedicated to preserving the history and culture of German Jewry. When later, as a rabbinical student, he heard from one of his teachers, Rabbi Leo Baeck,[29] the courageous leader of German Jewry during the Nazi period, that he was planning to give lectures in the German Federal Republic, Schindler recalled that he said to the elderly, now famous rabbi, "How can you go back? The hand you shake may be the hand that held the dagger that killed your brother." But true to his character, Baeck, a survivor of the Theresienstadt ghetto, responded, "It might also be the hand that stretched out and gave me a piece of bread." When Schindler did go back to Germany that one time, he insisted on speaking only English, though he had scarcely forgotten German, his mother tongue. At one point he did accept an invitation to give a series of three speeches in Germany only to cancel on account of a high fever, which one of his sons is convinced was psychological. Only very gradually did his attitude moderate after Germany began a program of reparations as a result of which his mother received a regular monthly check from the German government. To his wife he said on one occasion, "If we had thought about it, we would have had a sixth child [by that time they already had five children] on account of the Holocaust, one for each of the six million Jews who perished."[30]

Schindler was honorably discharged from military service in 1946 and, with the help of the GI Bill of Rights, eagerly reentered the City College of New York. In a German letter, composed in Hebrew characters to his sister and brother-in-law in New Jersey, he wrote, "After the dirt that we went through during the last months, I shall kiss the steps of every university and educational institution."[31] He wrote that he was, however, little qualified for university since the only skill he currently possessed was a background in photography.

Once again Schindler was a student, now majoring in social science. This time his grades were almost all A's and B's.[32] To supplement his studies at CCNY, he took evening courses in Hebrew language and literature at the Jewish Institute of Religion, the rabbinical seminary founded in 1922 by Rabbi Stephen Wise in in New York, and also at the Conservative Jewish Theological Seminary. Among the faculty at CCNY Alexander was especially drawn to Oscar Janowsky, the Polish-born professor of European history and Jewish studies who had coined the long popular statement "Jewish education is a mile wide and an inch deep." Called upon to write a recommendation for his student, Janowsky described him as "serious of purpose and [possessing] maturity beyond his years."[33] Under Janowsky's tutelage, Schindler wrote a history honors thesis titled "From Discrimination to Extermination: The Evolution of the Nazi Government's Anti-Jewish Policy 1933–1945." The subject was not chosen out of mere academic curiosity. Following his personal experience as a child and what he discovered in Germany immediately after the war, Schindler was determined to learn as much as he could about how what occurred to the Jews could have happened. The thesis, which earned him a *cum laude* upon graduation, concentrated on two sources: the transcripts of the multivolume trial proceedings of the Nuremberg tribunal and the *Reichsgesetzblatt*, the official journal containing the laws of the Nazi state. The thesis traces the development of anti-Jewish legislation but extends the analysis beyond the laws to the moral deterioration of German society, noting that concentration camp officials could shout with Hermann Goering: "I have no conscience! My conscience is Adolf Hitler." In the final paragraph of the 184-page thesis, Schindler concludes: "What is the value of this analysis? Why bring to light again the darkest chapter of human history? Because there is a hope that mankind will recognize the true consequences of blind hatred and race-frenzy. . . . Why repeat this agony? Because it is our duty to speak for the dead."[34]

During his years at CCNY—in all likelihood at the urging of his father and possibly because his father thought Alexander was the better writer in the English language—Alexander Schindler wrote two biographical articles that both pointed to a subject that would occupy him almost obsessively during his public career: bringing the message of Judaism to the non-Jew. They were published in the *United Israel Bulletin*, a bimonthly periodical founded in New York City in 1944 by the journalist David Horowitz and dedicated to spreading a universal understanding of Judaism.[35] The first Schindler article was titled "From Rome to Israel: The Life-Story of Aimé Pallière,"[36] and told of this Catholic Frenchman who—influenced by Elijah Benamozegh, the prominent rabbi of Leghorn in Italy—gravitated toward Judaism. Pallière had published the story of his pilgrimage in a volume that appeared in an English edition in 1928 with the title *The Unknown Sanctuary*, translated from the original French by Louise Waterman Wise, the wife of Rabbi Stephen Wise. In his introduction to Schindler's summary of this volume, the editor of *United Israel Bulletin* noted that Alexander Schindler's father, Eliezer, had long been an admirer of Pallière, who became an active supporter of Judaism, although he did not officially convert. Eliezer had popularized Pallière's work by translating sections of it into Yiddish. His son's biographical sketch, descriptive rather than analytical in character, added no new information to the account, but it was so affirmative of this heartfelt religious odyssey that when Pallière learned of it he sent a handwritten note to the editor of the bulletin expressing his gratitude for the pleasure that reading Schindler's piece had given him.

The second article told the story of another non-Jew who had been drawn to Judaism, Nahida Ruth Remy Lazarus,[37] the wife of Moritz Lazarus, the prominent Jewish philosopher, cofounder of *Völkerpsychologie* (ethnic psychology) and supporter of the Liberal Jewish seminary, the Hochschule in Berlin. Like Pallière, Nahida Remy composed a spiritual autobiography, which Schindler read presumably in the original German. Deeply religious, Remy had for a time entered a convent but soon became skeptical of miracles and of tortures in hell. She left the cloistered environment and moved ever further away from orthodox Christianity. Eventually, she discovered Liberal Judaism, with its emphasis on ethics rather than dogma and its refusal to pray what was not sincerely believed. As a feminist, she insisted on a more egalitarian religious service. Unlike Pallière, she decided upon a formal conversion to Judaism. Inspired by the story of Ruth, she adopted the biblical heroine's name as her own. In writing these two sketches, Alexander Schindler became acquainted with how two intelligent and sincerely religious individuals, a man and a woman, could become attracted to Judaism and add to its legacy. One must therefore conclude that his interest in bringing non-Jews into Judaism had its origins as early as his college days, long before he would seek to make it a program of Reform Judaism.

Schindler had decided to become an attorney, but in his senior year changed his choice of career to the rabbinate. Janowsky wanted him to become an academic, but Schindler recalled of himself that he was, "much more of an activist, so it's a good thing that the Reform rabbinate was there for me."[38] For rabbinical studies he might have chosen the Jewish Theological Seminary or the liberal Jewish Institute of Religion, both of them conveniently located in New York. That he decided instead to study at Hebrew Union College in Cincinnati was, he claimed, his father's idea.[39] We don't know the reasons behind that decision. Perhaps his father thought exposure to the Midwest would broaden his son's Americanism; perhaps Schindler himself wanted to get away from parental influence. His application for admission to the College, dated as early as January 8, 1947, was for the College's Lay Student Department, an indication that likely at that point he was thinking of Jewish scholarship rather than the rabbinate. In explaining why he was applying, Schindler wrote of his "deep interest in Jewish scholarship in general and Reform Judaism in particular, and the firm belief that through my studies at the H.U.C. I will, eventually, best be able to serve progressive Judaism in America."[40] The application listed an academic and a rabbinical reference. The first, not surprisingly, was Oscar Janowsky; the second was Paterson, New Jersey's Reform rabbi Max Raisin, a graduate of Hebrew Union College, and chosen perhaps because he was one of the earliest Reform rabbis to be a strong advocate of Zionism. The applicant's non-Jewish interests were listed as music and photography. By the time he entered HUC two years later, in the spring of 1949, Alexander had decided for the rabbinical program and, apparently as a result of his extra studies in New York, been granted advanced standing. After evaluation by the College's psychiatrist who noted, according to College records, that the incoming student had "done well in difficult situations,"[41] Schindler moved into HUC's lavishly endowed dormitory in Clifton, the Cincinnati suburb that also harbored its university. During his student years Schindler served part-time pulpits in the very small towns of West Point, Georgia; Logan, West Virginia; Williamson, West Virginia; and Petoskey, Michigan. At the same time, he served as counsellor at the B'nai B'rith Hillel Foundation of the University of Cincinnati and as Jewish chaplain at the Longview State Hospital for the Mentally Ill, where he helped organize the Jewish Social Service Program. Despite these additional duties, Schindler managed to complete the rabbinical school curriculum more rapidly than usual, in only three and a half years.[42]

Although he was already twenty-four years old when he came to Cincinnati, the faculty judged this veteran of the war to be less than fully mature, at least initially. One professor noted that "Schindler was observed driving his automobile across the grass in a most careless manner."[43] Another observed charitably that he "gives indication of growing up." On one occasion he participated in a prank that left the school's president, Nelson Glueck, forlorn when some students—including Schindler and perhaps his fellow student, friend, and later associate Balfour Brickner—had surreptitiously rolled his automobile from the college to Glueck's home. Schindler himself admitted that he "was not known as the most reverent of students."[44] His assignments were undertaken just shortly before they were due. The grades he received in his classes varied greatly, apparently based upon how much interest he had in a particular course. On one major examination, he managed to do better than any of the other students and consequently received a $50 prize.[45]

When it came time to select a topic for his senior thesis, Schindler did not choose to write in the area of history, as might have been expected based on the subject of his CCNY thesis. Instead, perhaps thinking now in practical terms of usefulness in a rabbinical career, he selected a topic in homiletics, asking the professor of homiletics Israel Bettan to be his adviser. Not surprisingly, Schindler decided to make use of his German knowledge in choosing as his subject a German Jewish religious leader, but remarkably he did not choose a Reform or Liberal rabbi. Instead, he settled upon Solomon Plessner (1797–1883), a popular Orthodox preacher, a *magid*, known as an avowed opponent of liturgical reform.[46] Plessner had published eight major collections of sermons, so Schindler had ample material with which to work. Not only did he read through them, but he also found descendants of Plessner whom he was able to interview. His admiration for this unlikely subject was immense. He writes of Plessner, "Young and old gathered about him, to enrich their knowledge and to warm themselves at the fire of his enthusiasm. And the poor also came." He was "mourned by friend and opponent alike as a proud son of his people."[47] One may wonder how much of Schindler's apparent identification with Plessner resulted from projecting his own values on those of his subject. For example, he attributes to Plessner the idea that "no matter how blatant the voice of the Zeitgeist, the preacher must speak up, fearlessly, courageously, ever seeking the applause of God and history rather than the applause of the masses."[48] In Schindler's view, Plessner's sermons represented a significant milestone between the innovative exegesis of the medieval *darshan* (interpreter of Scripture) and the homiletics of the modern preacher. To be sure, Schindler could also be critical of his subject. Using an argument typical of Reform Judaism, he noted of Plessner that "he failed to realize that the advocates of Reform were merely justifying changes which had been decades in the making and which were the direct outgrowths of the spiritual unrest of the times."[49] More interestingly, he criticizes Plessner for being hostile to mysticism, a notion not popular in contemporary Reform Judaism, but one to which, as we shall see, the young Schindler was warmly sympathetic. Whatever the mild critique, the thesis conclusion is unreservedly positive and can be taken as a personal hope for Schindler himself and his career. He writes of Plessner, "He was a good Jew—no higher praise could be bestowed upon him. His sermons manifest a love for his people, a pride in his faith, an uncompromising devotion to his ideals, an ardent joy-filled adoration of his God."[50]

CHAPTER 2
Ascending the Ladder

IN THE SPRING OF 1953, at the age of twenty-seven, Alexander Schindler was ordained a rabbi on the Cincinnati campus of Hebrew Union College–Jewish Institute of Religion, potentially the most prominent member of the graduating class. In the early days of the College, a large proportion of ordinees was foreign-born; in 1953 that was true for only 15 percent.[1] Alexander spoke with a noticeable German accent, which might have been a professional disadvantage, but in fact did not hinder him in finding a suitable position. The customary recommendations he received and the interviews to which he was likely subjected seem to have gone very well, for he received a highly desirable placement as the assistant rabbi of Temple Emanuel in Worcester, Massachusetts. This congregation, founded in 1920 and part of the Reform Movement since 1937, was one of the largest in the country, with a membership that rose from 610 families in 1948 to more than 1300 in 1957. Its constituency was mostly German Jewish, solidly middle-class, and active in community affairs. The congregation had built a new synagogue building in 1949 and harbored a renowned religious school, which met three times a week and served nearly a thousand students. Men covered their heads during services, Jewish holidays were celebrated for two days, and children were expected to miss school in order to attend holiday services. Most unusual for the Reform Movement, it prided itself on a daily lay-led minyan, which began to meet in 1954. Its cantor, until 1955, was the talented German Jewish composer of synagogue music Hugo Chaim Adler.[2] The temple had been served by Rabbi Levi Olan, one of the most prominent Reform rabbis of his generation and an active leader in interfaith activities. His successor, Joseph Klein, who led the congregation for close to thirty years, from 1949 to 1977, was also a long-time editor of the *Central Conference of American Rabbis Journal*. Klein took particular pride in inspiring young men in his congregation to study for the rabbinate, successfully sending at least eight prospects to Hebrew Union College. Among them, in due course, would be Rabbi Eric Yoffie, Schindler's successor as president of the Union of American Hebrew Congregations. For Schindler, the newly employed novice rabbi, Klein became an immensely appreciated mentor.

Like assistant clergy in general, Rabbi Schindler was given charge of serving the congregation's youth. In this capacity his native ebullience and lack of stiff formality made him extraordinarily popular. He served as the adviser of a very successful youth group with content-full Jewish programs and he soon became nationally known as an inspiring leader for Reform Jewish young people. Recalling his early years in the rabbinate, Schindler noted that the better part of his time was spent "running from camp to conclave to conclavette."[3] Four times he served as dean for the National Federation of Temple Youth's summer leadership institutes, sometimes also serving as a song leader. He even spent part of his honeymoon taking Jewish youth from the Massachusetts region on a trip to Montreal. Looking back upon his experience as a leader of the youth, he called those times, perhaps somewhat nostalgically, "the happiest days of my career."[4]

A few months after his arrival, at a Friday evening service on October 2, 1953 Schindler was installed as "assistant rabbi," which was his proper designation, although the temple bulletin made no distinction between him and Klein, consistently referring to both men simply as "the rabbis." The Torah portion for the week of his installation was *B'reishit*, Genesis 1:1–6:8, appropriate for his new beginning and coincidentally the same as for his bar mitzvah fifteen years earlier. His installation sermon, given in the presence of his mother and father, cited various appropriate rabbinic passages, all of them in the Ashkenazi pronunciation that was universal in those days. Most unusual was the performance of a Yiddish song composed, of course, by his father.

Schindler had no illusions about the impact of the sermons he delivered at Emanuel. Jokingly, he told a reporter, "Preaching a sermon is about as effectual in actual benefit as dropping medicine from the top of a skyscraper on a crowd below and hoping it will do some good."[5] Nonetheless, he believed the role of the rabbi as preacher was significant and that it differed from the role of the scholar in the classroom. Although he was himself very much engaged in teaching during these early years of his rabbinate, he questioned whether text study should replace the sermon in a religious service. The question arose: "Do we have the right to transform the worshipful atmosphere of the service into the educational study group?"[6] For Schindler, the sermon was art form no less than it was admonition, rebuke, or instruction. Long before he became a rabbi, while living in Manhattan, he had visited the Cathedral of Saint John the Divine in order to learn the art of skillful oratory. For Schindler, the sermon became an oratorical performance: carefully crafted, delivered with humor, verve, and content elevated by emotional crescendo.

Some of the few extant sermons from Schindler's early years are worth examination in order to understand his personal views, whether or not they succeeded in affecting those of his listeners. They touch upon themes that would remain prominent in his consciousness throughout his life: some political, others religious or even theological. It was the age of McCarthyism and its attendant fears, and of Julius and Ethel Rosenberg, executed as spies for a Soviet Union in whose Communist restructuring of society they firmly believed. Against this background, Schindler gave a sermon that can be seen as a veiled response to the tense political atmosphere of the time. In it, he explicitly rejected the notion that Judaism was a religion of revolution and the Jew a radical. Very much in contrast to the political activism that would characterize the Union of American Congregations during his tenure as president, Schindler's sermon advocated a reflective conservatism. To his listeners he said, "Judaism is not even particularly interested in the structure of society; its paramount concern is the individual who makes up society. It seeks to change, not the established social order, but the human soul within that order, whatever it might be. Our spiritual leaders have always taught loyalty to the government as a primary obligation of the religious Jew."[7] He goes on to suggest that "the basic conservatism of the Jew" is justified because "no revolution has ever benefited the Jew."[8] Insofar as Jews enter the political arena, Schindler concludes, the proper counsel is "against radical social upheaval" with a preference for seeking "the world's salvation in evolutionary constitutional change."[9]

In these early days of his rabbinate, the State of Israel was not foremost on the minds of American Jews. Few Jews had visited the ancient homeland. It had been successfully established and no war was imminent. But two moral issues were on the minds of thoughtful Jews: the problem of the excesses of Jewish terrorists and the problem of the Arab refugees that had been displaced when the state was created. Two of Schindler's early sermons raise these issues. In his Chanukah sermon, a few weeks after his installation in 1953, he chose to stress a necessary rededication, not like that of the ancient Jerusalem Temple but rather of the Jewish spirit disturbed by "reports of extremities and excesses"[10] during and immediately after Israel's War of Independence. Without mentioning the Swedish diplomat Folke Bernadotte by name, Schindler here speaks of "the assassination of a man of peace"[11] and other morally questionable actions in the years that followed. In his view, such departures from Jewish morality called for an accounting, a *cheshbon hanefesh*, on the part of Jews everywhere, and not in Israel alone. However, Schindler adds—as he would frequently add in later years when his voice was heard far more widely—that Jewish self-criticism did "not give others the right to criticize us. Let no non-Jew raise his voice against the Jew—whether he wear the collar of a clergyman or the frock of the diplomat."[12] The checkered history of the critics on the outside gave them no right to find fault: "Where were these same right honorable gentlemen when millions upon millions of Jews were gassed, burnt alive and buried alive.... They did not speak up then. Let them remain silent now."[13]

Unlike his sermons addressing Jewish terrorism, Schindler does not evince any Jewish responsibility or guilt with regard to the Arab refugee problem created in 1948. His sermon on the subject is based on the then current Israeli narrative of the Palestinians' departure as entirely provoked by Arab agitators and not by Jewish Israelis. That conclusion served to relieve any pangs of Jewish conscience: "No, we need feel no sense of guilt as far as the Arab Refugee problem is concerned. For the responsibility of the Arab states is the central issue in the refugee debate.... Theirs is the initiative for its creation ... theirs is the onus for its endurance. And above all—theirs is the capacity for its solution ... They alone hold the key to the past and gateway to the future."[14] Its solution was up to the Arab leaders, "vegetating in Capri or on the French Riviera," who "choose to perpetuate the plight of their brethren as a political expedient."[15] Schindler, together with nearly all Jews of that time, believed that it was the responsibility of the Arabs to integrate the refugees in their own countries even as Israel integrated destitute Jewish survivors from the Holocaust in Europe and refugees from Arab lands.

CHAPTER 2: *ASCENDING THE LADDER*   23

Alexander Schindler in the year of his ordination, 1953. *Courtesy of the Schindler family.*

Alexander Schindler had not always been a believer in God. In directing himself to confirmands of the temple, home from their university studies and honored at a Shabbat service in the congregation, their young rabbi chose to speak to them in a sermon titled "Good-Bye God, I'm Going to College."[16] To strengthen the faith of his young listeners, he chose to confess before them his own religious crisis at CCNY, presumably before his army experience and his visit to Dachau. Here he recounted that he had accepted his father's admonition to be firm in faith but quickly spent that faith along with his allowance check. "After my first whiff of philosophy and the sciences, I quickly rejected the religious attitudes transmitted by my parents, abolishing God entirely along the way. I felt certain that this disbelief was the true mark of the grown man and with pride I joined the company of self-styled atheists."[17] He had lost not only belief in God but also "I had little to say for Jewishness as a religion. And I felt sooo sophisticated and mature."[18] His atheism had been a sort of liberation. His ability to refute all the philosophical arguments for the existence of God had made him feel "happy." What led him, not long thereafter, to a positive attitude to religion was not, however, explicitly faith in God. The sentences that follow in his sermon mention God only once; they dwell instead upon the spirituality and intellectuality that Judaism offered. He had come to believe that science might be complemented by religion, not destroyed by it. Religion could supply meaning, which was as valuable as fact; ritual could invest life with holiness. Moreover, the religious community could provide a sense of belonging and the study of Jewish texts supply religious understanding.

Rabbi Schindler did not deal frequently or at any length with the theological problem of evil, made urgent after the Holocaust. However, in 1954, relatively early in his Worcester years, he did speak in a *Yizkor* (memorial) sermon of Judaism's "ardent faith in the immortality of man."[19] Here he expressed the view that the belief in God and the belief in immortality went hand in hand: "One without the other is quite meaningless, and both are necessary if life is to have any meaning."[20] By implication, life after death could therefore counterbalance the tragedies of this life on earth. However, it is possible that he believed more deeply that there really could not be any answer. His illustration for that opinion, which came to him as "a moment of discovery, a moment of revelation," dated back to an experience during his years in the military:[21]

> It happened during the Second World War. Our company was quartered in an Italian farmhouse somewhere in the Po valley. It was a cold wintry day, a day filled with violence, the violent storms of nature, the violent ragings of men. Bombers thundered overhead; the rumbling of deadly guns could be heard. Suddenly, a little boy, perhaps five or six years old, scampered across the courtyard; he was badly frightened by the presence of strangers; tears trickled down his cheek. His mother appeared. She said nothing. She merely opened her arms and smiled. The boy ran to her. No longer afraid, he stopped his weeping; he was safe, he was at peace.

Schindler did not apply this perhaps overly dramatized recollection directly to the Holocaust, but he does say that it made a profound and lasting impression upon him. It taught him "the strength of silence."[22]

Among Schindler's early thoughts on religion there is also the topic he had already addressed in his sketches of the lives of Aimé Pallière and Nehida Remy, the subject that would play a central role in his professional life at the apex of Reform Jewish leadership: the question of proselytism.

In a published article, at a time when he had as yet published very little, Schindler discussed the newly critical attitude among some Christian thinkers with regard to missionizing Jews. Here he applauds the new attitude among leading Protestant theologians, Paul Tillich and Reinhold Niebuhr in particular, who wish to abandon the centuries-long effort to convert the Jews. It is, Schindler notes gratefully with regard to Niebuhr, "the first time in 2000 years . . . that a leading Christian thinker suggests that God speaks to Jews even in our day."[23] Yet with all of his appreciation for prominent Christian theologians who advocated an end to proselytizing Jews, during those same early years of his rabbinate Schindler was propagandizing that contemporary Judaism should move in the opposite direction with regard to Christians. It should reassert itself as a missionizing religion. In a sermon delivered during the tercentenary of Jewish life in the United States, celebrated in the years 1954–55, Schindler maintained that Judaism was not "a parochial religion whose sole interest is self-perpetuation within Jewish ranks, but rather a missionary faith giving its adherents the task of carrying its truths beyond the bounds of the Jewish people in the fervent hope that in the not too distant future men everywhere will recognize that the God, worshiped and proclaimed by Israel, is One, that He alone is God, who was, who is, and who ever will be."[24] Schindler does not regard Jews proselyting non-Jews as merely secondary, but as a primary preoccupation. "The mission of Israel provides us with a *raison d'etre*; it alone gives meaning to Jewish striving and Jewish martyrdom, to our history of pain and degradation."[25] Expressing a thought that he will echo again and again at a later time when his impetus will render the issue broadly discussed in Jewish life, Schindler concludes that advocating for Judaism among non-Jews is the necessary conclusion for all Jews who take pride in their Judaism. Not to do so reflects the sad admission that "we ourselves have come to believe that we have no message."[26]

On at least one occasion, as assistant or associate rabbi, Schindler was called upon to address a dialogue of ministers from varying denominations. In Paul Blanshard's then recently published severe critique of Roman Catholicism, Schindler found a precedent for his espousal of mutual understanding together with passionate critique. Competition[27] among religions, he suggests, can be productive, indeed necessary to sustain pluralism when—as Schindler believed to be the case in the mid-1950s—ethnic pluralism was giving way to ethnic integration. What follows in his address—representing positions that Schindler would continue to hold—is the espousal of two divergent trajectories. Decades before the rise of the Religious Right in America, against which he would later speak out vigorously, Schindler here argues that "we should never be afraid if the adherents of a particular faith seek to reshape the institutions of American culture according to their own scale of values, yes even if they seek to reshape America's laws to conform to *their* moral code."[28] Yet in the same speech, he insists that Judaism unequivocally opposes any effort to diminish the separation of church and state, such as the Religious Right would later advocate, especially in the area of federal aid to religious education. The former view makes room for Jewish political advocacy, which would soon play a larger role in Reform Judaism; the latter sets boundaries to the state's furtherance of religious objectives. He concludes with a caution to avoid the excess of competition that devolves into chauvinism. Perhaps what is most beautiful in Judaism, he sums up, is its "confession of uncertainty in the claim for exclusive truth."[29]

Not surprisingly, during his rabbinate at Temple Emanuel, Schindler was repeatedly accosted by members of the Sisterhood attempting to put an end to his prized status as a bachelor. That status ended not long after he met a young woman—not a member of the congregation—to whom he was immediately attracted. Rhea Rosenblum, born in 1933, was twenty-four years old, eight years younger than the rabbi. Raised in Manchester, New Hampshire, she came from a well-to-do home with parents who were both attorneys. Although her sister, a member of Temple Emanuel, had been convinced Rhea would never go out with a rabbi, Rhea agreed to meet Alexander on a blind date. The talented young woman was a 1955 graduate of Smith College who had spent an academic year abroad and, like Alex, enjoyed photography and classical music. After her new boyfriend reluctantly agreed to lose weight—a problem that, given his love of sweets, plagued him throughout his life—they married in her home on September 29, 1956, with Rabbi Balfour Brickner as the best man. The marriage occurred three years after her husband had become a rabbi at Emanuel. By the date of their wedding he had risen to the rank of associate rabbi, presumably with a commensurate salary increase that made

Alexander Schindler with his wife, Rhea Rosenblum, at their wedding on September 29, 1956. *Courtesy of American Jewish Archives, Cincinnati, Ohio.*

a comfortable wedded life affordable. The local Worcester newspaper described Rhea Rosenblum as "dark-haired and brown eyed, a vivacious homemaker who bubbles over with a contagious enjoyment of life."[30] Like her bridegroom, the bride's favorite sport was skiing. An activist like her husband, she immediately joined Jewish organizations in Worcester, including, as was to be expected, the Temple Emanuel Sisterhood.[31] In the conservative Worcester community, it was regarded as a bit scandalous when the demonstrative Alexander Schindler did not hesitate to hold hands with his new wife in public. Over the years, Mrs. Schindler learned how to bake challah, taught friends and neighbors how to set a Sabbath table, and instructed them on lighting Sabbath candles.

Schindler's tenure at Temple Emanuel, he recalled, was marked by a relationship of "uncommon spiritual harmony and friendship" with Rabbi Klein, which served to sharpen his religious vision. Yet in the spring of 1959, at the age of thirty-three, he decided to leave the congregational rabbinate in pursuit of a broader horizon, accepting an offer to oversee a six-state area as executive director of the New England Council of the Union of American Hebrew Congregations. After a few months, he moved his family (which had grown to include two children) to Newton, Massachusetts, where he would spend the next brief period of his life. Although Schindler remained connected to close friends in Worcester throughout his life,[32] it seemed time to move on and up.

Like other regional directors, Schindler's duties at the UAHC were to work with established congregations, form new ones, and advise the New England Federation of Temple Youth. Although NFTY in the early sixties was remarkably successful locally, regionally, and nationally for engaging teens, Reform Jewish college students did not enjoy similar support from the Movement. Because of his close relationship to young people, Schindler was asked to present his views on the subject to his rabbinical colleagues.[33] Alumni of the Reform youth movement, he noted in his brief address, thought back nostalgically to their days in Reform summer camp, but they were not at home in the interdenominational Hillel activities on campus they encountered when they sought to remain Jewishly connected. For Schindler, this was a problem that required an effective solution. Although he was dedicated to a Jewish identity that ultimately transcended denominational boundaries, he here expressed the view that denominational diversity was required in order to avert "a watered-down faith fully satisfying to none."[34] Positively, he suggested that, while not competing with Hillel Foundations, the Reform Movement should establish Reform "alumni groups," a proposal later taken up by the Movement but with only occasional success. Possibly in his capacity as regional director, Schindler had been able to encourage establishment of such groups in New England universities. We know only that he also hoped to create a college of Jewish studies in Boston to train religious school teachers for Reform Judaism, a task that he seems either not to have undertaken or failed to accomplish.

Probably his most notable accomplishment as regional director was to establish a "big brother" system, whereby each new congregation was teamed with an existing and well-established temple that provided it with lay and professional resources.[35] This was a time when Reform Judaism was expanding, though it was still smaller in size than its Conservative counterpart. In his regional capacity, Schindler was able to contribute to the Movement's growth. In later years he took great pride in the role he had played in creating and personally nurturing new congregations.

Schindler had been in his position as regional director for less than four years when in 1963 the president of the Union of American Hebrew Congregations, Rabbi Maurice Eisendrath, elevated him to a more central position as the Union's national director of education. In this role, his tasks included simultaneous service as the Union's main delegate to the joint Commission on Jewish Education, composed of representatives from both the Union and the Reform rabbinate. Thus, for three years Schindler became the effective head of the entire broad area of Reform Jewish education. It was a position that had grown in size and stature in the preceding years. For more than a generation, Emanuel Gamoran, a layperson with a strong Jewish and Hebraic background, had prompted a virtual revolution in Reform Jewish education. Class hours increased, Hebrew became more prominent, and adult study programs arrived on the scene. Zionism entered the curriculum, and peoplehood became the foundation for religion. Most important, the Union gained broad status as the principal publisher of religious school textbooks, some written by Gamoran or by his wife, Mamie. There was a new emphasis on the specifically Jewish in Jewish education, what Gamoran called "survival values," which reflected both the changing ethnic composition of Reform congregations and Gamoran's own Eastern European and Hasidic background. During his three years in office, Schindler—also of Hasidic stock—strove to deepen Gamoran's curriculum for Reform's congregational schools. He also developed his own philosophy of Jewish education, set forth goals, and launched at least one project of ongoing value to the movement: a Torah commentary composed in the spirit of Reform Judaism.

As the head of education for American Reform Judaism, Schindler confronted a theological divide deeper than it had been in earlier years. In the 1960s the Reform rabbinate contained prominent individuals who deemed themselves religious naturalists, rationalists, or humanists, among them Roland Gittelsohn of Boston and Levi Olan of Worcester and later of Dallas, Texas. But there was also a blossoming movement that was called "covenant theology," which likewise had its avid adherents, and that stressed the existence of a personal and historically faithful God. Among its leading figures was Schindler's almost immediate predecessor as director of education, the covenant theologian Rabbi Eugene Borowitz.[36] With regard to these two positions, Schindler declared himself clearly on the side of the supernaturalist covenant theologians. He saw his own Jewish philosophy as being closer to the traditionalist Conservative leader Solomon Schechter than to the naturalist thinker Mordecai Kaplan, who started what was then called Reconstructionist Judaism.[37] In 1966, Schindler told the Conservative Rabbinical Assembly that "Reconstructionism, nurtured in the bosom of the Conservative movement, in its theology, is far to the left of the current consensus within Reform."[38] And he told fellow Reform educators, "I count myself among them, whose approach to theology is more traditional, to whom God is the Creator, Revealer and Redeemer, who fashioned man and gave him the power to enter into a dialogue with the divine."[39] At the core of the Jewish tradition, he believed, lay the concept of "a continuing covenant with God."[40] Recognizing that no theology would bridge the gap between the two positions and placing himself firmly on one side, Schindler decided that the only common ground on which to propagate Judaism in the classroom was not theology (even as Emanuel Gamoran had derided "theology for tots" when taught in the lower grades), but rather—perhaps influenced by the writings of the Conservative theologian Rabbi Abraham Joshua Heschel—a Judaism of "numinous experience."[41] Clearly he drew on Martin Buber when he told a largely non-Jewish readership that "all learning must be made to serve the end of faith, this end alone, the principal object of being—to help the I encounter the Eternal Thou."[42] Put into language closest to Schindler's own thinking, the ultimate purpose of Jewish education was—expressed by terms taken from Hasidic thought—to instill in Reform Jewish young people a sense of "*kavonoh* [religious mindfulness in prayer] leading to *devekus* [clinging to God]."[43]

If Schindler was not a proponent of teaching religious school children formal religious principles, neither was he in favor of teaching much formal Jewish history, despite the attention he had himself devoted to study of the Holocaust and the influence it had on him. The Holocaust, too, he thought should be taught not as a purely academic subject but rather guided by questions such as "What can we say about the face of man after Auschwitz? And what about the face of God?"[44] The new curriculum toward which he was striving would shift the emphasis away from historical study and language mastery toward "the transmission of belief."[45] In advocating for the expansion of Reform Jewish education on the high school level—one of his foremost objectives—Schindler believed that effective communication with teenagers must focus on current religious and ethical issues through Judaism's unique lens, rather than present a history of the Jewish religion. In short, it was most effective to begin with the present and, only from there, proceed to evolution from the past.[46]

Schindler's critique of religious school education that was too much a narrative of Judaism's past and too little related to young Jews' concerns with their Jewish present was paralleled by his critique of rabbinical education, as he himself had experienced it in Cincinnati. In his student days, the Hebrew Union College faculty was mostly trained in Europe and largely devoted to pure scholarship of a positivistic nature, its interests and concerns far removed from those of the students. Invited to deliver a Founders' Day Address, Schindler deplored the emphasis on historical and linguistic minutiae to the neglect of relevant religious issues. As he expressed it in typical Schindler fashion, "The *daggesh chazak* [a Hebrew grammatical form] is never allowed to suggest the *pintele yid* [the Jewish spark within]."[47] Jewish scholars' strict focus on fact and their disinclination to deal with religious questions of value, for fear of crossing the line between the scholar and the apologist, represented, in Schindler's thought, a failure to play an essential role in shaping an effective religious leadership. Between the academy and the community, Schindler saw himself as representative of the latter.[48]

Necessarily, there were also practical issues that required attention. One of them was the thorny question of religious education within the public school. In 1962 the Supreme Court had ruled that states could not compose and encourage official school prayer. Citing John F. Kennedy in wake of the court's decision, Schindler affirmed the president's suggestion that we should instead "pray ourselves" both at home and in church.[49] Yet he approved of reference to religion in public schools as long as it was not sectarian indoctrination and was fully contained within the boundaries of moral values.[50] Another issue of ongoing concern during this time was academic standards in the religious school. No doubt due to Schindler's influence, the UAHC Biennial Assembly in 1963 passed resolutions calling upon member congregations to confirm only those students who had received a minimum of six years of instruction and that the study of Hebrew be made a requirement for confirmation to a point "sufficient at least to read and comprehend the Hebrew portions of the *Union Prayerbook* and the *Union Haggadah*."[51] Finally, there was the proper training of teachers. To this end, Schindler created a Union "Department of Teacher Education." He argued that Israelis did not necessarily make proper religious school teachers in a Reform institution. Yet, he also believed that the decisions of small congregations to hire non-Jews as religious school teachers, although perhaps not the ideal candidates for such positions, should be respected, especially when these teachers were married to a Jewish partner and when Jewish teachers were simply not available.[52]

Schindler liked to think of himself as one among the men and women who were dedicated to Jewish education. He claimed a close relationship with the National Association of Temple Educators and enjoyed multiple opportunities to speak before their conventions. Late in his career, he was pleased when the Association granted him the title "Reform Jewish Educator," which afforded him the right to add the initials RJE after his name; as he said, Jewish education was "among my first loves."[53] However, on one occasion Schindler misjudged the course of American Jewry. During the period of African American self-assertiveness and just before the Six-Day War, Schindler told his fellow educators he thought the present was revealing "a loosening, a dissolution of the ethnic strains which bound us once," which needed to be compensated through the reinforcement of religious ties "as a unifying bond in their stead."[54] Although he was himself a deeply ethnic Jew, Schindler thought it an age of diminishing ethnicity, when "the American Way of Life is not so open that divergent cultural components can easily be made a part of it."[55] Only religion remained immune to the pressures of conformity. The fulfillment of the Zionist dream made a political Zionist identity less relevant. And where it persisted, political Zionism robbed Jews of their reason for collective continuity in the Diaspora. Clearly that situation, questionable even in the mid-1960s, would change in the wake of Israel's extraordinary—and fervently hoped for—military success in 1967. And Schindler would himself soon come to recognize the large role that Israel played for American Jews.

If Schindler did not clearly see the rise of ethnicism in American society during most of his term as educator, he could hardly overlook the clearest marker of the 1960s—the anti-authoritarianism of the younger generation. In fact, he made that the subject of the final address in his position to the National Association of Temple Educators. So many of the rebels were Jewish, not the least of them Abbie Hoffman—who, Schindler embarrassedly admitted, had been one of his confirmands in Worcester. His response was not to denounce the youthful protestors, but to listen to them sympathetically while placing much of the blame on members of the adult community. Schindler noted that the adults were often hypocrites in failing to bring about a harmony of preachment and practice, for example in condemning but not protesting against the Vietnam War. To be sure, he rejected the arrogance of the youth, but he thought they could be won back to a Judaism that would focus on quenching their "uncommon thirst for spirituality."[56] Schindler also realized, late in 1967, that perhaps he and his listeners had been "premature in reading out ethnicity as a fact of American Jewish life. . . . The very same hippies who decline to serve in Vietnam were among the first to volunteer for Israel."[57]

Alexander Schindler made his most controversial educational proposal during his initial year as director of the Division of Religious Education: In 1963 he joined his colleague Rabbi Jay Kaufman in suggesting that the Reform Movement should support Jewish day schools.[58] This was, to be sure, not a new idea. Jewish day schools (or, "all-day schools" as they were sometimes called) had existed in Reform congregations in the nineteenth century when public education was generally poor, but they had died out some time ago. Then, in 1950, the subject had been brought up for debate before the CCAR, with Emanuel Gamoran presenting "a sympathetic approach" and Rabbi Victor Reichert of Cincinnati's Rockdale Temple emphasizing "its fallacy and dangers."[59] A few years later, members of the faculty and student body of the New York branch of Hebrew Union College–Jewish Institute of Religion asked for a "re-thinking" of the subject, and the idea was then urged by the New England Council of Reform Rabbis. Some Reform leaders had, in any case, begun to send their children to day schools, but to schools under non-Reform auspices. And a good many Reform congregations had started running daily nursery schools, though none had extended its program even as far as kindergarten. Then, in 1963 in response to the HUC-JIR faculty/student petition and by a vote of eight to three, the Commission on Jewish Education created a Committee on Day Schools and selected as its chair Rabbi Bernard Bamberger of New York's prestigious Congregation Shaaray Tefila. Finding the matter too controversial for formal action, the committee decided merely that "the subject should remain under continuing observation."[60] If a congregation were to decide on a pilot project, the commission could provide it with consultative assistance.[61] At no time had the Union formally come out against day schools, but neither had it moved forward toward their establishment. When the matter came to the floor of the UAHC Biennial Assembly in 1963, it was decided to submit the proposal once more to the Joint CCAR and UAHC Commission on Jewish Education, where Schindler, now the Union's director of Jewish education, could play a central role.

The multiple opponents of the project included both laity and some prominent Reform rabbis. The professor of Jewish education at HUC-JIR in Cincinnati declared the proposal to be irreconcilable with "the philosophy of Reform Judaism."[62] There were those who discredited the project by branding it with the alien and off-putting descriptive "parochial." Some raised the Movement's long-standing commitment to public schools, an integral element in its liberalism. Also raised was the fear that day schools would lock Jewish children into an intellectual ghetto and that their secular education would be reduced, making it more difficult for them to gain entry to a prestigious college. And, of course, there was the issue of the separation of church and state, which the Union regularly defended through its Religious Action Center in Washington. Finally, there was the expenditure that a full-scale day school program would impose on the Union's budget, possibly reducing availability of funds for what were regarded as projects more central to its mission. Such arguments carried sufficient weight for Rabbi Maurice Eisendrath, caught between the views of his lieutenants and their opponents, to simply urge calm: No definitive decision had been taken, he noted to a layperson in 1964 who had raised an alarm.[63]

Schindler and his supporters argued contrariwise that it was not enough for only rabbis to possess a thorough Jewish education; it was essential for the Reform Movement to possess a cadre of thoroughly educated lay leadership, as well. They were not suggesting day schools across the board, but simply that they would provide training for the lay elite that was sorely lacking. They were certain that attending a day school would imply neither an endorsement of undesirable segregation nor any infringement upon the church-state divide, as long as such schools would refuse financial assistance from the government. Moreover, as Schindler noted in a letter, numerous Jewish parents were sending their children to private preparatory schools or to public schools where nearly all of the children were Jewish, especially in the New England area.[64] The only difference with a Jewish day school would be the Jewish content of the curriculum.

In 1969 the issue again came before the UAHC Biennial Assembly. This time the plenum was asked to deal with a modest proposal presented by its Committee on Resolutions. The proposal merely called upon the Union not to reject the idea of Jewish day schools completely, but required no responsibility for bringing it to fruition: "Reaffirming our devotion to separation of church and state we strongly urge that full-time Reform Jewish schools be entirely supported by private and Jewish community funds."[65] There would be no "parochial hierarchy," and no authorization for the Union itself to establish such full-time schools. If such schools were to be founded by individual congregations, they were not to exclude non-Jewish children. The proponents of the resolution would have to be satisfied with the provision that gave Schindler's department the right to encourage the establishment of "pilot programs and experimental projects in full-time Reform Jewish education."[66] And yet, when a standing vote was taken, the resolution was defeated.

Thus, Schindler failed to commit the central body of Reform Judaism to taking any initiative on its own to create Reform Jewish day schools. Many years later, at the dedication ceremony of the Rashi School in Boston toward the end of his Union presidency and looking back on his years as the Union's head of education, he expressed regret that he had not been able to do more: "About the best that I could manage was to establish the Union Hebrew High School, which offered part-time Hebrew schooling twice a week and on weekend mornings."[67] Unwilling to abandon the idea of Reform Jewish day schools completely, he continued to push for its realization.⁶⁸ But in the end, even he did not insist on the Union itself undertaking the day-school task. In 1973, after assuming his new capacity as president of the UAHC—at a time when Congregation Rodeph Sholom in Manhattan could pride itself on its congregational day school—he wrote to its rabbi, Gunter Hirschberg, that whatever schools were established should be founded by congregations or private individuals: "The congregation, the concerned parents, these are the ones best equipped to plan and conduct a day school that best meets the needs of their own community."⁶⁹

The Union's role would remain consultative even as Reform day schools began to appear. By June of 1975, there were five of them with about seven hundred students;⁷⁰ ten years later, there were almost a dozen with approximately two thousand students.⁷¹ These day schools and those that followed were all locally initiated and supported. However, Schindler's role in enthusiastically propagating the idea of a more intensive Jewish education among Reform Jews had no doubt carried some significance. He continued to hope for a single central academy of study for Reform Jewish youth, through which the UAHC would create a leadership elite.⁷² But such an academy would have required a major investment on the part of the Union, and for that its leadership was not prepared. The idea remained Schindler's "dream."⁷³

Years later, well into Schindler's presidency of the Union in March of 1988, a Council of Reform Jewish Day Schools came into existence and worked closely with the UAHC. The previous lack of such schools, Schindler noted in an address at the founding conference of the group, had contributed to a severe shortage of rabbis. Young Jews who possessed only a religious school Jewish education simply lacked the fundamental Jewish knowledge and commitment needed to serve as a foundation for rabbinical students.⁷⁴ Schindler noted that he had given "frequent public voice" to his conviction that "only a full-time setting can provide our students sufficient opportunity to be fully schooled in their heritage."⁷⁵ And he used the occasion to launch into a severe critique of Reform Judaism for its failure to create a more particularistic Jewish identity. Jewish young people's growth as Jews, he charged, had "been stunted by our movement's readiness to develop a social conscience in our children and be content to call that 'Jewish identity,' our willingness to sum up the whole Torah, as did Hillel, with words about kindness to our neighbors, but without adding his injunction to 'go and study.'"[76] Delivering a parting blow at the persisting critics of Reform day schools, he exclaimed, "Those who fear that day schools will isolate and ghettoize our children may well themselves be operating under the burden of a ghetto mentality, a mentality that fears Jewish particularism as a handicap, an obstacle to mainstreaming in America."[77]

To be sure, Schindler's vision for Reform day schools was not devoid of elements traditionally characteristic of Reform. He believed that, unlike some Orthodox schools, they should be fully egalitarian, include the children of interfaith couples, encourage social activism, understand Judaism as a living and developing faith, and integrate Jewish with general studies.[78] Thus, Reform day schools would educate not merely knowledgeable Jews, but rather knowledgeable Jews for the Reform Movement.

Schindler realized, however, that it was not only intensive, Reform-oriented Jewish education—at least for an elite of Jewish young people—that was lacking. There was another significant deficit, as well: The Reform Movement lacked a Torah commentary of its own and had been forced to rely on commentaries of a strictly traditional, rather than a historical-critical, orientation. Schindler thought such a commentary was of special importance for Reform Jews since, as he put it, "It is our attitude toward Torah—our answer to the question 'What is Torah?' that marks the divergence between Reform and traditional Judaism."[79] Such a commentary would, he thought, endow "our pluralistic community with a necessary sense of ideological cohesion, providing that centripetal force which Reform Judaism requires to keep the periphery of our movement in touch with the center."[80] He claimed to be the progenitor of the Torah commentary project, writing of it many years later, after it had been successfully achieved, "I began this venture when I was first appointed to the directorship of the Commission on Jewish Education in 1963."[81] He was probably not the first to conceive the idea, but from the start he was involved in its realization.[82] Later he related that "at the very first rabbinical convention I attended after being appointed director of education, Gunther Plaut and I sat down and talked about the whole idea for a Torah commentary."[83] What is certain is that Schindler raised the money and that in his position as head of Reform Jewish education at that time, it must have been he who created what he called the "elaborate machinery of scholars, rabbis, and lay leaders" that enabled the project to move forward.[84] There were, Schindler notes, many trials and errors along the way, but he admitted to being fortunate in securing "the prodigious labors" of Rabbi W. Gunther Plaut, who became the commentary's principal author. According to an oral tradition, Plaut initially presented Schindler with a version that was little more than a compilation of traditional commentaries. Schindler rejected it, insisting that the commentary should reflect the critical thinking of modern biblical scholars and hence the approach to the Torah of Reform Judaism.[85] But, at the same time, it should not "out academician the academicians."[86] He recalled writing a twenty-page critique, which Plaut readily accepted. The process of preparation would take an unexpectedly long time to reach fruition, some eighteen years until the publication date of 1981. Then, within a decade, Schindler claimed, it was selling 100,000 to 125,000 copies annually and making a profit for the Union of $200,000 per year.[87] By then he had long been concerned with other matters and he was not himself a contributor to the volume, but Alexander Schindler surely deserves credit for developing a project that turned Reform congregations toward Torah study to an extent well beyond what had previously been the case.[88]

CHAPTER 3
Becoming the Voice of Reform Judaism

THE EARLY GENERATIONS of American Reform Judaism had been led collectively by dedicated lay leaders, most of whom lived in Cincinnati. In that city on the Ohio River, Rabbi Isaac Mayer Wise first brought unity to Reform institutions when, in 1873, he inspired the president of his congregation, Moritz Loth, to organize a Union of American Hebrew Congregations; two years later in 1875, Wise founded the Hebrew Union College, the first enduring modern rabbinical seminary in the United States. As head of the Hebrew Union College and also president of the Central Conference of American Rabbis beginning in 1889, Wise was the unifying personality within the Movement's spiritual leadership.

At that time the congregational union, under the control of its major donors, lay in the spiritual shadow of the seminary. It was Wise's rabbinical successors as presidents of the College, rather than the lay heads of the Union, who continued to be the collective spokesmen for the Movement. That was as true for Rabbi Julian Morgenstern in 1935 as it had been for Rabbi Kaufmann Kohler in 1915. The Union, although it independently produced religious school textbooks, remained principally the handmaid of the College. This arrangement came under severe criticism in 1941 when Rabbi Louis Mann of Temple Sinai in Chicago accused the Union of escaping the religious challenges of the time, failing to create new congregations in the larger cities, and finding satisfaction as little more than a "religious mail-order business" for its textbooks. The UAHC seemed plagued by a torpor that deprived it of eminence among American Jews.

The lay leadership now decided to select a stronger leader, in hopes of bringing new vigor to the Union. Following a short period as its director, Rabbi Nelson Glueck gave up the position, and in 1943 the choice for new leadership fell upon the ambitious and energetic Rabbi Maurice Eisendrath, then of Toronto, Canada.[1] He was initially given the accepted title of "director" that had been held by his predecessors, making him subservient to the lay chairman of the board. However, it was not long before the enterprising Eisendrath was able to exchange that title for greater prestige and authority as the Union's "president." Glueck, a Biblical archaeologist more interested in pursuing his own research and expanding the seminary than in directing the course of American Reform Judaism, became the leader of HUC. Thus, the Movement's center of gravity shifted from College to Union, and so it remained.

Eisendrath came to the Union at a fortuitous time. During the Eisenhower years, the influence of liberal religion in America, seen as essential for maintaining morale in the struggle against Communism, was growing rapidly. As Jews moved to the suburbs they joined this trend, creating new synagogues in larger numbers. Reform temples appeared where they had not previously been, especially in the West. Attendance and activity within older and newer temples were high, to the point that one sociologist wondered whether the suburbs might not become a "gilded ghetto."[2] From 1949 to 1971 the number of American Reform congregations climbed from less than four hundred to more than seven hundred; membership, it was claimed, had surpassed one million. With this increase in size, the Union was able to expand its program. Crucially—albeit after a protracted conflict with Cincinnati laity—Eisendrath was able to transfer the Union's headquarters to New York, thus enabling it "to swim in the mainstream of Jewish life in America."[3]

Eisendrath was an appropriate and effective leader for the Reform Judaism of his time. He was deeply committed to a strong universalism along with a weak Zionism. A strict rationalist, he believed in a minimum of traditional observance and focused on prophetic Judaism's commitment to social justice.[4] Eisendrath was willing to antagonize constituents, even at the risk of congregations dropping out of the Union, when he took highly controversial positions on causes in which he strongly believed. For example, he expressed his opposition to the Vietnam War early, openly, and vigorously. In 1965, to the biennially gathered leaders of the Movement he declared: "We transgress every tenet of our faith when we fight on another's soil, scorch the earth of another's beloved homeland, slay multitudes of innocent villagers."[5] In 1961, and over concerted opposition, he was able to force a vote in favor of establishing what was to become the Religious Action Center of Reform Judaism in Washington, an institution that has remained central for the Movement. With increased income, he was able to expand those portions of the Union's staff that directed its auxiliaries as well as its education, camping, and regional support programs. His leadership style was distant, evoking respect more than love. He was a man who valued privacy and was not comfortable with small talk, but he was an effective—if rather florid and alliterative—orator and an indefatigable organizer. To maintain the supremacy of the Union over the College, he engaged in an ongoing struggle over common funding with the College's president, Nelson Glueck. After slightly more than a decade in office, he thought it proper to select a vice president, who would be a likely successor when the time came. For this position he chose Jay Kaufman, a highly talented young rabbi. However, when Eisendrath continued to linger in office, Kaufman became impatient and he left the Union in 1965 in order to become executive vice president of B'nai B'rith.[6] Two years later, Eisendrath turned to his director of education, Alexander Schindler, to fill the vacant vice presidency. It is possible Eisendrath made this choice with the thought that the new vice president, after proving himself while in the president's shadow, would at some point become his successor.

When Schindler assumed the vice presidency in 1967, it was at a time when Eisendrath had begun to lose some of his earlier vigor. By the following year he had made the decision to retire in 1973. As his health increasingly deteriorated, he allowed his new vice president to handle the largest portion of the Union's day-to-day organizational management. This meant dealing with staff, budgetary matters, and the various lay boards of the Union. Eisendrath gave his vice president a remarkably free hand, although Schindler was careful not to impose his own views on issues that lacked advance approval by Eisendrath. Such issues, he deemed, were still in "Maurice's ball park."[7]

After he had been in the office of vice president for about four years and had thoroughly acquainted himself with the Union's workings, Schindler convened the UAHC staff at the Union Camp in Warwick, New York, for an undisturbed retreat devoted to serious discussion of the Union's future. He opened the gathering with a lengthy speech reflecting views he had gathered from the participants and blending them into his own vision of the Union's future.[8] He expressed his conviction that in multiple respects American society was "mutating" more rapidly than ever before, to the point that "all of us are beginning to suffer a new kind of illness, a *mal-de-mer* brought about by our inability to gain inner balance on these seething seas of change."[9] There were now many more older members in Union synagogues; Reform Jews took mini-vacations and departed to weekend homes, wreaking havoc with religious school attendance; lifestyles were becoming more diverse. In Schindler's words, "More people are doing their own thing in more and more ways."[10] What then could Reform Judaism offer them?

Schindler's answers reflect opinions that he had developed earlier, beginning in his Worcester days, and that he now wanted to bring to the national organization. In his view, rapid change made religion, which provided a solid foundation, more needed than ever. Even as the external world had become less stable, the inner world of the individual had not. Religion spoke to that inner world, within which "a thousand years are but as yesterday when it is past."[11] It retained its moral mandate and its "need for that insight which emanates from its mystic core."[12] As he had said earlier to Reform educators, he now repeated to the Union staff: What Reform Judaism needed was a turn to "the numinous, a consciousness of the holy, *kavonoh* leading to *devekus*." Moreover, the Reform Movement, Schindler urged, while not neglecting its universal message, should shift in the direction of particularism. The balance, he thought, was well expressed in the metaphor "to affix the mezuzah to the door of our people even while we make certain that these doors remain open to the world."[13]

Similarly, Schindler asserted that the Union should balance ideology and action: "Our innovative efforts should grow from midrash to *maaseh*, beyond theory to practice."[14] Specifically, the Union should enlarge its Israel program, "if only because it is the best vehicle for the nurturing of Jewish identity at our command."[15] Educational efforts should take advantage of technological innovations, make more extensive use of camping, and provide better support for day schools. The Union should encourage more intimate synagogue buildings: "The barrier between the pulpit and the pew must be broken. . . . The hierarchical order of temple life is obsolete."[16] Only at the end of his speech did Schindler hint that this shift in emphasis was necessitated not only by the quest for a new vision but, perhaps more profoundly, by widespread despair. He concluded, "If we despair, despair will be the harvest. If we stand by our tasks, resolutely pledged to pursue them, the impossible will yet be possible."[17]

To understand why the characteristically optimistic Schindler should even mention despair in his address to the Union staff, we need to look more broadly at Reform Judaism during the early 1970s. Already in the mid-1960s a malaise had begun to drift over the American Reform Movement. A widely discussed article had predicted that American Judaism, rapidly assimilating and declining in commitment, was on the path to increased indifference and eventually to disappearance from the American scene.[18] The rapid growth of Reform Judaism during the early decades after World War II had in fact given way to a perceived stagnation. Only a handful of new congregations were entering the Union; membership lists of individual congregations either remained static or slightly declined; ten Reform congregations merged with Conservative synagogues in their area, though nine out of the ten chose Reform affiliation.[19] Reform laypeople who had earlier devoted themselves to their congregations were now often found in the leadership ranks of Jewish federations, which were expanding their activities and becoming the foci of Jewish loyalty and communal engagement. Whereas in earlier times Reform Judaism had been the dominant denomination among non-Orthodox Jews, it was now being overtaken by the Conservative Movement. Religious school populations diminished as the "baby boom" generation moved on to college. This shrinkage resulted in financial stress on the Union's budget; its debt had grown to half a million dollars, and in 1970 alone Schindler thought the annual deficit might reach $200,000.[20] It was small comfort that similar trends were unfolding in liberal, mainline Protestant Christianity and even in Catholicism. There, "churchgoing declined steadily year by year during the 1960s, and the proportion of Americans who thought religion was losing its influence grew as the decade progressed. Terms such as post-Protestant, post-religious, and secular city found their way into common parlance."[21] Only on the far right and far left was the Christian religion still flourishing. American society's commitment to self was overwhelming its commitment to community, inducing Reform Jews, like their liberal Christian counterparts, to attend religious services in gradually declining numbers and leaving rabbis to address ever smaller numbers on Friday evenings (the principal service of the week). Newly ordained rabbis had difficulty finding positions.

The Reform rabbinate was in a pervasive crisis of despair. In response,

Levi Olan, the CCAR president in 1968, initiated a sociological study to determine the views of its members and their congregants. Popularly known by the name of its principal author as the Lenn Report, it shocked many when it showed that only 53 percent of the rabbinical respondents would choose their profession again if they had the opportunity and only 34 percent were completely happy with their choice.[22] While most had remained qualifiedly traditional in belief and practice, and even moved further in that direction, an increasing number had gone decisively in the direction of humanism. (The latter was especially true among Hebrew Union College students, some of whom, though insecure in their faith, had chosen a theological deferment to avoid the Vietnam military draft.)

As the number of interfaith marriages had increased rapidly in the 1960s,[23] the Reform rabbinate found itself deeply divided on how to respond. The chief issue, which absorbed and severely divided the Reform rabbinate for decades, was whether or not Reform rabbis should affirm interfaith couples by officiating at their weddings. The Lenn Report indicated that 41 percent of CCAR members had made the decision to perform interfaith weddings, under varying conditions, while 59 percent did not do so under any circumstances. Two-thirds of Reform congregants approved of their rabbis' participation.[24] Among those most bitterly opposed to any rabbinic sanction of interfaith weddings was Joseph Klein, who had been Schindler's senior in Worcester. Klein was convinced that a rabbi who conducted interfaith ceremonies was being "used" to placate more traditional members of the family and was "contributing to the ultimate destruction of Jewish life, for he is participating in the destruction of the Jewish family and the Jewish home."[25] To Schindler he wrote, "Of course you know my position. I feel very strongly that our whole Reform Movement is being endangered by the men who officiate at mixed marriages without prior conversion."[26] Klein favored a CCAR resolution that would do nothing less than prohibit members from officiation.[27] Two prominent Reform rabbis, David Polish and Roland Gittelsohn, were among those who raised a different objection: The refusal to officiate would "contribute substantially to our current struggle for acceptance in Israel as a legitimately Jewish alternative."[28] In 1982 the Responsa Committee of the CCAR added to the arguments of the opponents the highly controversial conviction that, even if the result of non-officiation should be smaller numbers, "it is far more important to have a strong commitment from a smaller group than a vague commitment from a large number who are at the very periphery."[29]

On the other side of the issue was Schindler's boss as president of the Union. Eisendrath was troubled by what he regarded as the "intolerance implicit in the decree that the rabbi should under no circumstances conduct a marriage ceremony, even for a loyal member of the congregation where a Jewish partner is marrying a non-Jew, especially since this rigidity will not deter those determined to wed."[30] Vehemently agreeing with Eisendrath was Rabbi Eugene Mihaly, professor of midrash at HUC—and someone to whom Schindler frequently turned with questions of Jewish law and tradition. In a lengthy responsum of his own, Mihaly declared that any attempt to restrain rabbis from performing interfaith weddings was against the spirit of Reform Judaism.[31] When the CCAR adopted a resolution at its 1973 convention discouraging rabbis from officiation, Mihaly created the Association for a Progressive Reform Judaism, composed of rabbis who felt that there should not be even the mildest rejection of the position taken by colleagues who affirmed officiation.[32] Their position was strengthened by awareness that approval of such officiation by the laity was considerably higher than among the rabbis, reaching nearly two-thirds.[33] Over time, rabbis largely came to embrace the position that rabbinical officiation was permissible—for some, even desirable—if the couple promised to raise their children as Jews.

From the beginning of his rabbinate until the end of his life, Schindler was an opponent of rabbinical officiation at interfaith weddings. It was one of his most deeply held convictions. He realized that, because of his position, his views carried more weight than those of the average rabbi and he was not averse to using that influence. As he wrote with regard to officiation: "It represents a potential drain on the numeric strength of the Jewish people and on its inner commitment. Whether I like it or not, my officiation would be seen as a seal of approval and would therefore become encouraging of intermarriage. If I participate, I give license to those who say, 'Well, the rabbis are officiating, why in heaven's name is there anything wrong with intermarrying?'"[34] When one of his more traditional colleagues, Rabbi Simeon Maslin, issued a booklet intended to support those Reform rabbis who did not officiate, Schindler was among more than one hundred signatories. Along with Rabbi Gunther Plaut, at the time president of the CCAR, he was "glad to add my *Haskamah*—my endorsement."[35] But he felt the necessity to add that his endorsement was strictly personal and did not reflect the Union's institutional consensus. He could not commit the Union to take an official stand, even though he acknowledged that most of its staff did not subscribe to Mihaly's views. It was also important for Schindler not to give the dispute too much publicity, lest the matter should come to a Biennial Assembly of the Union where someone—probably a layperson—would introduce a resolution unilaterally affirming rabbinical officiation.[36] He was also convinced that on this subject each rabbi had to make an individual decision: "The rabbi's conscience must remain unfettered."[37] Hence a congregation, while legitimately raising the question in interviewing a candidate for its rabbinate, did not have the right to determine for the rabbi "what he should or should not do."[38]

A few years later, Schindler wrote of his own personal practice in regard to officiation: "When I know the couple, at least one of them, when I am dealing with the child of dear friends or even with family members, I will attend the wedding if I can and express some words of mazal tov and good wishes at the reception or dinner following the ceremony. I leave the door open and do my best to bring the couple closer to Judaism. I seek to make them aware that we are willing to welcome them, to help the non-Jewish partner learn about Judaism, to assure them they are both welcome at the synagogue."[39] Schindler believed that his presence would reinforce the notion that the couple was not Jewishly rejected.[40] When, in 1986, one of his daughters married the son of a Lutheran minister, the ceremony was conducted by a justice of the peace. Schindler was present and "said some words, as did her father-in-law, after the couple had been pronounced man and wife."[41]

Highly distressing to many Reform rabbis during the years of Schindler's vice presidency and thereafter was that while congregants understandably rated "being an ethical person" as ranking highest in their Jewish consciousness, they placed "synagogue worship" at the very bottom of their list.[42] Apparently, the low attendance at services was anchored in a value system that did not favor active participation in worship services—which rabbis regarded as their central rabbinical role. Moreover, in addition to this gap between clergy and congregants, rabbis were suffering a certain loss of prestige as university scholars, rather than congregational rabbis, were rapidly becoming the principal exemplars of depth in Jewish learning.

Schindler responded to these findings of the Lenn Report by admitting that "we are in ideological disarray.... We need to decide, and more quickly than with deliberate speed, what we believe as Reform Jews, why we believe it, and how—beyond theory—this belief can be transmitted into the life style of our congregants.... And to some things we must muster the courage to say 'No.' The risk of schism inheres in such an effort. The contrary risk is greater still. When anything goes, when each man can do what is right in his eyes, we hazard something more than fragmentation of the edges. We risk the disintegration of the core."[43] With all of Schindler's desire to extend Judaism outward, he expressed a parallel and continuing concern with maintaining inner unity. Other rabbis agreed and moved toward a new platform for the Reform Movement that would document a new commonality, intended to coincide with the centennial of the Union in 1973. But initial efforts at a successful formulation failed, and only in 1976 was "Reform Judaism: A Centenary Perspective" adopted by the CCAR.[44] Largely the work of Rabbi Eugene Borowitz, it—for the first time in an American statement of Reform ideology—firmly stressed ritual and prayer as well as moral "obligations." The new platform was more in line with Schindler's philosophy of Judaism than were the earlier Classical Reform statements, which had neglected practice in order to give greater centrality to belief and ethics.[45]

On the heels of the Lenn Report, which focused principally on the rabbinate, came the UAHC-sponsored "Fein Report," with questions focused wholly on the laity.[46] Like its predecessor, it too showed that Reform laypeople believed that it was far more essential for a Jew to lead an ethical life than it was to attend services, in this case even on the High Holy Days—especially among younger respondents. The report also indicated declining commitment to marrying within the faith, especially among the youth, where such commitment stood at less than 10 percent.[47] Moreover, congregants had come to perceive the rabbi in a narrower role, principally as the purveyor of life-cycle events rather than as the preacher whom one regularly came to hear at worship services on Friday evenings. Whereas

Schindler had expressed hope for the future through the deepening of an individual's religious quest, this new study's authors suggested a different direction: the revival of Reform Judaism could be achieved by rebuilding an explicitly longed-for sense of community within a fragmenting, excessively individualistic general society. Although he continued to stress the importance of the individual, Schindler must have liked that proposal since it conformed to his own broader view.[48] He favored giving this second study wide attention.

Although as vice president Schindler was not yet in a position to respond to the crisis by striking out boldly on his own, he did express personal views on specific subjects of concern to the Reform Movement. One of these was the alienation of Jewish youth from the Reform temple. The 1960s had been a period of youthful revolt, spurred by the civil rights movement and the Vietnam War. Within Reform Judaism the "generation gap" seemed to be expanding during the Nixon presidency, as some Jews of the older generation shifted in the direction of political conservatism. Schindler, who had always felt close to Jewish young people, argued for a solution that the older generation was to bring about for the sake of the younger. He urged the older adult community to "look beyond their unkempt hair, their extravagant dress and their outrageous manner of speech."[49] The younger generation's rebellion, he maintained, was against religion only when it was too narrowly conceived: "They reject institutionalism with its swollen pride and its divisiveness."[50] If members of the older generation wanted to maintain a spiritual connection with the younger, then it was incumbent upon them to "join the young in their condemnation of racial discrimination, poverty, and the war in Vietnam."[51] To Schindler's mind, the protest of youth was nothing less than "what religion, at its finest, has always been about."[52]

For Schindler, that "religion at its finest" centrally involved faith in God and the practice of individual personal morality as well as social morality. Both were contentious topics during these years. The "death of God" debate, arising in the 1960s, had gained prominence in the mass media, having spread from theologians and philosophers to the general public. Though it began within the sphere of Christian theology, it reached the Jewish community, especially after *The New Yorker* devoted three successive issues to the subject. As surveys showed Jews to be more disbelieving than either Catholics or Protestants, the revived notion of a God who had died or never existed found resonance in their ranks and required a response from Jewish religious leaders. For his part, Schindler argued that, unlike Christianity, modern Judaism had long made its peace with secularism, had abandoned unsupportable theological ideas, and yet had been able to maintain a sense of the sacred. He wrote, "Sometimes I think that about the only place God might really have been dead is in the seminaries and the learned tomes of theologians."[53] Here again, for Schindler it was the young people, with their firm commitment to the sacredness of human life, who were religious in a deeper sense than many of their church- and synagogue-going parents.[54] And it was not the rational in religion that touched their minds, which remains attractive, but the mystical, the Hasidic, that "sets their souls on fire."[55]

Along with the death of God debate came a fresh discussion of personal morality. The old prescriptive variety—based on text and tradition—was being challenged in public discourse by a new constellation termed "situation ethics," which subjected moral decision-making to the particular circumstances of the time, place, and individual.[56] Speaking to his rabbinical colleagues, Schindler affirmed his attraction to this mode of ethical thought: "I like this 'new morality,' as I perceive its mood. I respect its openness. I appreciate its hope. I respond to its essential dynamism and its insistence on passionate involvement. As a system of thought it may not be sufficient for Judaism but its major thrusts that focus on contextual considerations and especially its celebration of individual responsibility—these certainly are congenial to our ethos."[57] Schindler also regarded this present-focused morality as a bridge stretched toward those who stood outside the community of faith, a bridge leading from moral action inward to religious belief. Placed between libertinism and legalism, it was, he thought, conducive to Judaism—at least in its Reform variety. However, he was also critical. Situation ethics exalted love as the ultimate moral principle. For Schindler, that was a dangerous proposition, for love in the human psyche, he believed, was intrinsically related to lust, "and when the former is professed, the latter, more often than not, is purposed."[58] He concluded that as important as context is for Jewish moral action, Jewish tradition acts as a brake upon untrammeled individual prerogative. It is neither fully heteronomous nor fully autonomous, but seeks to balance

Rabbi Maurice Eisendrath with Rabbi Schindler. Rabbi Erwin Herman stands between them. *Courtesy of American Jewish Archives, Cincinnati, Ohio.*

the two. Judaism is a religion that recognizes the worth both of commandments and of morally responsible free choice.

Maurice Eisendrath, too, was severely disturbed by the degree of discontent that the sociological studies were revealing within the Reform Jewish world. But whereas Schindler tried to put positive spin on it, the UAHC president chose rather to be defensive or simply to give up. "It requires consummate *chutzpah*," he told fellow rabbis, "an extraordinary degree of audacity, to report on any of our Establishment institutions in this day of widespread denigration of whatever they are striving to accomplish."[59] If the criticism of the Union and the College, reflected in the Lenn Report, were at all valid—which Eisendrath did not believe to be the case—"then it is indeed time for a change, for many changes, in very truth."[60] For that reason he had authorized the Fein Report. And change was already set in motion; the time had come for Eisendrath to retire: "Just two days ago, the Board of the UAHC unanimously adopted my recommendation to elect our high-minded, warm-spirited colleague, Rabbi Alexander Schindler, President of the UAHC as of January 1, 1974."[61]

That decision, however, was not uncontested. There were Reform lay leaders who believed that—with both Hebrew Union College and the Central Conference of American Rabbis headed by rabbis—the Union should revert to lay leadership, as had been the case before Eisendrath came into office. If one testimony is to be believed, Eisendrath himself "had always known of the strong undercurrent of opposition to his having assumed the presidency and that he recognized the need for a change once he passed from the scene."[62] In any case, there was very strong lay opposition to Schindler being promoted to the Union's highest office. The president of a major Reform congregation communicated to all fellow temple presidents his belief that "it was a mistake for the lay people to abdicate their responsibility" when they had allowed Eisendrath to become the UAHC president.[63]

Initial opposition to Schindler as president came not only from the laity.[64] In a much discussed article, Rabbi Eugene Borowitz, while not criticizing his colleague personally, attacked the centrality that Eisendrath had given the Union within the Reform Movement. The organized Reform rabbinate had "been dwarfed by the growing activity of the Union"; it "had displaced the CCAR as program leader of Reform Judaism."[65] Whereas lay opposition to Schindler's candidacy was based on his being a rabbi, Borowitz's milder objection was the opposite: He was not enough of a rabbi. Though Schindler had been an assistant and associate rabbi, he had never served a congregation of his own. Neither he nor the incoming leaders of the College and CCAR (who likewise lacked sufficient congregational experience) possessed the broader vision that transcended their institutions.[66] It may be unkind, but nonetheless not unthinkable, that Borowitz, who had been a senior congregational rabbi, was unhappy that he had not been selected for one of the three positions.

When the Union gathered for its 52nd General Assembly in New York, from November 9 through 13, 1973—its centennial year—Maurice Eisendrath was prepared to deliver his final presidential sermon before his scheduled retirement on December 31. However, it was not to be. On the first day of the assembly, on Friday afternoon, Schindler went to Eisendrath's hotel room to wish him "Good Shabbos." The outgoing president then reportedly said to his designated heir, "I'm so glad that the Union is in your hands. Carry on."[67] Shortly thereafter, Eisendrath was stricken with a fatal heart attack only hours before he was due to speak. His vice president made the announcement to the shocked thirty-five hundred delegates and their guests. Not wanting Eisendrath's final message to be lost, Schindler then delivered the presidential address himself, allowing his predecessor's words to be heard one last time. They resonated the rhetoric that typified the man who had led the Union for three decades: "The world needs Judaism—its *menshlichkeit* instead of the machismo of today's ubiquitous violence; its optimism in the face of despair; its *rachmanut* [mercifulness] in the face of human callousness; its reverence for the life of the mind in defiance of emotionalism run riot; its love of learning and passion for justice; its intoxicating toast, *l'chayim*, "to life"; its hunger for peace as the apex of God's kingdom; and its partnership with God in setting the world aright."[68]

The gap in presidential leadership lasted only three days. On November 12 at Temple Emanu-El in New York, Alexander Moses Schindler, forty-eight years of age, was consecrated as the new president of the Union. He would now be the principal voice of American Reform Judaism. In place of Eisendrath, Rabbi Roland B. Gittelsohn of Boston—one of the most prominent rabbis in Reform Judaism—was chosen to enact a symbolic passing of the Torah to the initiate. In his address, Schindler articulated desires he had cherished earlier and that had set him apart from his predecessor. He called for an "end to minimalism"[69] and shared, as an example of greater intensity, his vision of at least one academy for full-time Jewish study under UAHC auspices. In contrast to Eisendrath's rationalism, he called, once again, for a reevaluation of the "mystical core" of Judaism, a shift in emphasis intended especially to appeal to the younger generation, some of whose members were drawn to a variety of cults or to Oriental religion. And he argued for a relationship to Israel that was not only political, but that radiated from within, "a deeper, more abiding bond of a common community of faith."[70] He concluded with a self-description, a reflection on who he was and who he wanted to be. The language, which some praised for its poetic quality, and the mild German accent were very different from Eisendrath's stentorian unaccented tones. Schindler said, "Above all, I commend to your benevolence a man who wants only to be your brother, who loves this people Israel with an abounding love, who wants to walk with you, so that together we will find and deepen conviction in our bewildered and bewildering world."[71] Most extraordinary—especially within the Reform citadel of Temple Emanu-El—was the inclusion of the Yiddish song *Netzach Lied*, a composition by his father that extolled the eternality of the Jewish people. It mattered not that the song had originally been written for the Tze'irei Agudat Yisrael, the youth of Orthodox Judaism.

Among those affected by the consecration address was a reporter from the National Religious Party of Israel, who conveyed his impressions for his party's newspaper, *Ha-Tzofeh*. Needless to say, he did not express any solidarity with Reform Judaism—as usual, he referred to Reform rabbis as *rabbaim* and not properly as *rabbanim*—but the article was nonetheless unusually positive, in particular with regard to Alexander Schindler. The reporter believed the selection of the new president represented an extraordinary turning point in the history of the Reform Movement: "It was easier to believe that a Jewish refugee from Germany would be appointed Secretary of State than that a Jew of Eastern European origin, the son of a Belzer Hasid and poet for Agudat Yisrael, would be chosen as president of the Reform rabbis in the United States."[72] The anonymous writer was gratified that Schindler spoke of *ahavat Yisrael* (the love of the Jewish people), that—in contrast to previous Reform leaders—he had taken a clearly Zionist stand, and that he had spoken out against widespread ignorance of Jewish sources. He concluded that Reform Judaism "had come a long way" and that it was important to pay attention to the vast number of American Jews who stood on the threshold of totally losing their religious and national Jewish identity. Schindler, he rejoiced, represented a thrust in the direction of reintegration within the Jewish people. This extraordinarily favorable reception of Schindler's election in the Israeli Orthodox press was, less surprisingly, echoed in the religiously more neutral *Jerusalem Post*. In an interview conducted in Israel, its reporter was pleasantly surprised to hear Schindler tell him "in his erudite but accented English" that he did not seek to cut himself free of his roots, "but on the contrary he nurtures them and seeks to transplant them, suitably adapted, into the context of the New World and the new Judaism as he sees it."[73]

The unexpected sudden demise of Maurice Eisendrath—who at the time of his death was about to continue his career of leadership by assuming the presidency of the World Union for Progressive Judaism—and the joyous inauguration of Alexander Schindler took place in the wake of the shock unleashed by the surprise attack initiating the Yom Kippur War. Concern for the State of Israel, which Schindler deemed "in a large measure the arena in which the destiny of the Jewish people is settled,"[74] would soon and unexpectedly assume a greater centrality in his professional career than it had for Eisendrath. Within a month of his consecration, he embarked on a three-day trip to Israel along with Matt Ross, the chairman of his board, and other American Jewish leaders. The group met with leading politicians of various parties; possibly this was the first time that Schindler met Menachem Begin. They journeyed through the Sinai and dined with Prime Minister Golda Meir. Schindler's general impression, as he reported it, was depressing: "The mood in Israel is bleak. The sorrow of loss is very great; not a family is untouched by tragedy; indeed, all Israel is an enlarged single family which now mourns."[75] There was fear that the proposed peace agreement emerging from Geneva would now be less to Israel's advantage than it would have been before the war. Visiting a field hospital, Schindler heard the parent of a lone wounded soldier responding to his words of consolation, "Don't you know that there are more than two thousand mothers in Israel who envy me?" This trip no doubt played a role in bringing the new Union president into closer personal acquaintance with Israeli political leaders, as well as the associated American Jewish leadership from across the religious and ideological spectrum. That would prove to be useful only a few years later. Schindler ended his report with an announcement of greater commitment: "Our fall 1974 Board meeting will be held in Israel."[76] Yet on the eve of departure for that meeting, ten months later, Schindler expressed a critique of the hitherto uncritical relationship of American Jewry to Israel, especially as it had developed following the Six-Day War of 1967—a critique that he would repeat in various forms thereafter. He told the Board members:

> Again we record, without any satisfaction whatsoever, that there were in the leadership ranks of Reform Jewry those who forewarned that Israel could *not* survive by the strength of her arms alone, that she must come to terms with her neighbors as best and as soon as she can. If we have a regret, it is that we did not give voice to such views with sufficient force, that we too were captured and enraptured by the euphoria which prevailed, and that we told our brothers in Israel *not* the truth as we saw it but rather what we thought would please them to hear.[77]

But Schindler did not yet express this critique publicly on the Board's Israel trip. When he introduced Prime Minister Yitzhak Rabin during a meeting in the K'nesset, he defined the Reform Movement as *ohavei Yisrael*, noting institutions it had founded in Israel such as the Leo Baeck School in Haifa, and taking pride in the formation of the first Reform *garin*, a group of young people determined to found a Reform kibbutz in the Aravah. He urged that Reform Judaism be granted full privileges in return for increasingly establishing itself in the state.[78] Schindler was convinced that political and fiscal bonds with Israel were insufficient. If there were to be deeper ties, they would have to rest upon common religious values.[79]

The Reform Movement's plan for development in Israel at this time, however, proved to be a source of intense internal conflict. Shortly before Schindler assumed the Union presidency, it was decided that an American Reform rabbi, Herbert A. Friedman, would be appointed as the chief fundraiser for Reform Jewish expansion in Israel. Friedman had achieved a record of remarkable success in his capacity as CEO of the United Jewish appeal. In 1971, his family moved to Israel, where he continued to work part-time for the UJA but also took on a position created for him as director of planning and development for HUC-JIR and the World Union for Progressive Judaism. He promised to use his well-established contacts with wealthy Jews to raise funds for a "world center" for the Reform Movement in Israel where Rabbi Richard Hirsch, earlier director of the Religious Action Center in Washington, had just relocated as president of the World Union.[80]

Schindler was never an opponent of Reform development in Israel, but he lacked the fervent enthusiasm for the project displayed by Friedman and Hirsch. Diverging views over how to raise and disburse funds for Reform Judaism in Israel resulted in conflict with Friedman and strained the long-lasting friendship that Schindler enjoyed with Hirsch. Returning from a trip to Europe, he suggested rather pugnaciously to Hirsch that the World Union should rather undertake a major effort in France, where he thought it criminal not to act: "You know how stubborn I am and once I've set my mind on something, I won't give in until it is achieved, so you might as well make life easier for yourself by coming up with some ways and means for proceeding here."[81]

The conflict with Friedman concerned the latter's excessive demands for compensation and expenses while he was expending, in Schindler's opinion, too little effort.[82] By the end of 1976, Schindler had severed Friedman's financial arrangement with the College and the World Union.[83] The strains with Hirsch arose from the latter's insistence that the UAHC apply more of its budget to the establishment of a physical "world center" of the Movement in Jerusalem; whereas Hirsch wanted buildings, Schindler believed program should have priority over property. Moreover, neither he nor the Union's Board was willing to jeopardize American activities in order to increase support, beyond a certain measure, for expansion in Israel.

Meanwhile, settled back in his New York office on the top floor of the "House of Living Judaism" at 838 Fifth Avenue—directly opposite Temple Emanu-El in Manhattan—the new president found himself heading an organization in financial distress. The crisis in oil prices and the stock market crash, which began in 1973, led to a recession that severely affected the UAHC budget. Unhappily, expenditures exceeded income. Schindler noted that one reason for this was that the synagogue was not being given priority in the Jewish philanthropic community. Instead, donations were being made to the local Jewish Federation at the expense of the national Reform Jewish Appeal. Israel's spiritual and ideological centrality in the early 1970s, which Schindler supported not less than other American leaders, was having negative consequences for his own organization.[84] And yet, Schindler was a savvy enough politician to know that contributions increase when a deficit budget is combined with hopeful prospects. Thus, at the same time that he was complaining about insufficient donations, he was also pointing to an apparent recovery. The "decade-long decline and stagnation in membership growth"[85] had been halted, he claimed; many of the Union's 715 synagogues were growing again, albeit only slightly. There was also now an increasing number of American Jews who identified as Reform; there were "hundreds" of synagogue *chavurot*, groups devoted to more intense Jewish living; and there was a 30 percent increase in the number of Jewish youngsters attending UAHC youth programs in the United States and in Israel. Beyond statistics, he noted that Watergate, the economic crisis, and the American failure in Vietnam had produced a disillusionment that resulted positively in a search for "newer and truer values, for deeper personal meaning."[86] This spiritual quest, he believed, had resulted in the more favorable statistics.

Only in urban-center congregations, especially in areas of New York, was decline in membership continuing. Eisendrath's move to the metropolis had not brought appreciably larger numbers of New York's Jews into the Reform fold. But like his predecessor—who had been very interested in having the Movement focused where it could be in close contact with the larger Jewish community—Schindler did not regret the decision; indeed, it was quite the opposite. Although he had been ordained in Cincinnati, he thought that it was a mistake for the College-Institute to invest so much money there; it should have moved with the Union to New York or to some other major center of Jewish life, he thought: "The faculty members of HUC by and large have no feeling of what is going on in the mainstream of the Jewish people and there's the pity."[87] However, the president of the College-Institute during Schindler's time, Alfred Gottschalk (whom Schindler disdained), though like Schindler a German-born New Yorker, was not about to give up the elaborate and impressive campus that had been expanded by his predecessor, the well-known biblical archaeologist Nelson Glueck. Moreover, the Cincinnati campus continued to attract students who found the life of a smaller midwestern city more conducive to intensive learning than the hectic atmosphere of New York. Schindler indicated that, were he to be invited by the rabbinical students, he would always be willing to accept an invitation to speak in Cincinnati.

There were also strains within the organization itself. Schindler appointed Albert Vorspan, a highly talented layman, to be his vice president. Vorspan had already served the Union under Eisendrath, building the Movement's social justice program and at times helping to draft his speeches. Although politically he was more to the left than Schindler, Vorspan became not only the new president's highly effective associate and mentor in matters of social justice, but also his confidante and, it seems, the only Union official who was also a close personal friend. They both had large families, liked telling jokes, and enjoyed smoking good cigars.[88]

But beneath these two top executives there was discontent among at least some lower members of the staff. One anonymous individual, who had been on the staff since early in the Eisendrath years, complained to Schindler and Vorspan of the Union's "level of mediocre performance,"

Rabbi Schindler with his loyal assistant Edith (Edie) Miller. *Courtesy of American Jewish Archives, Cincinnati, Ohio.*

of executives who, wanting to be loved, engaged in favoritism, and of the resulting credibility gap between the top level of administration and all the levels beneath it. The conclusion was drawn: "We have run ... the Union as though it were a family-owned candy store on the corner. In fact, the Union runs itself—and us."[89]

Perhaps with such criticism in mind, Schindler appointed a remarkable woman to be assistant to the president. Edith (Edie) Miller, an active member of the Stephen Wise Free Synagogue in Manhattan, was a Jewishly knowledgeable feminist. As a member of the Task Force on Rabbinic Families, she railed against the notion that a woman who married a rabbi should be satisfied with her role as a rebbetzin. It was "a sad state of affairs," she believed, "when people are thus relegated to but one role in the minds of others," overlooking the many other contributions that they could make if regarded as "total persons."[90] In 1975, when chairing a special liturgy committee of the New York Federation of Reform Synagogues, she told the group that "we can no longer accept the use of masculine terminology on the basis that it is 'generic' and covers all humankind. We want language which utilizes words encompassing male and female together and as one."[91] Miller had at one time worked for Eisendrath, but she left, along with Jay Kaufman, to join the staff of B'nai B'rith. After Kaufman's early death, she returned to the Union. Miller knew the UAHC—its structure, activities, and policies—so well that she could and did act as Schindler's liaison to his staff, to the Reform lay leadership, and to other Jewish organizations.[92]

The early years of Schindler's presidency also involved at least one instance in which he attempted to use his limited authority to influence an American political matter. In 1974, General George S. Brown, who had attained the highest office in the American military, gave public expression to distinctly antisemitic tropes before an audience at Duke University. In putting forth his view that military aid to Israel was due to Jewish pressure, he said of American Jews, "They own, you know, the banks in this country, the newspapers. Just look at where the Jewish money is."[93] In angry response, Schindler wrote to then president Gerald Ford that "General Brown's explosion was defamatory, malicious, false, and betrays so colossal a defectiveness of judgment that one has to tremble at the knowledge that such a mentality occupies the chairmanship of the Joint Chiefs of Staff."[94] In the interest of America, Schindler wanted Brown fired immediately. In a personal letter, Ford replied that although he did not plan to ask for Brown's resignation, he had "publicly rebuked the General and privately conveyed to him in no uncertain terms my disapproval of his comments."[95] Whether Ford's rebuke or Brown's public apology were due in any degree to Schindler's letter is unclear.[96] But for Schindler, the exchange marked entry into a political sphere where he would soon play a march larger role.

CHAPTER 4
Spokesman for American Jewry

THE ESTABLISHMENT of the State of Israel in 1948 created a new situation for the Jews of America. As the largest Diaspora Jewish community and as citizens of the country on which the new state depended for political and financial support, American Jews felt an obligation to play an unprecedented mediating role between governments. They had relied on the American constituents of the international World Zionist Organization and the World Jewish Congress for that purpose, but these institutions were not structured to play a unified representative role.

During the early years of Israeli statehood, the foremost international Zionist leader was the European Nahum Goldmann, who served for a time simultaneously as the president of both the WZO and WJC. It was he who, from the Jewish side, now felt the need for closer political contact between American Jews and the American government, especially its State Department. However, the initial impetus for this closer contact came from outside the Jewish community. As Schindler recalled it, the American secretary of state, John Foster Dulles, called Goldmann in for a meeting during the Suez crisis of 1956 and showed him his calendar, which listed appointments with seventeen different "spokesmen" for American Jewry. "Look here," said Dulles, "either you people get yourselves organized, or I won't see any of you."[1] Goldmann too was considering a single Jewish organization that could speak for the interests of American Jewry as a whole, especially in regard to Israel. Although an active Zionist, he believed that world Jewry—not Israelis alone—should play a role not only in Diaspora Jewish affairs but in those of Israel, as well. Goldmann was only too happy to respond to American pressure with the establishment of an unprecedentedly broad umbrella American Jewish organization, which became known as the Conference of Presidents of Major American Jewish Organizations (Presidents' Conference). In his autobiography, Goldmann related, "I succeeded in convincing the then president of B'nai B'rith, Philip Klutznick . . . as well as the leader of Reform Judaism, Rabbi

Maurice Eisendrath, to join me in convening a conference of the presidents of all the major Jewish organizations in order to create an informal forum for the discussion of all questions bearing upon [the relationship between] America and Israel."[2] In a memoir written on the occasion of the UAHC centennial in 1973, Eisendrath confirmed his role, even according himself equal standing with Goldmann in the work of founding the organization. That Maurice Eisendrath—and with him the Reform Movement—were among the founders of an organization in which the UAHC would be only one member among others testifies to the fact that already in Eisendrath's time, during the 1950s, Reform Judaism was reaching out beyond its own organizational periphery to the larger American and world Jewish communities.

Eisendrath also noted that his decision to join the effort had led to a rash of resignations from the Union's Board, probably because there continued to be opposition within the Reform leadership to expanding Union activities beyond the realm of Reform Judaism itself.[3] The same reluctance manifested itself at that time in opposition to Union membership in the American Section of the World Jewish Congress. Even as Alexander Schindler backed Eisendrath with regard to Reform's association with the Presidents' Conference, so did he justify membership in the World Jewish Congress. Writing as vice president of the Union in Eisendrath's name, he revealed what he regarded as a fundamental necessity for Reform Judaism:

> The Congress, marginally noted, is also the only organization in the international sphere in which the Reform Jewish community does not have some kind of second-class citizenship. In many quarters we are totally ignored. Not so in the ranks of the World Jewish Congress. After all, the Congress was founded by a Reform rabbi—Stephen Wise—and moreover, while its present president, Nahum Goldmann, is not a Reform Jew, Reform Jews are in the highest level of the Congress leadership, and such names as Joachim Prinz and Philip Klutznick are bandied about as likely successors to Nahum Goldmann.[4]

The Presidents' Conference developed gradually, from a loose association devoted almost solely to strengthening the American government's support for Israel and consisting only of the presidents of the largest American Jewish organizations, into a more structured forum with broader aims. The Union of American Hebrew Congregations was among the fifteen founding members, one of the seven that were not specifically Zionist organizations. Not only did Eisendrath himself attend the meetings, but so did Jay Kaufman, his vice president until 1965. In a note to Eisendrath, Kaufman revealed a surprising rumor: "Again and again voices are being raised requesting that Rabbi Eisendrath accept the presidency of the Presidents' Conference. I expect there will be a strong démarche to achieve this end."[5] Such an initiative did not materialize, in all likelihood because, given the Reform Movement's earlier anti-Zionism and also Eisendrath's initial coldness to it, the Zionist delegates would not have supported it.

Nonetheless, it is important to note that at least within some circles, Reform was no longer regarded as ineligible for broader communal responsibilities. As a delegate to the Conference, together with Eisendrath, Kaufman had already deepened Reform involvement in the organization. Without reluctance to make known his views regarding the Conference structure, Kaufman had argued, for example, that its purposes should be expanded beyond Israel-American relations, that its domination by the Zionist organizations be diminished, and that its membership be limited for greater efficiency.[6] When Schindler became vice president of the UAHC two years later, he assumed Kaufman's role as a delegate, familiarized himself with the Conference's work, and also shared some of his own opinions and critiques. He regarded the organization as mostly a waste of time, little more than useless talk: "Our endurance is tested, especially by those eternal, infernal 'general debates' whose rules are that there are no rules. Anyone can speak on any subject he pleases—whether germane to the discussion or not—for as long as he pleases. Young Israelis disdainfully designate such debates as *Zionut*, associating the term with interminable talk and little action; they prefer the direct, unvarnished speech of a Dayan. Conferees are of an older generation; they still respond to the rhetoric of [Abba] Eban."[7]

Even before he became its chairman, Schindler was working to make the Conference fairer and more effective. During the time that Herschel Schacter, an Orthodox rabbi, served as chairman of the Conference (from 1967 to 1969), Schindler joined with Rabbi Wolfe Kelman, the director of the Conservative Movement's Rabbinical Assembly, in expressing "outrage" in regard to the Conference's nomination procedures. Non-Orthodox delegates had been promised chairmanships and vice-chairmanships, but the promises had not been fulfilled. Writing to "Dear Herschel," Schindler concluded bluntly, "In a word, my friend and colleague Herschel, we have just about had it, and because I know that you are a thoroughly decent human being, you will understand our chagrin and dismay."[8]

Yet another issue of concern to Schindler already at this stage of his relationship with the Presidents' Conference, and a matter that he would bring up again and again, was its passive role vis-à-vis Israel. In this complaint he was encouraged by Joachim Prinz, who had served as president of the Conference immediately before Schacter. Prinz—a liberal rabbi, though not institutionally associated with Reform Judaism—suggested to Schindler in 1970 that when Schindler participated in an upcoming CCAR meeting with then Israeli prime minister Golda Meir, he should make her aware of the discontent felt by the Presidents' Conference at having to take orders from the Israeli embassy. Prinz asserted—and presumably Schindler agreed—that taking orders made the Presidents' Conference "politically useless.... It would be catastrophic," he added, "if the Central Conference [of American Rabbis] would have a convention and indicate that its only concerns are with religious and cultural matters."[9]

By the time Schindler was installed as president of the UAHC in November 1973, he had gained sufficient status within the Presidents' Conference to be regarded as a contender for its chairmanship. But not only did he need first to establish himself as president of Reform's Union, he also had to win over the Israelis. Apparently, he rapidly made progress on that front. An Israeli reporter, David Landau, noted that "a well-placed official in Jerusalem, closely involved in Israel's ties with U.S. Jewry, admitted to me that the establishment here favored Rabbi [Israel] Miller, but added: 'No one here would be unduly sad if Rabbi Schindler won the vote.'"[10]

However, the time for Schindler's ascendancy to that position was not yet ripe. The same reporter noted that Schindler, unlike Miller, had spoken out publicly against President Nixon in connection with Watergate and also against the US's position on Vietnam, contra Israel's political position of support for the Vietnam War. It was not until after he had been president of the UAHC for a little over two years, from November 1973 to January 1976, and Gerald Ford had replaced Nixon, that Schindler was unanimously elected chairman of the Presidents' Conference. By that time he had expressed strong views on its work, so that his Reform association and approach to Israel were well-known, as were the issues he might propose and stress as chairman. Schindler had complained that the Conference was poorly organized and that its policies tended to take the form of short-term reactions rather than long-term planning. It was clear that giving him the presidency would mean fundamental changes in the structure as well as the function of the organization.

Upon the completion of Israel Miller's term in January 1976, Schindler became the first Reform rabbi to head the Presidents' Conference. Neither his Reform affiliation nor his political views stymied his election. Nor did the expenses for exercising his role, amounting to an estimated $20,000 to $30,000 a year—mainly for travel—which would have to come either from a personal discretionary fund or from the Union's budget.[11] That he was so easily chosen was no doubt due in large measure to his demeanor, which shattered the stereotype of the Reform Jew who prided himself on his roots in the German Reform tradition, possessed little sense of Jewish peoplehood, and gave higher priority to a domestic social justice program than to worldwide Jewish concerns. In these regards Schindler was different. He told Landau, "I symbolize the evolution of the Reform Movement."[12] The reporter was surprised at the way Schindler spoke to him:

> Strange though it seemed to me, Rabbi Schindler, graduate of the Hebrew Union College of Cincinnati, Director of the Reform Movement's educational programme these past several years, and now the Movement's president, talks like a *"hassidischer yid* [a Hasidic Jew]." He fixed our interview for "Thursday evening, *im yirtse Hashem* [God willing]," and his rich and sparkling conversation is spiced with the phraseology of the Talmud and related literature.[13]

In this interview with an Israeli reporter, Schindler was clearly striking a pose, but it was not an unnatural one. He did come from a Hasidic background and he was a believer, though a shaky one, in divine providence. What is beyond question is that Eisendrath could not have made a similar impression.

Schindler was broadly acceptable to the institutional representatives who chose him for the important chairmanship position not only from a religious perspective but also politically, since he had been able to demonstrate the acuity that the position required. For example, he had met with top American and Israeli officials and participated in multiple briefings with Henry Kissinger, on which he reported confidentially and in detail to the membership of the UAHC Board.[14] He had shown himself a staunch advocate of Israel in its struggle with the inimical forces of Egypt and Syria, and with the power-seeking ambitions of Yasser Arafat. He had called the brutal dictator of Uganda, Idi Amin, a "Haman" and had labeled the French "harlots" for embargoing arms to Israel. But perhaps to the displeasure of some members of the Presidents' Conference, he had also insisted that with regard to Israel, "dissent should never be equated with disloyalty." Speaking to the CCAR during a meeting in Jerusalem, he questioned: "Must I indulge in annexationist fantasies to prove that I am a passionate Jew? Must I applaud this government's every act to demonstrate my love for Israel?"[15] Schindler hoped to provide Israel with "a perspective born of distance."[16] The problem of the relationship between American Jews and Israel was, in Schindler's eyes, far deeper. It was not simply that American Jewry had little if any say in Israeli affairs; it was that for many Jews, perhaps even for some Reform Jews, Israel had become "a surrogate synagogue."[17] For Schindler, Israel was to be understood as central within the Jewish people, but not to the point of diminishing the parallel centrality of the synagogue for American Jews.

Yet despite this emphasis on the dual perspective, Israeli government and American Jewry, as well as on the danger of diminishing the centrality of the American synagogue in favor of Zionist identification, Schindler concluded his speech to fellow rabbis in Jerusalem with a commitment that later he would not fully uphold:

> And so we shall come here, and we shall bring our children here. Some will be here for a time, and some for always. Here we shall build our synagogues and schools and camps. The very center of our movement will be established here. And on the easternmost site of that center there will be a synagogue. And the eastern wall of that synagogue will be made of glass, even the wall of the ark against which the Torah scrolls will be framed. And through that glass we shall see the walls of our holy city, and the Tower of David, and the mount where waiting for God was born.[18]

These somewhat conflicting views—commitment to Israel but also the right to criticize its policies, upholding the centrality of the State of Israel but also of the American synagogue—did not diminish Schindler's prospects for becoming the principal spokesman vis-à-vis Israel for almost the entire American Jewish community.

On January 14, 1976, the representatives of thirty-two American Jewish organizations elected the president of the UAHC to be likewise and simultaneously chairman of the Conference of Presidents of Major American Jewish Organizations. This was the first time since the Conference was founded in 1956 that an official leader of Reform Judaism was accorded that honor and responsibility. In accepting the office, Schindler noted that his election reflected the ever-growing commitment of Reform Judaism to the peoplehood of Israel and to the well-being and security of the Israeli state.[19] Within hours of his election, Schindler was characteristically frank when interviewed by Dan Margalit, the Washington correspondent of the Israeli newspaper *Haaretz*. His predecessor, Israel Miller, had been criticized for his subservience, frequently "obeying" recommendations that came from Jerusalem. Miller believed that the problems facing Israel were too complex for him to deal with and that they were better left to the Israelis alone.[20] It was widely believed at that time that Henry Kissinger, aware that such was the feeling in the Conference, had said, "Why should I talk to the Presidents' Conference when I can get it firsthand from [Israeli ambassador Simcha] Dinitz?"[21] Schindler, now fifty years old and full of enthusiasm for his new responsibility, gave voice to a differing approach. He aimed "to tell Israel the truth as the Conference sees it, not just as it thinks Israel would like to hear it."[22] The Conference would cease simply taking orders from Jerusalem, behaving, by analogy, like the lowly caretaker of a synagogue: "If you act like a *shammas*, you get treated like a *shammas*."[23] As long as Schindler held the office, the Conference would be more than an extension of the Israeli government. There would no longer be a difference between what members of the Conference said among themselves in closed consultations and what they told the Israeli government. The welfare of Israel would be the central consideration, but it would not be the only one.

Within weeks of his election, Schindler took a public position regarding the situation of the Jews in Soviet Russia that was not to the Israelis' liking. Soviet Jewry was a cause close to Schindler's heart, as he wrote letters to US government officials on behalf of individual Jews who were denied exit visas. On one occasion, he wrote to Secretary of State Kissinger in a Jewish vein, asking that he intercede on behalf of two Refuseniks, framing it as a modern example of the religious commandment of *pidyon sh'vuyim* (the redemption of captives).[24] During the Second Brussels Conference on Soviet Jewry, February 17–19, 1976, Schindler was one of the principal Jewish leaders to address the delegates. In what was termed "a stormy speech,"[25] he argued not only for the free emigration of Soviet Jews, a position universally agreed upon, but also for their right to migrate to the country of their choice rather than to Israel alone. Moreover, Schindler asserted that world Jewry should assist in the revival and revitalization of religious and cultural life for those Jews who chose to remain in the Soviet Union. He suggested establishing a modern rabbinical seminary and teacher training institutions in the USSR, and the free admission of Western Jewish scholars to deepen the process.[26] This thinking ran contrary to the prevalent view in Israel that the dominant, if not exclusive, effort should be made to increase Soviet *aliyah* to Israel, not migration to America or Europe, and that effort should not be diverted by encouraging Soviet Jews to remain in their current communities. Even the Labor Party's Abba Eban, generally favorable to Diaspora Jewry and opposed to pressure tactics (such as withholding funds from emigrants who chose to settle elsewhere than Israel), was of the opinion that Soviet Jews who left Russia with an Israeli visa, but then "dropped out" and settled in Europe or the United States, did "great disservice to the central interests of the Jewish people."[27] Schindler did not share that view.

At the invitation of the Romanian government, Schindler also traveled to Romania, where he met with government officials and leaders of the Jewish community. While there, he was favorably impressed with the rights Jews enjoyed and their many flourishing institutions. But, as he related to a congressional committee upon his return, although Jewish rights in Romania were on par with those accorded to other minorities and he and his colleagues favored the continuation of favored nation status for Romania, "yet the concept of human rights, as we perceive it in its fullness, must encompass the right of emigration."[28] That right had not been given.

Schindler's election cast him into an American political milieu not conducive to his own political philosophy. He was a liberal Democrat, but the administration with which he had to deal was Republican, under President Gerald Ford. Its chief Jewish contact was the wealthy Republican businessman, philanthropist, and prominent Jewish leader Max Fisher. Yet Schindler successfully cultivated a friendly relationship with Fisher, an indication of his ability to deal amicably even with individuals who differed with him on fundamental issues. In the case of Fisher, friendliness was easier for Schindler since he believed that Fisher identified as a Reform Jew. Working together, they were able to arrange a meeting on Israel issues with President Ford. The new chairman selected and sent for Fisher's approval a proposal for a sixteen-person Jewish delegation that included individuals with a broad range of Jewish affiliations, as well as two women—a total of only half of the members of the Conference. He regarded this smaller group as "a kind of informal 'upper house'" that could represent American Jewry in meetings with high government officials more efficiently than the Conference as a whole.[29] In preparing for the meeting, Schindler also took it upon himself to approach individual senators on political matters, especially those with whom he had some ideological connection, including Joseph R. Biden, Democratic senator from Delaware.[30]

The meeting with President Ford took place in the White House on March 17, 1976, with a group ultimately consisting of seventeen Jewish representatives, led by Fisher and Schindler. The government was represented by President Ford, Secretary of State Henry Kissinger, and the assistant to the president for national security affairs, Brent Scowcroft, among others. In their initial presentations, Ford and Kissinger asserted the government's "desire to maintain a special relationship with Sadat," who was then distancing himself from the Soviet Union, while at the same time withholding large-scale arms sales to Egypt and standing by United Nations Security Council Resolutions 242 and 338 guaranteeing Israel safe borders. When Ford and Kissinger finished, Fisher only noted that "some would say this meeting has a Teutonic aspect with Kissinger and Schindler."[31] Then, the Conference chairman presented the first Jewish response. Although expressing appreciation for the overall thrust of American policy in the Middle East and admitting that the sale of six C-130 transport aircraft to Egypt would not affect the military balance of power, Schindler's reply indicated severe misgivings with the Administration's position:

> Still we are afraid and we are apprehensive. We fear it is the beginning of a process. The symbolic aspect scares us. We buy the approach of supporting moderates so we support economic aid to Egypt and we do not oppose the nuclear agreement [with the Soviet Union]. But we are worried about the [sale to Egypt of] six C-130s as being the start of a much larger process. Why does Egypt need arms? Its only enemy is Israel. Israel must fear not only Egypt but all the Arabs. Arms can be transferred from one to another. . . . Israel needs to maintain qualitative superiority with planes like the F-15 [tactical fighter bomber].[32]

After other members of the delegation had the opportunity to express their views and Ford and Kissinger were able to reply in some detail, Ford concluded the ninety-minute meeting by saying to the Jewish representatives, "You need to trust me. My view will be the same in the future as in the past on Israel."[33] Schindler was not, however, willing to trust the Republican president.

This first diplomatic encounter for Schindler in his new role cannot be described as a Jewish success. *Haaretz* called it a "cold meeting": "Not only did the Jews leave empty handed, but it had been largely publicized."[34] The latter was a mistake made, perhaps, because Schindler publicly declared the meeting a success. The reporter was of the opinion that such open diplomacy harmed the prestige of the Presidents' Conference and that the new chairman should try a more restrained style.[35] Yet Schindler remained forceful and committed to making the work of the Conference public. His impetuosity would prove offensive and perhaps counterproductive at a later time, when he applied it in negotiation with Ford's Democratic successor, Jimmy Carter.

Not long after this consultation with the American political leadership, and upon the invitation of Prime Minister Yitzhak Rabin, Schindler took off for Israel. There he reported on the meeting to Rabin and sought to assure the Israelis—despite his own misgivings—that there was no reason for panic with regard to United States policy, even if difficult times might be ahead. Likewise, in encounters with a broad spectrum of Israeli politicians and intellectuals, Schindler sought to assure them that

American Jewry was intent on strengthening the solidarity with Israel that he judged to be most necessary at this time.[36] Although William Scranton, the new ambassador to the United Nations, in his first speech before the UN Assembly, blasted Israel's approval of new Jewish settlements in the West Bank, Schindler discounted the speech as one written for the ambassador by the State Department. Though Scranton seemed a less enthusiastic supporter of Israel than his predecessor, Daniel Patrick Moynihan, Schindler judged him the more knowledgeable on Middle Eastern affairs. Schindler tried to convince Israelis of Scranton's good intentions, and he earned kudos from the U.S. ambassador to Israel, Malcolm Toon, for mediating between the Americans and Israelis. Shortly after his return from Israel, Schindler met with Scranton and later invited him to speak to the Presidents' Conference.[37]

Apparently, Schindler had performed his function in Israel very well. After hearing multiple voices commenting on the visit, Zalman Abramov, a conservative Israeli politician and friend of Reform Judaism, wrote to Schindler that his style of action represented a novel and welcome phenomenon to many Israelis, especially when Schindler extended his contacts beyond political officialdom. He had successfully taught Israelis that American Jewry was not omnipotent and that it had to function within the framework of the American national interest.[38] Rabbi Richard Hirsch, president of the World Union for Progressive Judaism, likewise reported to Schindler from Jerusalem, noting that he had been "exceptionally well received"[39] in Israel. The people with whom Hirsch had spoken about the visit all agreed "that you are a considerable improvement over the past leadership, that you articulate well and speak 'dugri' (that's an Arabic word meaning 'straight')."[40]

In their syndicated column, famed journalists Rowland Evans and Robert Novak likewise took note of Schindler's trip and came to a similar conclusion. They expressed surprise that an American rabbi, chairman "of a potent pro-Israel lobbying organization,"[41] should have warned Israelis on a state-owned television network that they should harbor no illusions regarding American policy. It was clear, they reflected, that America would not back Israeli expansion into the West Bank, especially after US Ambassador William Scranton had just reiterated the American position that Jewish settlement there was illegal. According to the two journalists,

Schindler had not suggested, as one might have expected, that the future would see greater harmony between the two countries, but rather that there would be greater friction. In their view, he had intimated to the Israelis that "after eight years of occupation, it is time for a change."[42] Schindler, who was no fan of the conservative-leaning Evans and Novak column, regarded their account as "somewhat distorted,"[43] but did not explain what specifically he meant by that. Writing to Alfred Gottschalk, president of the Hebrew Union College–Jewish Institute of Religion, he expressed an astounding pessimism regarding both the American and Israeli Jewish communities. He called Gottschalk's attention to Genesis 32:8–9, which reads: "Jacob was greatly frightened; in his anxiety, he divided the people with him into two camps, thinking, 'If Esau comes to the one camp and attacks it, the other camp may yet escape.'" Did Schindler really believe that one of the two communities might not survive, leaving only the other to carry on the Jewish legacy? Or was this reference no more than a very loose albeit clever metaphor? "I hope your Bible is not too dusty," he concluded.[44]

As with his new approach to American Jewry and Israel, Schindler also favored the free expression of dissent within the Presidents' Conference. To encourage it, he called a special meeting, sponsored by the Presidents' Conference and attended by more than one hundred Jewish leaders. The first speaker, Rabbi Eugene Borowitz of HUC-JIR, spoke in favor of encouraging dissent from Israeli policies; Rabbi Fabian Schonfeld, former president of the Orthodox Rabbinical Council of America, argued against that position; and Rabbi Arthur Hertzberg, president of the American Jewish Congress, presented a summary of the discussion. The overwhelming view following the session, Schindler reported, favored untrammeled free expression on Israel issues, provided that it was voiced only within the Jewish community. "But when Jewish dissent 'goes public'—that is, when criticism of Israel's policies is expressed in the daily press or in the halls of government, it was the near-unanimous opinion that the result is to give aid and comfort to the enemy and to weaken that Jewish unity which is essential for the security of the Jewish state, and, indeed, of the Jewish community of America."[45]

Schindler realized that even if he did not blindly accept every position of the Israeli government, in his role as chairman of the Presidents'

Conference he could not simply echo the UAHC's highly critical stance on certain Israeli policies, even if it closely paralleled his own. At the same time, he was of the opinion that his chairmanship should not hinder Reform leadership from formulating views that contradicted public statements of the Presidents' Conference. On the contrary, as he told the UAHC Board at its meeting in May 1976:

> Why should we express such critical judgments in public, and especially at such a delicate time? The immediate answer is as follows: the government of Israel, trapped in a very difficult—if not impossible—coalition system, is being subjected to fierce pressure to declare the West Bank non-negotiable because it is "divinely endowed." It is very important that within Israel and within the Jewish world, there be moderate countervailing views to balance the extremist pressures....
>
> I do not want the fact that I am the Chairman of the Presidents' Conference to be in any sense a constraining force on the Union. My newer, added post perforce serves to restrain my own public voice; I have a sense of responsibility to the office which I hold and my public statements must reflect the consensus of the Conference's constituency. But this more personal responsibility does not bind the Union nor do I want it to bind the Union. I want the Union to be what it has always been, a fearless spokesman for the truth as it conceives it, both within the Jewish community and on the larger American scene.[46]

However, in Schindler's eyes there was a limit even for the UAHC. In 1973, a small group of rabbis and intellectuals had formed an Israel-oriented organization named Breira, meaning "alternative." Among its leading members were two prominent Reform Jews on the Union's staff, Rabbi Balfour Brickner and Rabbi David Saperstein.[47] The group, which considered itself Zionist, favored recognition of the Palestine Liberation Organization if it were to recognize Israel, a view that ran directly counter to Israel's official policy at that time. Very early on, it also supported the concept of a two-state solution, Israeli and Palestinian. By the mid-seventies, Breira had close to a thousand members and was publicizing positions critical of the Yitzhak Rabin government in the general as well as the Jewish press. Despite its relatively small size in the American Jewish landscape, Breira's activities concerned Prime Minister Rabin—far more than its numbers justified—and led to disproportionate resistance. American Jewish hawks on Israel subjected it to severe attack, attempting to silence its voice, even as Israeli doves lent it support. Disturbed by the effort to squelch any critique of Israeli policy, the Reform rabbis passed a resolution affirming their commitment to free speech within the American Jewish community, but they stopped short of endorsing Breira.[48]

Schindler decided that such free speech, representing various sides of Israeli issues, belonged in the Presidents' Conference. He invited both Breira and its far-right counterpart, the expansionist Gush Emunim ("Bloc of the Faithful") to address the delegates, but he wanted such discussions to remain within the Conference—or at least not be officially publicized by it. "I don't mind dissent being leaked out but I do mind ads published in newspapers or demonstrations in front of t.v. cameras," he said.[49] Breira did publish such ads but, Schindler claimed, so did the far-right Jewish Defense League and Gush Emunim. He defined his own position as "a dove," since he believed in a step-by-step process toward peace. But he thought Israel should not budge until it received more commitment to peace from the Arabs. Schindler did not specify why he personally refused to join Breira, despite the fact that his views on some matters were close to theirs. Probably it was a combination of not fully agreeing with all the positions of an organization judged radical at that time, and his disagreement with its tactics in bringing non-Jewish readers of the general press into the discussion.[50]

While he may not have wanted to associate himself with Breira and thus invite the ire of American Jewish hawks, Schindler consistently criticized the one-way character of the relationship between Israel and American Jewry. American Jewry, he argued, unquestioningly accepted "dictation" from the state, and Israel assumed complete and unquestioning support from American Jews. Schindler wanted Israel to realize that on some issues liberal Jews, out of moral conviction, would disagree with Israeli policies. The Vietnam War was such a case. Israelis had told the American Jewish community they did not want to oppose American military action "because their perspective was that the same guns that faced us in Vietnam, faced us in the Mideast. They had every right to say that and I had every right to say I couldn't support the war because I had overriding concerns."[51] According to Schindler, it became easier for American Jews to disagree openly with Israeli policies after the mistakes that led to the near disaster of the 1973 Yom Kippur War. Until then, American Jews had felt "the Israelis knew best and you had to follow their lead" and "everything that Golda wanted, Golda got."[52] Further, Schindler suggested Israelis had made the diplomatic mistake of allowing internal disagreements to seep into foreign affairs. Their divisions, he intimated, were even more harmful to the Israelis' cause than those they claimed deleterious to their interests within the Diaspora Jewish community. Personal animosities within the Israeli leadership overshadowed national priorities: "When an American senator goes there, he hears from [Yigael] Allon not what Israel's foreign policy problems are but how bad [Yitzhak] Rabin and [Shimon] Peres are."[53]

Schindler sought to replace the one-way relationship with a new one of reciprocity. He said, "I don't think Israel should be silent when it comes to the US Jewish community. Just as I say we should tell them the truth, they have every right to tell us the truth as they perceive it. Neither side should feel obliged to follow the advice of the other but advice should be given."[54] That was a position former prime minister Golda Meir was willing to accept when she spoke to a meeting of the Presidents' Conference in 1976, even if she may have opposed it earlier.[55] But this perspective, intended to be broadly middle-of-the road, led only to Schindler's being clobbered by critics from both the left and the right. On the left, he was accused of censoring public Jewish debate because he accused organizations like Breira of bringing internal Jewish differences into public discourse beyond the Jewish periphery. With all of his commitment to openness, Schindler drew the line on what he called "public criticism whose *sole intent* it is to garner U.S. public support or even U.S. governmental support for a particular ideological position. This, it seems to me, constitutes '*messira*' [informing], which our tradition has always eschewed."[56] The left also questioned the Union's decision to join the World Zionist Organization. Was that step, which some perceived as restricting the independence of the Union, a matter of conviction, or was it simply to make its president more acceptable as chairman of the Presidents' Conference? That canard, at least, Schindler was easily able to dispel. The Union had joined the WZO back in 1974, two years before he became chairman of the Presidents' Conference. It was therefore not an act motivated by the desire to make his life easier among non-Reform Zionist groups within the Conference.

The criticism that came from the right is exemplified by a letter that

Schindler received from Rose Matzkin, national president of Hadassah, the Women's Zionist Organization of America. Not only did she come to the defense of Golda, a long-time heroine of Hadassah, but Matzkin did not consider dissent with Israeli policies a virtue—even when it was limited to within the Jewish community. She also disagreed with Schindler that American Jewry should have a say in Israel's policy decisions. Dissent, she suggested in a letter to Schindler, had unfortunately become "a new synonym for Breira."[57] Schindler's detailed response answered on both counts. He agreed that what Matzkin called his "flip statement" that Golda always got what she wanted was not good public relations. But he emphasized to Matzkin his conviction "that there was a kind of worshipful attitude toward Golda on the American Jewish scene, which led most among us to give her unquestioned obeisance."[58] As for dissent, Schindler considered it not one-sided disagreement with Israeli policies but rather "open discussion" expressing a wide range of opinion. "Joe Sternstein [president of the Zionist Organization of America] and Jacques Torczyner [a World Zionist Organization leader] have had as much say in the conduct of the Presidents' Conference, if not more, than they did in any prior administration. When I say open discussion, I mean open discussion for everyone."[59] Both men held decidedly hawkish views on Israel.

Schindler had an inclination to avail himself of such open discussion when he gave his own speeches. He had a penchant for catchy, shocking metaphors that drew the desired attention but were not always favorably received in every Jewish circle. In a speech at—of all places—a convention of the hawkish Zionist Organization of America, Schindler reportedly said, "Some American Jews have the feeling that they are cows to be milked, walked around a bit for some exercise and then let off to pasture. When I am in trouble, I do not want a cow. I want a man with the capacity for independent thought. Truth is the highest form of support for Israel."[60] In other contexts Schindler spoke of Israel as "a kidney machine" that, with frequent dialysis, kept some American Jews Jewish. Neither metaphor was appreciated in Zionist circles. The cow metaphor was wrongly interpreted to mean that Israelis wanted money from American Jews and nothing else. Golda Meir thought that with such damaging words Schindler was alienating American Jews from Israel.[61] In fact, Meir was now very much down on Schindler. In an article in the Israeli paper *Maariv*, she complained that whenever she had come to the United States in the past she had been asked to speak to the Presidents' Conference, but on her last visit Schindler failed to invite her—she had to invite herself. Once there, she presented Israeli policies and listened to reactions. She thought it a marvelous exchange. But she wrote that Schindler remained strangely silent, not saying a word. Petulantly, she exclaimed, "But no, I'm not worried about American Jewry. Schindler will not distance it from Israel."[62] Of course, that was never Schindler's intent.

Even within the Reform leadership there was shock at Schindler's language. Richard Hirsch could hardly believe that he actually said what he did. With regard to Schindler's use of the cow metaphor he wrote to his friend, "As it stands, it is not the kind of statement that in your capacity as chairman of the Presidents' Conference you should want to be associated with. . . . Be aware that the Israeli press (and the American, as well) are hungry for news of disunity. Any criticism of policy or any interpersonal rivalry is blown way out of proportion."[63] Hirsch sought to make Schindler better aware of how influential he believed the Presidents' Conference to be. In his view, it was "a vital instrument of American Jewry for supporting the cause of Israel on specific often life-and-death issues."[64] It was certainly of no less importance for Schindler, but he refused to acknowledge that support of Israel must be unquestioning or even blind.

With all the attention given to Schindler's unwillingness to accept Israeli policies without question, it is important to balance that picture with his genuine love of Israel as best expressed on yet another trip to the state—one that put him in Jerusalem the night Israel extracted the hostages from the skyjacking at Entebbe, Uganda, on July 4, 1976. He and his wife Rhea were asleep at the King David Hotel, the hostages on their way home, when they were awakened by the publisher of *Maariv* and told of the rescue operation. Hearing the good news, they were unable to go back to sleep. Together with other guests, they went to the hotel coffee shop, where they "spent the rest of the night laughing, singing and listening to the radio to snatch every bit of news."[65] In the morning, Defense Minister Shimon Peres gave the Schindlers passes allowing them to be present at the airfield near Lod for the arrival home. When he returned to the United States, Schindler paid tribute to the experience by writing, "My own predominant reaction was one of gratitude and relief. At its core was the recognition that an elemental aspect of the Zionist expectation had been fulfilled: When Jew was separated from non-Jew for 'special handling,' when once again we were abandoned to our fate, one force could still be counted on to seek our protection—the State of Israel."[66] For all of Schindler's qualms about particular Israeli policies, he held the Palestinians and the Arab nations fundamentally responsible for the lack of progress toward peace. The Israelis held the moral high ground in the conflict. In the shadow of Entebbe, he wrote to the UAHC membership, "Arab nations freely supportive of terrorism have no claim on the moral conscience of mankind, certainly not a PLO which is so fully identified with this globe-encircling conspiracy."[67] He utterly rejected the double standard that many in the world had long been imposing upon Israel.

No less controversial and nuanced in Schindler's view was the relation of the Presidents' Conference to the United Nations. The previous November, the UN General Assembly had branded Zionism a form of racism, a position that nearly all American Jews condemned. Mincing no words, Schindler called it "a moral collapse . . . a dismal slide downhill, backwards to the morality of the Neanderthal caves."[68] But should the Jewish community therefore turn its back on the UN, or should it rather attempt to exercise whatever limited diplomatic influence it possessed through the Presidents' Conference—especially after the United Nations continued to lambast the Zionist enterprise and the Israeli state? A committee of the UN had just voted ninety to sixteen for a resolution to purge the Zionist presence from Palestine and to declare the establishment of Israel null and void. Ambassador Scranton declared that resolution unfair, futile, useless, and totally devoid of balance. On November 28, 1976, a year after the anti-Zionism resolution and following the newer resolution, the Presidents' Conference Council published a full-page advertisement in the Sunday edition of *The New York Times*. Under the huge letters "UN," the ad was titled "The Farce Turns Ugly." The opening paragraph began: "Americans have long ago come to regard the debates in the General Assembly of the United Nations as a kind of theatre of the absurd in which the role of villain has been assigned to Israel." In the lower right-hand corner of the advertisement, a box appeared where readers who wanted to know how they could help were asked to share their concern by sending personal information to Rabbi Alexander M. Schindler, the chairman of the Presidents' Conference. The advertisement suggested readers should include a contribution "to carry the message to others around the country and around the world."[69]

This anti-UN appeal to the broad public aroused anger among some liberal Christians and some liberal Jews. For both, the UN—for all its failings—was virtually held sacred, the instrument for a future of universal peace. Schindler received a letter from a Unitarian Universalist supporter of the UN, married to a "man of Jewish ancestry," expressing outrage and even calling the "scurrilous" advertisement "political pornography."[70] She recalled the positive role Abba Eban had played at the UN and regarded it as "shameful that the many positive accomplishments of the UN are ignored by zealots who should know better."[71] She was particularly upset by the appeal for funds and called upon Schindler to send an apology for the advertisement to the UN's secretary general, Kurt Waldheim.[72] No doubt to her surprise, the letter writer received a personal response from Schindler that began, "I must admit that I share some of your concerns. *The New York Times* advertisement for the Presidents' Conference was prepared and placed during my absence from the country. . . . I would have deleted some of the wording which caused you distress."[73] He then went on to express his conviction that the UN was "frightfully stacked against Israel." Yet even as the UN's denunciation of Zionism and of Israel's right to exist did not turn Schindler away from the Jewish state, neither did the UN's blatant anti-Israelism induce him to abandon the United Nations. He ended his letter on a typically positive note: "While I feel strongly regarding Israel and the United Nations, I still feel strongly that we must ever continue to hope that the U.N. will become the organization that the world had hoped it to be and we must continue to work toward that end."[74] Upon the recommendation of Ambassador Scranton and "with great pride and pleasure," Schindler in May 1977 accepted election as a director of the United Nations Association.[75]

Schindler noted that within American Jewry there was a degree of uncertainty about which of the two candidates to support in the American presidential election of 1976. In terms of foreign policy and especially the Middle East, he believed Jews would very much favor President Ford, but most of them did not see eye to eye with him on such troubling matters as the "collapse of the cities, the economic crisis, crime, civil rights and government invasion of privacy and civil liberties."[76] For American Jews, he remarked, "Israel is not our only concern. . . . Jews are citizens of this land. They feel strongly about domestic issues, and as a result their attitude toward the Chief Executive is ambivalent."[77]

Perhaps initially Schindler also felt this ambivalence. Although he had not always agreed with Henry Kissinger, he believed that this fellow Jew had Jewish interests at heart. After the election, Schindler was sorry to see Kissinger leave office, telling a Presidents' Conference tribute dinner that the Jewish community would remember him "with exasperation tinged with affection."[78] Schindler could not forget that Kissinger had once said in his hearing, "How can I as a Jew do anything to betray my people?"[79] But there was no question about Schindler's decision at the voting booth. His concern for America's internal issues was determinative, so he set his hopes on Jimmy Carter.

Although Carter may have agreed with Schindler on domestic issues, he would prove to be more problematic than Ford with regard to Israel. Shortly after Carter's election, Schindler received a warning from Morris J. Amitay, the executive director of the American Israel Public Affairs Committee (AIPAC), the group devoted to lobbying in support of Israel. Amitay called attention to the appointment of Zbigniew Brzezinski, who replaced Kissinger as presidential national security adviser, describing him as "an academic, whose published works on the Middle East issue are not encouraging."[80] Amitay also expressed concern for Carter's description of himself as a Christian—"a fact, which while not in dispute, is usually not put forward publicly as a qualification for high office!!"[81]

Schindler did not share Amitay's concern about Carter as a religious Christian. To the Union's Board he wrote that although Carter described himself as a born-again Christian, he thought it "unjust and paradoxical for religious Jews to look askance at a presidential candidate because he is deeply religious."[82] Moreover, as governor of Georgia, Carter had scrupulously adhered to the principle of separation of church and state, to the point that his opponents accused him of being an atheist. But of course it was necessary for the Presidents' Conference, and the Union as well, to retain a neutral stance in the presidential election. Both organizations

Alexander Schindler with President Jimmy Carter, ca. 1976. *Courtesy of the Schindler family.*

would want to be in the good graces of whoever won. Schindler met personally with each of the candidates, including even Alabama governor George Wallace.[83] He wrote, "Someone has to be the winner and identification with the wrong side will send us into hot water. It is advantageous to have Jewish leaders active in both campaigns, and that we have. In addition, we have established as many lines of communication as possible with Carter since the lines of communication with Ford are fairly well established."[84]

But the neutral stance did not apply to Schindler's own actions. During the course of 1976, whatever doubts he had about Carter gave way to active support. To Stuart Eizenstat, a top official in Carter's campaign, he offered to be of assistance: "I'd like to do something and if you are interested in having a gathering in Westport, I hereby offer, unofficially, the services of a great organizer—my wife, Rhea. Do let me know if you'd like to do something in our town."[85] To a UAHC supporter in Los Angeles, he confessed that after his initial doubts were removed, he began working very closely with the Carter campaign people. Still, he cautioned, "I hope you appreciate that all of this has been done unofficially and quietly and I would not wish you to share it with others. I am in almost daily contact with the Atlanta headquarters and have been for some time now."[86] If Ford had won, he later said, with typical hyperbole, he would have had to become "the leader of the opposition" in the Presidents' Conference or even to resign from it.[87]

On September 30, 1976, at the head of a large delegation of Jewish community leaders, Schindler met with the presidential candidate at a Ramada Inn near Boston's Logan Airport. After describing American Jewry to Carter as a proud and self-confident community in an America that had been good to it, but also as part of a people that had suffered grievously during the Holocaust, Schindler posed the question: "What do we want in a president?" Tongue in cheek, he answered his own query: "I suppose we would really like someone who will always agree with us. But barring that, we want a man who will tell us the truth and who will then act upon that truth himself."[88] Schindler went on to speak of the religious bond that united Carter with religious Jews. Carter, in turn, thanked Schindler for explaining so eloquently "the character of the Jewish people in this country and around the world."[89] At this point in their relationship, it seems that Schindler had won the presidential candidate's favor.

With Carter's election in November, Schindler had high hopes for "a moral renewal for America." He reiterated his conviction that he was not troubled by Carter's religious professions. In fact, he perceived in Carter's concept of rebirth something "akin to the spiritual rebirth of which the Prophets spoke," and he discerned in the president-elect nothing less than "a man of clear potential for greatness."[90] When, shortly after his election, Carter determined to pardon all those who had avoided service in the Vietnam War—a step that would have been most gratifying to Maurice Eisendrath—Schindler wrote directly to Plains, Georgia, that such an official proclamation, however controversial, would be an expression of moral leadership and help heal the trauma of the war. Either out of a genuine sense of closeness of spirit or simply to fit the religiosity of the addressee, he closed the letter to Carter with language more common to Carter than to himself: "God bless you."[91] A few months later, when Carter appointed the civil rights leader Andrew Young as the American ambassador to the United Nations, Schindler felt he had chosen "a man of courage and intellect, of deep compassion and broad understanding."[92] Most importantly, Young seemed a warm friend and ardent supporter of

Israel, as well as a diplomat who spoke respectfully and sincerely when meeting with the Presidents' Conference.

It did not take long for apprehensions about Carter to arise, even in Reform circles. However, Schindler sought to exculpate the new president with an analogy from Jewish history: Even as Jews in Tsarist Russia had consistently ascribed pogroms to lower officials, not to the Tsar himself, so too did objectionable policies originate with officials in Carter's administration and not with Carter himself. Any sentiments critical of Israel or endangering it did not arise from the top rank of the new administration, but from "pro-Arab Carterites" beneath it. In Schindler's words: "They came from the bowels of the State Department and the Pentagon, from briefing papers—God knows when written and from individuals of slanted views.... Moreover, they must be seen against every positive stance which has been taken by the Carter administration vis-à-vis Israel, e.g., PLO, and also vis-à-vis Soviet Jewry, where I expect more progress under Carter than ever before."[93]

However, when in March 1977 Israeli prime minister Yitzhak Rabin came to Washington in order to meet with Carter, the two men revealed sharp differences of opinion. Unlike Kissinger, Carter favored creating an overall solution for the Middle East rather than working step-by-step, which some considered a less realistic and potentially more dangerous program. The new president also argued for restitution for the Palestinian refugees. Unlike Carter, Rabin did not believe in an independent Palestinian entity—whose area of settlement Carter shortly thereafter referred to as a Palestinian "homeland"—but rather favored a combined Jordanian-Palestinian state. Moreover, Rabin was opposed to any recognition of the Palestine Liberation Organization, which still refused to recognize Israel. He was also not in agreement with Carter that all settlements in the West Bank were illegal. The Carter/Rabin meeting—perhaps really a confrontation—raised anxieties within the American Jewish community. Schindler gathered a delegation from the Presidents' Conference to learn more about that meeting from the new secretary of state, Cyrus Vance. They received an assurance that the special relationship between the United States and Israel had not been damaged, but, on the contrary, remained strong.[94]

On April 6, 1977, Schindler met with Zbigniew Brzezinski, Carter's national security adviser. In advance, he sent a telegram to Carter in which he identified President Sadat of Egypt as the most moderate leader of the Arab world and noted that he strongly supports economic aid to Egypt, though not any supply of military equipment. William B. Quandt, who served on the US National Security Council, read the telegram and then advised Brzezinski to remind Schindler of Sadat's need to demonstrate tangible gains as a result of his break with the USSR and his shift to the West. According to Quandt, this shift was clearly in Israel's interest, while Sadat's downfall would not be. The implication was that Brzezinski should argue, against Schindler's conviction, that the sale of armaments to Egypt was in fact good for Israel.[95]

Another meeting with Cyrus Vance followed in September. This time the mixed Jewish delegation was unified and well prepared, and the meeting apparently went well. Schindler later recalled that he was moved and a bit surprised when Rabbi Moshe Sherer, president of the Charedi Agudath Israel, informed Vance that everyone stood behind Rabbi Schindler. Displaying his rarely absent sense of humor, Schindler added, "I nearly fell over. In his own *shul* he never calls me 'rabbi.' But when we're fighting for Israel we're all one."[96]

By that time the main problem for Schindler—and for American Jewry—was no longer Carter and his administration, but rather the newly elected Israeli prime minister, Menachem Begin. Begin's right-wing philosophy and political program stood in sharpest contrast to those of Schindler, the Union of American Hebrew Congregations, and the majority of American Jews. Begin was an ideological disciple of the militant Russian Revisionist Zionist Ze'ev Jabotinsky, and like Jabotinsky, he was a man of the political right, a doctrinal anti-socialist, and a fervent nationalist. His Likud bloc's program in 1977 declared that the Jews' right to the totality of their land—the entire West Bank of the Jordan, if not its East Bank as well—was eternal, and none of it should be surrendered.[97] He had believed that only by military force against the British mandate authorities could the State of Israel come into existence. His record as head of the Irgun, the Jewish terrorist organization noted especially for its memorable bombing of the King David Hotel in 1946, made Menachem Begin, insofar as American Jews knew of him at all, an extremist whose views contradicted their vision of a politically moderate, peace-seeking Jewish state. For a generation, American Jews had developed their relationship to Israel via the more flexible Labor Party, whose leaders—from Ben-Gurion to Golda Meir—had become their popular heroes. Suddenly, they were confronted with an Israeli leader who contradicted their cherished values.

When, on May 17, 1977, the Likud bloc won the Knesset election, and a month later, on June 20 of that year, Menachem Begin became prime minister, American Jewry was thrown into turmoil. There was shock and disbelief. Would American Jewry's carefully nurtured relationship with Israel be able to exist within the gulf between the new Democratic American president and the highly conservative Israeli prime minister? And what of its own carefully nurtured relationship to Israel—would that be undermined by what was expected to be a nasty confrontation? Would American Jewish identity, long supported by its admiration for Israel, begin to falter, thereby surrendering to the seductive assimilation of American culture? Finally, would Alexander Schindler—the Reform rabbi whose political views in multiple areas differed fundamentally from those of Begin, and who was an advocate of straight talk between American Jews and Israeli leaders—be able to overcome these differences and sustain a productive relationship that mattered to both sides? Schindler's immediate response to the results of the election, as was only to have been expected from the Conference chairman, was: "The people of Israel have chosen a new Parliament in a democratic expression of the nation's will. We congratulate the country's leaders and pledge to them the support and commitment that the American Jewish community has given since the day the Jewish State was born."[98]

To be sure, Schindler had not exactly fancied all of Begin's recent predecessors as Israeli prime minister either. While he held Shimon Peres in high regard, the same was not true for Yitzhak Rabin. The latter, he believed, never really cared about Diaspora Jewry and treated its representatives with a lack of genuine respect. He went so far as to suspect that "Rabin viewed the Presidents' Conference as not so much an instrument to marshal support of America's Jews, but rather to 'manage' them, to keep them out from under foot."[99]

It is not entirely certain when Schindler and Begin first met. It may have been in February 1976, at the Second Brussels Conference on the subject of Soviet Jewry, held shortly after Schindler became chairman of

Rabbi Schindler with Prime Minister Menachem Begin, 1977. *Courtesy of American Jewish Archives, Cincinnati, Ohio.*

the Presidents' Conference and before the victory of Begin's party. Begin's official chronicle reports that the Brussels Conference went beyond its immediate subject of Soviet Jewry and "accepted the proposal of the Reform rabbi Alexander Schindler that 'our right to the Land of Israel is not subject to dispute.'"[100] Perhaps there were additional earlier meetings, for the relationship between Schindler and Begin had warmed by the time of the Likud victory, to the point that when Schindler sent Begin a telegram of congratulations and support, the triumphant incoming prime minister responded with a cable calling Schindler "dear friend Alexander" and concluding "... yours in friendship and respect."[101]

Within a few days after the Likud victory and even before Begin became prime minister, Schindler was on his way to Israel at the urging first of Begin's son and then of Begin himself. He described it as a "dramatic gesture."[102] The American government, represented by Carter's chief domestic policy adviser and self-affirming Jew Stuart Eizenstat, also thought such a trip to be a good idea. Not so, however, the Israel Embassy. The Israeli ambassador in Washington, Simcha Dinitz of the then still-regnant Labor Party, commented, "Why should Alex commit himself so soon? It is unseemly for him to do so. Why so great a hurry? Begin may not even be able to form a government. Besides, he is not well."[103] Knesset member

Zalman Abramov agreed, noting that Begin was "rigid and will never change"; even if he should become prime minister, "he won't last long."[104]

In Israel, Schindler was able to chat with Begin in the hospital where he was recovering from a heart attack, and the two continued their conversation a few days later in Begin's impressively modest home. A mutual admiration quickly developed between the two men. One of Begin's aides confirmed that Schindler had proven himself to be more European than American, "very smart, and a good politician."[105] Schindler, in turn, was impressed by Begin's "sense of responsibility for the Jewish people as a whole."[106] He was more Jew than he was Israeli, more patriot and statesman than simply a politician seeking power.[107] Schindler wrote that Begin possessed a soul fired by the *n'kudah y'hudit*, the *pintele yid*—which meant for Schindler the tiny inner Jewish spark that defines every Jew, no matter how distanced from Jewish practice.[108] A profound rapport—which today we might describe as "chemistry"—developed between them. What struck Schindler more than anything Begin said was how Begin, the person, made him feel. He sensed that this adamant ideologue was a man of integrity with a love for the Jewish people and a mystical love for its land. Schindler told Begin that American Jewry required a new Israeli government very quickly, one with a strong parliament and a broad ideology. For American Jews to remain united in support of Israel, he reported after his trip, "we needed a government with which we could identify ourselves, and a narrow coalition of the radical right and the religious grouping would not give us such a government."[109] He expressed his hope that the new government would be encompassing and that it would include parties to Begin's left. Schindler was also impressed that Begin listened to what he had to say and that he did so with respect: "For the first time I had an Israeli leader say to me, 'You know, you've got a point.'"[110] Begin's attitude was the more remarkable since Schindler refused to act grateful like a cow, as Schindler had earlier claimed American Jews were expected to act in response to Israeli milking. On the contrary, Schindler made it clear that Begin's recent appearance at the controversial West Bank settlement of Kadum while carrying a Torah scroll was a divisive provocation. Nonetheless, when Schindler returned home from Jerusalem, he told officials of the American government and representatives of American Jewry that he believed Begin would make the necessary transition from radicality to responsibility as he moved from candidacy to incumbency. Schindler honestly believed that Begin's desire now was for peace, despite his militant background. Not less important, especially to Schindler's constituents at home, was Begin's affirmation of Diaspora Jewry. Regarding Begin, Schindler wrote to fellow Reform rabbi David Polish, "There is a much greater sense of peoplehood which emanates from him than ever did from Rabin."[111] The two men's closeness despite their differences prompted a reporter from the Israeli newspaper *Maariv* to declare them an "odd couple."[112]

Not surprisingly, opposition to Schindler's positive evaluation of Begin came from the ranks of his own Reform Movement. After all, were Begin's views not an utter betrayal of Reform ideals? Close associates within the UAHC felt that Schindler had been deceived, and that his favorable view of Begin only encouraged the latter's obduracy. This seems to have been especially true of an anonymous critique by a leading figure in the Reform Movement's social justice program—probably the UAHC vice president and politically more radical Democrat Albert Vorspan. His dissenting view was that, in supporting Begin, Schindler was "betraying him and those causes which we had always stood for together."[113] Schindler also received criticism from a conservative source when he was quoted in a press statement as saying, "A united American Jewish community will remain committed to support the policies of the democratically elected government of Israel."[114] Professor Charles S. Liebman, who wrote to Schindler from the Jewish Theological Seminary, claimed that such a statement of a priori acceptance of whatever Israel does could raise a charge of dual loyalty against American Jews.[115] Schindler did not disagree but ascribed the unfortunate statement to inattention: "I am keeping so many balls juggling in the air that my children rightly complain that they have no father."[116] He had not examined the press release with sufficient care. In fact, he would, as he had always argued, maintain his right and that of the Presidents' Conference to independent judgment regarding Israeli policies.[117]

Persuading the American news media and government that Begin's ascent to power was not a catastrophe was a no less difficult task. *Time* magazine infamously quipped that "Begin" rhymed with "Fagin," the unsavory Jewish fence in Charles Dickens's *Oliver Twist*—a comparison that quickly made the rounds. The press, Schindler noted, was putting forth slanderous references to Begin as an "extremist" while calling PLO chieftain Yasser Arafat and Syrian president Hafez al-Assad "moderates."[118] Some thought that the American government might use Begin's election as a wedge to divide American Jewry, thereby gaining at least some Jewish support for an American-imposed peace plan.

At least initially, approaching the American government as an advocate of Menachem Begin must have been a difficult, if not ironic, diplomatic endeavor for the liberal Schindler. He had never been a supporter of Begin's politics and must have felt some inner doubts—if not about the person, then certainly about Begin's expansionist program. But he also had doubts about the new Democratic government in America, in particular the problem of Brzezinski, who was suspected of being more critical of Israel than was the president.[119] Given the uncertain period of the interregnum before Begin entered the prime minister's office, Schindler saw it as his primary and highly necessary task to prevent erosion of support for Israel within the American government.

Jimmy Carter, too, was shocked by the Israeli election results. "I had not dreamed that Menachem Begin, once declared by Great Britain to be a foremost terrorist leader in the region, would win the election that May and become Israel's leader," he recalled.[120] But then, a month after Begin formed his government on June 21, the prime minister and his wife Aliza came to the White House on July 19 for a formal kosher dinner hosted by President Carter. Shortly in advance of his arrival, Schindler led fifty-three Jewish leaders to the capital for a dialogue with the president and senior government officials. Among those present was Stuart Eizenstat, who took copious notes on the meeting. Describing Schindler as "eloquent but tart," he recorded that during the two-hour meeting, the chair of the Presidents' Conference "complained that while Israel was being publicly pushed, the Arabs were not being asked to commit to making peace with Israel."[121] Speaking to Carter, Schindler said, "The world isn't used to your open diplomacy. It stiffens the back of Israel and raises the expectations of the Arabs, which, once frustrated, will retard rather than bring peace."[122] In the course of that meeting, Schindler the politician, whether sincerely or for effect, suddenly became Schindler the dramatic rabbi. Unexpectedly, he blessed Carter with the Hebrew prayer for heads of state, to which the president responded with "Amen." He further declared that Carter "was the vessel of two thousand years of Jewish history. We come here with open hearts and grateful hearts."[123] Then, revealing his love of jokes, he aroused general laughter when he said, "So why do we come here if we are so happy?" He answered himself by saying to Carter that Jews were not used to the open diplomacy that the president espoused; it made the Jewish community nervous. American Jewry was beginning to fear a "tilt" in American policy toward the Arabs, and they were afraid it would result in an imposed peace settlement.

Eizenstat judged the meeting to have been successful: "If time could have been frozen after this extraordinary meeting, much of the tension in American-Israeli relations would have dissipated. But events would raise the temperature back to the boiling point."[124] Schindler thought it best to fly to Israel immediately and inform Begin of the American point of view on the current situation before the prime minister flew to Washington.

Despite their differences, the initial dinner meeting between Begin and Carter in Washington was evaluated positively by both sides. Begin thought that the president seemed pleased by his willingness to offer the Palestinian residents of the West Bank a measure of autonomy through the establishment of an "administrative council," even if withdrawing Israeli sovereignty was out of the question. For his part, Carter thought Begin genuinely wanted peace. He thought there was value in Israel's now having a stronger leader who was better able to negotiate than Yitzhak Rabin had been. He even concluded that, overall, Begin was much more flexible than he and his staff had feared. As a personality, the new Israeli leader was "quite congenial, dedicated, sincere, and deeply religious."[125]

Schindler now had less of a problem with Begin than with Carter, whose views were represented by Secretary Vance, with whom Schindler met in a closed meeting in October 1977. The administration was becoming ever more ready to acknowledge the PLO, which Schindler called "a worldwide conspiracy of terror."[126] Step-by-step the Carter government was gradually shifting its position, and an escalation seemed to be taking place: from speaking of a Palestinian homeland, then of an entity confederated with Jordan, and, most recently, of the legitimate rights of Palestinians. The last, Schindler believed, opened the door to bringing the PLO into a negotiating process that would lead to an independent Palestinian state run by an organization dedicated to the destruction of Israel. In addition, a PLO-led government would provide a base for Soviet penetration.[127] Not long thereafter, President Carter did respond positively to Schindler's and his constituents' principal concern by stating in a press conference that the PLO, in its refusal to recognize Israel, had "ruled itself out" of the Middle East process.[128]

However, by February of 1978, the peace negotiations between Israel and Egypt—which had looked so hopeful after Anwar Sadat's visit to Jerusalem the previous November—were facing formidable barriers. Begin wanted to retain the Jewish settlements in Sinai, a proposition clearly unacceptable to Sadat, as was Begin's self-rule proposal for the West Bank. On February 8, Carter invited nine American Jewish leaders for supper in order to bring American Jewry into the discussion. He spoke about the "illegal" settlements, the need to continue negotiating while there was still momentum, and his view that Israel should be ready to withdraw from the West Bank and the Gaza Strip. Carter recalled that he "spelled out the relative flexibility of Sadat's position and the intransigence of Israel."[129] Then, after the meeting, he jotted into his diary a reference to Schindler that consisted of a highly derogatory comparison between the Reform rabbi and the other Jewish leaders: "With the exception of Schindler, who always acts like an ass, the rest of them were constructive."[130] By the time this comparison became publicly known, Schindler had died, so we cannot be certain how he might have provoked so negative a reaction on the part of the president and how he would have reacted to it once it became known. But it seems not unlikely that Schindler's outspokenness, his tendency not to qualify but rather to speak *dugri*, as Richard Hirsch had put it, must have offended Carter. We do know that Schindler left the meeting "feeling that the administration was beginning to orchestrate a campaign against Begin. I didn't want Jimmy Carter to bamboozle the Jewish community the way FDR had."[131] No doubt the confrontation made it more difficult for Schindler to play an effective diplomatic role on behalf of American Jewry during the Carter administration. He gravitated more and more toward Begin.

Schindler's relationship with Begin became still warmer, even as he was provoking Carter's contempt. Because he trusted Schindler, Begin drew him into his circles of confidanes. He related, "I met with Alexander Schindler, chairman of the Presidents' Conference. I . . . swore him to secrecy. He accepted that, and I revealed to him the entire plan in both of its parts [regarding Egypt and the West Bank]. He responded with enthusiasm and afterwards announced publicly that when the plan would become known, 95 percent of Jewish community would support it."[132] When, on one occasion, Carter had made a concession to Begin by using the expression "Judea and Samaria" for the West Bank, Begin was more than willing to give at least some of the credit to Schindler. Speaking to American Jews, Begin quipped that whereas some critics "had fumed over the 'Beginization of Schindler,'" what had actually happened was the "Schindlerization of Begin."[133] The prime minister noted that it was Schindler who had laid the groundwork for Begin's visit with the government and had kept the Jewish community united. Schindler emphasized why this was his duty as chairman of the Presidents' Conference when he said of Begin that "he is a worthy leader not only of Israel but of the entire Jewish people."[134] Schindler was determined to counter any attempt by Washington to divide the Jewish community or to pry away its support of Israel. Perhaps it was therefore Begin's obligation to thank him for that. What is remarkable is that Begin had come to see the relationship as more than a political necessity; beneath the political convergence lay a remarkable personal one. Begin did not hesitate to express warm appreciation for Schindler, calling him "Alex, my dear friend, Rabbi Schindler, my master and teacher."[135]

And yet the increasing closeness of their relationship did not diminish Schindler's willingness to hold Begin to account. Early in 1978, he stated once again that it was a "solemn obligation" to express dissent, adding now that such dissent was essential even if it should find its way beyond the Jewish community into the general press.[136] As for himself, he insisted to a reporter that he was not "just a mouthpiece for Begin. I can assure you . . . Begin knows different."[137] But as the negotiations for a peace treaty with Egypt became ever more tense, Schindler was increasingly engaged in speaking out in support of Israel, a necessity given the mounting pressure on the state to make territorial concessions and the newly projected sale of F–15 fighter aircraft to the Saudis. Schindler was most concerned about a Jewish community whose enthusiasm for Begin's government was in decline. Months were passing after President Sadat's dramatic meeting with the prime minister in Israel and there was still no resolution of their differences. The members of the Presidents' Conference decided that under these circumstances they needed the now experienced Alexander Schindler to continue in office for a few months longer, until June 30, 1978—beyond the expiration of his second one-year term. It was an unprecedented decision, reached by unanimous consent.[138]

The seemingly cordial relationship between Carter and Begin at their first meeting had by now evaporated. Begin thought himself under severe pressure; he believed it to be a very difficult time in his life. Schindler too was under pressure: Brzezinski complained that Schindler had called him an antisemite, a charge Schindler denied, though he admitted to calling Brzezinksi "antagonistic."[139] Perhaps as a result of these tensions, the government decided to weaken the chairman of the Presidents' Conference. *The New York Times* columnist William Safire later claimed that he had received a call from the White House asking him to attack Schindler.[140] On March 23, following difficult meetings between Begin and Carter and just before his return to Israel, Begin spoke at a meeting of nearly a thousand Jewish leaders in New York convened by the Presidents' Conference. He informed the gathering that he had been told both directly and indirectly that Israel was obstructing peace. His peace plan, calling for Palestinian autonomy, had been ignored. Speaking fervently, he called on American Jewry to provide support for Israel.

In response, Schindler, too, spoke with emotion. He praised Begin as "a leader who merits our support, a worthy leader of all Israelis." In a statement that included the right to independence of judgment—this time with regard to American policy—he vowed "to uphold the hands of Israel's leadership not only by preserving our unity but also by giving voice— strong unfettered voice—to our convictions. We shall speak the truth as we see it. When promises are broken we will say so. . . . When we sense that our country is selling out our idealism for petrodollars, we will say so. Whatever the evil is, we will call it by its real name and not justify it on the basis that it is something else."[141] Recalling the failure of American Jews to make their voices heard with sufficient force against America's restrictive immigration policies during the 1930s, he called upon American Jews of the 1970s to speak out publicly without fear against their government. "No longer will we allow ourselves to be beguiled by the blandishment of those who sit in places of power. . . . We will not commit the sin of silence a second time in the same generation."[142]

Although Schindler was not centrally involved in the difficult negotiations that produced the Camp David Accords of September 17, 1978, and led to the signing of a peace agreement between Israel and Egypt on March 26, 1979, he was not entirely absent.[143] At the encouragement of Menachem Begin, Schindler met with Anwar Sadat in Aswan on January 11, 1978, accompanied by the executive director of the Presidents' Conference, Yehuda Hellman, whom Schindler much admired. The meeting was widely covered in the Egyptian press, with some commentators resorting to ancient Jewish stereotypes bordering on antisemitism. During their conversation, Sadat complained that while he had "done everything possible" for advancing the cause of peace, Prime Minister Begin had given him "nothing in return." Nevertheless, he assured his guests "that Egypt guarantees the security of Israel."[144] Schindler, never one to be bashful, refused to accept that offer. He insisted that it was rather Israel itself that was the best judge of what its security required and that Egypt, being but one Arab nation, was not its only concern. Sadat did not disagree, but pointed out that Egypt, together with Sudan, represented "two-thirds of the Arab world" and that it was therefore key to resolution of the conflict. Acting as an intermediary between the parties, Schindler had, upon his arrival, presented Sadat with an oral message from Begin and upon his departure, he similarly took a message to Israel from Sadat. Questioned about the messages after the meeting, Schindler refused to discuss their contents. When he returned to Israel, from where he had set out for Egypt, Schindler told *The Jerusalem Post* only that he believed peace talks could succeed provided they dealt with practical matters and were conducted "out of the glare of international publicity."[145]

A few days later, on January 17, the negotiations on Begin's peace plan began. They did not go smoothly. Schindler tried to be realistic about the difficulties, though not without a belief in their ultimate success. They would be "long and arduous," he said, but in the end they would be successful. He even went so far as to call an Egyptian-Israeli settlement "inevitable," for both Begin and Sadat had "a powerful personal commitment to peace." The role of the United States, Schindler believed, was to act as a mediator rather than an arbitrator—to "unravel the snags" and keep both parties talking, rather than to propose its own solutions.[146]

Frustrated at the lack of progress, Sadat turned to the American Jewish community. In an open letter, he appealed to the Jewish sense of justice while complaining of the recalcitrance of the Israeli government, especially its failure to respond to his Jerusalem visit in a forthcoming manner. As the spokesman for American Jewry, Schindler, of course, needed to respond. Addressing the Egyptian president, he offered a clear defense of Begin's plan for the future of the occupied territories: "You have raised the question of the Palestinian Arabs. Prime Minister Begin's proposals offer them the opportunity of self-rule and self-identity—more autonomous power over their own affairs than they ever enjoyed before, including the years from 1948 to 1967, when the territory had been conquered by Jordan and there was no talk of Palestinian 'rights' or even of a Palestinian 'people.'"[147] In diplomatic language, he accused the Egyptian president of a take-it-or-leave-it attitude and an unwillingness to work toward mutual concessions—which, Schindler insisted, was the way a democracy operated. When Sadat came to the United States shortly thereafter to meet with President Carter, it was thought that he might want to meet with representatives of American Jewry. Schindler welcomed Sadat's visit to America but ruled out such a meeting, believing it inadvisable for the Jewish community to play any role as intermediaries, certainly not as "surrogates" for the Israelis.[148] Schindler did, however, continue to act as an adviser to the American government. Together with eight other top American Jewish leaders, he was invited to a private White House dinner with President Carter and Vice President Walter Mondale, where the topic was Sadat's visit. Here Schindler again stated his view that negotiations between Israel and Egypt should continue face-to-face, while America should act "as honest broker and mediator but not as an arbiter."[149] Above all, the PLO should be left out of consideration. Schindler's very last act as chairman of the Presidents' Conference was to cable Secretary Vance from Jerusalem, on June 30, 1978, assailing the State Department's assertion that the United States "does not consider the PLO a terrorist organization."[150]

It was rumored that the unprecedented extension of Alexander Schindler's term as chair of the Presidents' Conference was "dictated" by Menachem Begin.[151] Be that as it may, shortly after conclusion of the extended term, on July 6, 1978, the prime minister hosted the rabbi at a formal banquet in his honor at the Jerusalem Plaza Hotel. Before 250 invited guests, including members of the government, parliament, and diplomatic corps, Begin praised Schindler especially for his civil courage. Noting again that he and Begin had been called an "odd couple," Schindler responded by admitting their differences of approach to religion and politics, but insisting that "I, a man from the Left and a Reform rabbi to boot, he from the Right and a traditional Jew, share a passionate conviction: that the Jews of the world are one—one and indivisible."[152] Their souls were bound together, he claimed hyperbolically, as were those of the Biblical David and Jonathan. Politically, they agreed to oppose the demands that the PLO be made a negotiating partner and that negotiations should lead to an independent Palestinian state. The negotiations with Sadat were indeed deadlocked, but there was no reason to give up hope. Schindler then recalled for Begin a story from his youth that he thought relevant for the present moment. When he was a little boy, Schindler's father had taken him to Warsaw where they visited the *shtiebl* of the Umaner Hasidim, the devotees of Reb Nachman of Bratzlav. He remembered that carved into the wood of the synagogue's ark was not the usual Hebrew inscription *Da lifnei mi atah omeid*, "Know before whom you stand." It was rather an inscription in Yiddish: *Yidn zait sich nisht misya-esh*, "Jews, do not despair." Schindler concluded his talk with an expression of belief in *netzach Yisrael*, which he interpreted not as God, the Eternal One of Israel, but rather as an expression of "the invincibility of Israel." He ended his speech on a theological note, saying "God has promised us this land."[153]

On the same trip to Israel, the Hebrew University likewise honored Schindler just a few days earlier. It bestowed on him its coveted Solomon H. Bublick Public Service Award, a prize given in alternate years to an Israeli and a person from abroad who, during the two years preceding, had "made an important contribution to the advancement and development of the State of Israel."[154] It was an award first given in 1949 and previously bestowed on David Ben-Gurion, Harry Truman, Herbert Lehman, and Nahum Goldmann, among others. It consisted of a sterling silver plaque and a monetary sum, and it was given to Schindler as "a distinguished American rabbi," in part for his "deep and abiding commitment to the role of education in Jewish life" and also for his consistent work as "a sensitive interpreter of America and American Jewry to the people of Israel."[155]

Clearly proud of the acknowledgments he received, Schindler understood the two honors as a tribute that reached beyond himself. Writing to members of the UAHC Board, he expressed his feeling that "in no small measure I served as a symbol of the American Jewish community generally and the Reform Jewish community in particular, so that these honors are for you as well."[156] He went on to observe a truth: His serving as chair of the Presidents' Conference, though it took away a very large portion of his time from the duties that he owed the Union of American Hebrew Congregations (which no doubt had been noticed, perhaps with some dismay), "the happenstance of my chairmanship clearly served to destroy the stereotype of Reform as 'a thing apart' from the body Jewish."[157] Drawing more upon aspiration than demonstrable fact, he expressed his view that there had been a dramatic change for the better in how Israelis viewed Reform Judaism, noting, "We are seen as a force to be reckoned with."[158] As evidence, he cited the influence he was able to bring to bear against a proposed change in the Israeli Law of Return that would have disadvantaged Reform and Conservative converts by not considering them Jews under Israeli law. Schindler had sent a sharp protest to his friend Begin: "It would be a direct slap in the face to all non-Orthodox Jews saying, in effect, that our money and our energies are good enough but we and our children are not!"[159] A spokesman from Israel's Liberal Party, a constituent of the ruling Likud coalition, thereupon made a public announcement that his faction would oppose such an initiative in order to fulfill a promise made to Rabbi Schindler, and the proposed change in the law did not come about.

That fall Schindler was fully back at the UAHC working, as he wrote, to strengthen it, "which is no less vital to the creative continuity of our people than is the work in behalf of Israel."[160] The Union had jumped on the bandwagon of Schindler's publicity; it too honored him with a tribute dinner, which drew some seven hundred guests and raised about $300,000 for its budget and that of the Hebrew Union College–Jewish Institute of Religion. No longer would Schindler stand in so bright a limelight as during the two and a half years of his Presidents' Conference chairmanship. Now he turned his attention inward: to analyze, criticize, and seek to expand his own Movement. He did so in ways that were no less controversial than his insistence on American Jewry's right to dissent from Israeli policies.

CHAPTER 5
Reaching Out

BY THE TIME Alexander Schindler rose to leadership in the Reform Movement, the most severe problem it faced, next to religious indifference, was the fear of demographic decline due to interfaith marriage. Jewish partners in the majority of interfaith unions rejected or minimized Jewish identity and practice, and in most cases their children were not raised as Jews. Moreover, the percentage of interfaith marriages was steadily increasing. During the period from 1900 to 1920 only 0.8 percent of American Jews intermarried; from 1966 to 1972, the figure had risen to over 30 percent and the shift was gaining momentum.[1] There was some consolation in the fact that the non-Jewish partners were more frequently the women, who were more favorably inclined to raising their children as Jews than were non-Jewish husbands. Less consoling was the discovery that not only average Reform Jews but even the children of the Movement's topmost leaders were marrying someone of a different faith. Although the parents of the leaders had almost unanimously opposed their children marrying a non-Jew, by 1987 only slightly more than half the current leaders deemed themselves bothered "a great deal" by the prospect that their offspring would marry someone from a different religion.[2] Even when the non-Jewish partner converted to Judaism (which during the 1970s occurred in about 30 percent of cases)[3] and the couple sought Jewish religious identification, most frequently in Reform temples, the interfaith couple was often frustrated in its attempts to feel fully accepted by members of the congregation.[4] Some observers began to consider more seriously whether the interfaith marriage rate, along with such factors as late marriage and decline in birthrate, did not augur for a diminishing Jewish population in America, especially among secular Jews and adherents of Reform Judaism.[5]

In earlier generations, interfaith marriages could be easily ignored. "As recently as thirty years ago," wrote Reform Rabbi Sanford Seltzer in 1984, "some critics were still able to dismiss them as examples of aberrant behavior and describe couples in an interfaith marriage as rebellious, neurotic sons and daughters who were getting even with their parents by marrying outside of their faith."[6] Such an explanation no longer held. Yet Jewish leadership, especially in more traditional circles, continued to condemn interfaith marriage, and in some cases parents even severed relationships with their straying children. Efforts to strengthen Jewish education had a limited restraining effect, but they were insufficient to curb the general trend. In the Reform Movement, too, there was much hand-wringing and little positive initiative. Against this background, Schindler concluded that the trend of interfaith marriage was increasingly damaging Reform Judaism and required a radical response. Rather than simply voice concern, he determined to set forth a multipronged plan.

Within the Central Conference of American Rabbis, as noted above, discussion had long centered on whether its members should officiate at interfaith marriages. For rabbis, that was the most immediate and relevant issue. However, when interfaith marriage came up in 1962, a proposed resolution asked broader questions: "Is it possible to keep a significant percentage and perhaps the majority of mixed couples within the Jewish community? Can we, through a maximal effort and the mobilization of our considerable resources, save the children of mixed marriages for Judaism?"[7] But the CCAR did not have the resources in funds and staff to undertake such a task. If it were to be accomplished, the initiative would have to come from the UAHC.

The Union would not take action for another dozen years. In 1974 the West Coast director, Rabbi Erwin Herman, initiated "Project Outreach," intended to increase involvement of unaffiliated Jews in urban areas. Though launched in a part of the country where lack of affiliation was more prevalent than in the east, the initiative seems to have had little effect and it was not adopted nationally. It was therefore not until Alexander Schindler's address to a meeting of the Union's Board of Trustees, held in Houston on December 2, 1978, that "outreach" advanced from an abstract idea to an actual program.[8] Significantly, Schindler's address occurred only a few months after he completed his term as chair of the Presidents' Conference. His energies could now be redirected from foreign relations to his Movement's regeneration and expansion. In his presidential address, Schindler indicated his intention to offer a resolution for the creation of an agency within the Union that would "earnestly and urgently confront the problems of intermarriage" and seek to turn "the tide which threatens to sweep us away into directions which might enable us to recover our numbers and, more important, to recharge our inner strength."[9] The previous evening, Leonard Fein, a Brandeis University political scientist, social justice advocate, and Schindler's close friend, had confronted the Board with the troubling statistics. It was clearly time, Schindler concluded, to face a situation whose reality could not be altered, but whose consequence could. Interfaith marriage, Schindler noted in his address, was "the sting that comes with the honey of our freedom" in America's open society. Prevention of interfaith marriage was not working; therefore, the best option was to integrate interfaith couples more effectively into the Jewish community, attracting them with a warmer welcome and encouraging them to raise their children as Jews. Put succinctly, rejection of intermarriage should not mean rejection of the intermarried.

This welcoming attitude to religiously diverse couples was the least controversial proposal within Schindler's address. From urging a more complete welcome, he proceeded to suggest that the non-Jewish partner should be permitted to "join in most of our ceremonial and life-cycle events."[10] He gave examples: to sing in the choir, to recite the blessing over the Sabbath and festival candles, and to handle the Torah; upon death, the non-Jewish partner should be allowed burial next to his or her spouse in a Jewish cemetery. This suggestion set off extended discussions in individual congregations as to where the limits on non-Jewish participation should be placed and resulted in a wide variety of local policies. It is a subject to which we shall return.

Schindler's third recommendation went further yet: a child born of a Jewish father and a non-Jewish mother should—despite the standard halachic position that one's Jewish status follows matrilineal descent—be regarded as Jewish once that child has been Jewishly educated and gone through the bar or bat mitzvah ceremony. This was not a novel position within the Reform Movement. According to a note in the 1961 *Rabbi's Manual*, Reform Judaism accepted a child of a Jewish father and a non-Jewish mother as Jewish without a formal conversion "if he attends a Jewish school and follows a course of studies leading to Confirmation."[11] Schindler brought the issue up anew—either to stoke controversy, as he liked to do, or to create new awareness of the issue at a time when such situations were becoming more prevalent.[12]

His final suggestion was no less, and perhaps even more, controversial: "I believe that it is time for our movement to launch a carefully conceived Outreach Program aimed at all Americans who are unchurched and who are seeking roots in religion."[13] That is to say, Reform Judaism should seek new adherents not only within the Jewish community, but also beyond it. Schindler did qualify the proposal by stressing that proselytizing was not at the top of his agenda. His priority was "making Jews of the non-Jewish partners in an intermarriage."[14]

What motivated Rabbi Schindler to put forward these proposals? It could be argued that he was by nature an intrepid innovator, that he enjoyed stirring things up, and that he craved the greater attention brought by radical proposals than by innocuous, incremental, and balanced suggestions that stayed close to broadly accepted views. But it can also be argued that, as a refugee from Nazi Germany, Schindler was acutely conscious of the losses that the Jewish people had suffered in the Holocaust and the need to restore their numbers. Furthermore, the Reform Movement was not expanding as rapidly as it had during the early Eisendrath years and the Union required a larger financial base lodged in solid congregational membership. Finally, Schindler earnestly believed in the power of Reform Judaism to win over non-Jews on the periphery of the Movement, such as those who had married a Jewish spouse. If they could be made aware of the principles of the Jewish faith and the beauty of its practices, they would become active Jews through conversion—or at least they would instill a positive view of Judaism in their children.

In response to Schindler's address, the Union's Board of Trustees overwhelmingly approved a resolution that sought to intensify formal and informal educational programs within the synagogue, thereby creating a stronger attachment to Judaism. In addition, the resolution stimulated congregations to welcome interfaith couples and encourage the conversion of the non-Jewish partner. Finally, it sought to "bring the message of Judaism to any and all who wish to examine or embrace it."[15] The resolution did not include acceptance of Jewishness by patrilineal descent; that was regarded as an issue to be broadly discussed by the laity, but best settled by the rabbis. Most importantly, the adopted resolution called for a task force composed of members of the Board to consider implementation of the president's recommendations.

The Schindler proposals set off a discussion that swelled, ebbed, and swelled again during the course of his presidency of the UAHC. Not long after his address, he could report with satisfaction that response to it was running about nine to one on the positive side. Approving calls and letters were coming from non-Jews as well as from Jews of every shade of thought and affiliation.[16] Schindler told *The New York Jewish Week* that although he had prepared six thousand copies of his address, the printing was exhausted within a few days. It had become, he claimed, the most widely discussed topic on the internal life of American Jews. A filing cabinet drawer was rapidly filling with letters from people inquiring how they could become Jews. The incoming chair of the Board, Donald Day, called the pronouncement "historic" and used the occasion to congratulate Schindler upon the Board's unanimous decision to bestow a new and presumably more favorable contract upon the president.[17]

Except for the suggestion that synagogues be more welcoming to persons who had converted to Judaism, the Schindler proposals also provoked broad critique. The very idea of outreach seemed to stand in dangerous opposition to "inreach," which focused on Jews by birth or conversion. Would it not be better to concentrate on this group, rather than on those who had chosen to wed a non-Jew—let alone bring in non-Jews who had no personal connection to Judaism other than through their spouse? Critics worried that outreach would serve to dilute Jewish consciousness within the community rather than to intensify it. The most serious argument against outreach was that it would diminish conversion to Judaism. If non-Jews felt fully at home in the synagogue, if they were treated as equally accepted members of their congregations, then why should they bother to go through a process of conversion that involved organized study and solemn commitment? Schindler was well aware of this challenge and deplored what became an unintended consequence of outreach: the decline of conversion ceremonies in Reform congregations. In 1984, he could still claim, without citing specific evidence, that the rate of conversions to Judaism had "tripled over the past five or six years."[18] In later years, he no longer made that claim and instead acknowledged that outreach had led to a decline in conversions. "By making non-Jews feel comfortable and accepted in our congregations," he told an interviewer, "we have sent the message that we do not care if they convert. But that is not our message."[19] He thought non-Jewish partners should not be left to take the initiative with regard to conversion, suggesting instead, "We need to ask. We must not forget to ask."[20]

Until the end of Schindler's presidency in 1996, his 1978 proposals remained a topic of discussion within the American Jewish community; rabbis and laity alike staked out positions on his proposals. In the face of dissent, Schindler tried at times to play down the proposal for outreach, especially when he was charged with unduly allocating funds to the project that might better be used elsewhere. "Most of our resources here at the Union are devoted to the task of Jewish education," he wrote in defense of the proposal. "We operate eight camps in various areas of the United States where thousands of young people come each and every summer and throughout the year. . . . The patrilineal program was but one small element of a much vaster effort."[21] The "vaster effort," as Schindler understood it, was strengthening the Jewish community, both in its numbers and its intensity.

The Outreach Program may have been relatively small in expense and widely acceptable within Schindler's constituency, but its legitimation of patrilineal descent caused deep outrage, even in Reform circles. Rabbi Jakob J. Petuchowski, a professor who taught liturgy and theology at the Hebrew Union College–Jewish Institute of Religion in Cincinnati, was more concerned than most of his colleagues with how Reform Judaism could strengthen ties with its more traditional rivals. To his mind, the unilateral declaration recognizing the Jewish legitimacy of patrilineal descent was "a conscious step taken by the Reform rabbinate to establish Reform Judaism as a sect on the periphery of Judaism."[22] He warned that non-Reform rabbis would, as a result, look askance at the Jewishness of any Reform Jew. Rabbi Moses Cyrus Weiler, who had moved from Johannesburg to Jerusalem, noted that the acceptance of male lineage was bound to produce negative repercussions in the Diaspora and especially in Israel. For the fledgling Reform Movement in Israel, it would "break the desired united front of the non-orthodox, specifically with our Conservative brethren."[23] With this consideration in mind, the Israeli Reform rabbis, unlike their colleagues in the United States, refused to accept the validity of patrilineal descent in determining Jewish identity. Specifically, they feared it could bring about a change in the Israeli Law of Return that would require eligibility for immigration be limited to those converts who had undergone Orthodox conversion. It would also make it more difficult for Reform rabbis in Israel to gain recognition for the marriages and conversions they performed.[24] Canadian Reform rabbis likewise chose to reject patrilineal descent.

When the Central Conference of American Rabbis met in June 1982, Schindler was given the opportunity to make his case for patrilineal descent. He spoke of instances where interfaith marriages had led to divorce and the non-Jewish parent had gained custody of the children; as a result, the children were raised as Christians and the patrilineal Jewish parent, because not recognized as Jewish, had no recourse in a court of law. Such cases were becoming more frequent. Moreover, the children, even when raised as Jews by the patrilineal parent, never felt fully Jewish either in religious school or summer camp because their status as Jews was not officially recognized.

Although Schindler's proposal opposed centuries-old Jewish law, he could point out that in Biblical Israel and for a time thereafter, Jewish descent through the father had been the accepted norm. The fact that his suggestion was not entirely novel, but rather a return to ancient practice, gave Schindler's proposal a certain historical standing. Nonetheless, it still marked a significant break with the later development of Jewish law and with current practice. Although he was well aware that his suggestion would create a deep rift with traditional Jews, that outcome was insufficient to deter him. He preferred to give greater weight to the human anguish in the growing number of interfaith families caused by the current determination of status. Borrowing a metaphor from Mordecai Kaplan regarding the relative authority of Jewish law, Schindler concluded his message to the rabbis assembled:

> Let us not become sycophants, truckling for favor by becoming what we are not. It will not avail us. We will only demean ourselves and lose our distinctive character. Our fathers and our mothers did not forge Reform Judaism to have us trade it in for a tinsel imitation of Orthodoxy. We owe Halacha a vote and not a veto and we ourselves that self-respect and integrity which holds fast to our finest values and our most cherished beliefs.[25]

Although Schindler very much wanted non-Jewish partners in interfaith marriages to convert to Judaism, he was not prepared to deprive children in such a marriage of being recognized as fully Jewish because the Jewish parent was so only by patrilineal descent and not by matrilineal as required by regnant halachah.

A year later, when the assembled rabbis adopted a resolution on the subject, they did add a provision that was not spelled out in Schindler's original proposal: they insisted that the Jewishness of a child born of an interfaith marriage, though resting presumptively upon the Jewishness of either mother or father, would have "to be established through appropriate and timely acts of identification with the Jewish faith and people"[26] before the individual would be fully recognized as a Jew. However, while the Union Board had been favorable to patrilineal descent, American Reform rabbis were divided. After going through a long committee process and plenary deliberation at the March 1983 CCAR conference, the 550 rabbis present supported the essence of Schindler's proposal—made almost five years earlier—by a margin of three to one.[27] A few months later, the decision was affirmed in a responsum issued by the CCAR's Responsa Committee.[28] But those Reform rabbis opposed to the resolution continued to express their views. The highly respected David Polish posed an argument, frequently heard: "It makes it possible for intermarrying couples to enter upon their marriage with full psychological comfort and with religious satisfaction that their children will in all events be Jewish. Then why convert?"[29] Interestingly, among those in support of Schindler's position was a leading American Zionist, Professor Ben Halpern of Brandeis University, who wrote, "Yet, whatever difficulties it may entail, the Reform [affirmation of patrilineal descent] is one that a secular Jewish loyalist can only welcome. It signalizes an openness to all who choose to be Jews, and to all the forms in which their Jewishness authentically finds expression, which we must applaud."[30]

In defending his position during the course of a public discussion that would continue to the end of his life—his last article on the 1978 proposals appeared less than two years before his death[31]—Schindler described his position on patrilineal descent as motivated foremost by "the demographic imperative facing the Jewish people today."[32] Writing for a broader leadership, and perhaps with Conservative Jewish readers in mind, he called it a "halachic innovation" that gained authority from earliest practice, as had been recently described by the respected professor of Jewish history Shaye J. D. Cohen, then teaching at the Jewish Theological Seminary.[33] Here and elsewhere, Schindler liked to refer to the irony that Nikita Khrushchev's grandchild was halachically considered Jewish by birth because born of a Jewish mother, while David Ben-Gurion's grandchild, born of a non-Jewish mother, required conversion. In the last analysis, for Schindler, the subjective aspect trumped the halachic.[34]

Thoughtful discussion of Schindler's views on patrilineal descent was not limited to Reform Jews, but came, as well, from outstanding representatives of Conservative Judaism and Modern Orthodoxy. Robert Gordis, a leading Conservative rabbi, chose to cite a famous statement from Yehuda Halevi's *Kuzari*: "Your intention is praiseworthy, but your action is unacceptable."[35] Rabbi Irving (Yitz) Greenberg, more than most Orthodox Jews, was concerned with preserving Jewish religious unity among its religious denominations and therefore expressed his concern that patrilineality would, regrettably, open a rift among them. But his moderated response took note both of the proposal's virtues and what he believed to be its unfortunate consequences. He wrote, "Adoption of the [CCAR's] resolution is a triumph for ethics, feminism, sociology, and Americanism and a defeat for halakhah (Jewish law), Klal Yisrael (the totality of Jewish people), and respect for tradition. Above all, it is a warning of stormy weather ahead for Jewish unity and community."[36] Greenberg expressed the hope that dialogue among the denominations would result in a halachic solution to what he recognized was a real problem. That, however, was a vain hope; a universally acceptable solution was not likely to be found either within an Orthodoxy, where Greenberg was regarded as an outlier, or within Schindler's Reform Judaism, which gave subjectively experienced ethical concerns precedence over received Jewish law. The left and the right would remain divided.

Schindler was, of course, quite aware that Reform Judaism would not be accepted as legitimate by Orthodoxy under any circumstances. That view was confirmed a few years later by a letter he received from an Orthodox rabbi, stating baldly, "Our Torah does not advocate patrilineal descent; we cannot change Torah law, as you *well* know, Sir."[37] Schindler was certain that efforts made by Conservative Judaism to gain Orthodox acceptance were likewise in vain. It was therefore not true that Reform was entirely responsible for what some regarded as deleterious religious division within the Jewish people. Schindler never admitted to that charge, arguing instead that Judaism could tolerate internal Jewish pluralism. Moreover, the unity of the Jewish people had survived a more consequential innovation when Reform Judaism, generations earlier, had decided not to require a religious divorce before remarriage. "Eliminating the *get* [certificate of Jewish divorce] was something that could not be dealt with from a *halakhic* viewpoint. Children of those who have divorced without a *get* are considered *mamzerim* [of illegitimate birth] under traditional halakhah and cannot marry other Jews. By comparison patrilineal is minor."[38]

Despite his vehement rejection of the notion that Reform decision-making should bow to Orthodox disapproval, Schindler looked for any support that his views could obtain from more traditional Jews. Among them was Conservative Rabbi Harold Schulweis, who called the patrilineal notion "a right move," adding, "I think it has enough traditional background biblically, and I think pragmatically it is of the greatest importance."[39] Even in his opposition, Greenberg had at least recognized the ethical basis for Schindler's view. That was not true, however, of mainstream Orthodox for whom contemporary halachic practice was unassailable.[40] No less in opposition, if not as vehemently so, was Conservative Judaism, whose United Synagogue of America passed a resolution in 1991 that made the rejection of patrilineal descent a standard of the Conservative Movement and urged both the Reform Movement and the small Reconstructionist Movement, which had adopted patrilineal descent as early as 1968, to reconsider their positions, lest religious Jewry be further divided.[41] Schindler replied to that development by noting that "recent studies show that 85 percent of American Jews accept the patrilineal principle, including a substantial majority of the Conservative laity and even a plurality of Conservative rabbis."[42] Moreover, the proposal was a step in the direction of greater equality of men and women within Reform Judaism. To defuse the argument that patrilineal descent was merely an accommodation, Schindler noted that children of Jewish mothers and gentile fathers, according to the CCAR resolution, would also need to participate in public acts of Jewish affirmation in order to be fully recognized as Jews.[43] In this regard, he believed, Reform Judaism was being not less, but rather more stringent.[44]

Schindler's most radical proposal—and also the one with the least effect—was to seek converts in the non-Jewish world who had no connection to the Jewish community. This was the case despite the fact that seeking converts—like patrilineal descent—had precedents in Jewish history. In ancient times, proselytizing non-Jews for the sake of enlarging Judaism had been a common goal. The Christian Bible, Schindler was aware, notes that the Pharisees traveled far and wide to make a single convert (Matthew 23:15). Wanting to provide a relevant Talmudic text in his favor, he could also cite Rabbi Elazar in *P'sachim* 87b: "The Holy One, blessed be He, exiled Israel among the nations so that converts might join them."[45] During the Middle Ages and into the modern period, Jews were usually prohibited from proselytizing in both Muslim and Christian countries. Yet, there was an extraordinary exception when at least the elite leadership of the Asian Khazar kingdom chose conversion to Judaism. More recently, Rabbi Leo Baeck, who taught at the Hebrew Union College while Schindler was a student there, had advocated a Jewish mission to gentiles even before World War I, while he was a rabbi in Germany. It is "for us a commandment of self-preservation," he had argued, "since recognition by others will awaken pride of possession in our own ranks."[46] Following the devastation of the Jewish community in the Holocaust, Baeck continued to advocate for missionizing, emphasizing the importance of replacing those Jews who had been lost. Schindler, who frequently quoted Baeck in his speeches, fully agreed. Increasing awareness of the Holocaust had already brought the subject of proselytizing into broader discussion during the 1950s, when the CCAR expressed its approval of such a move.[47] At that time, like Baeck, even Conservative rabbi Robert Gordis thought that an influx of men and women from other backgrounds would have a salutary effect upon the Jews themselves. "Perhaps," he wrote, "the time has come to renew the active missionary role of Judaism, now dormant for nearly two millennia."[48] A decade later, at the UAHC Biennial Assembly in 1965, Rabbi Eisendrath urged that Reform Judaism seek converts among "unsynagogued and unchurched" Jews and Christians.[49] Not long thereafter, a survey of Protestant churches revealed that strong denominations and congregations were those that possessed missionary zeal; they were eager to tell the good news to all. Weak churches, by contrast, thought in terms of dialogue rather than proselytism.[50] At least in Christian circles, it was apparently the case that seeking converts not only increased ranks from the outside, but also strengthened those already within.

For Alexander Schindler—who, as we noted in an earlier chapter, had long cherished the cause—actively advocating for the proselytization of non-Jews was not in 1978 a new ambition. However, as with his other proposals, he brought the topic into broader discussion. It differed from his other suggestions, however, as in this case non-Jews, no less than Jews, participated in the discourse.

Christian attitudes on mission to the Jews were at that time moving in two directions. On the one hand, the Catholic Church in 1965 had promulgated its Declaration on the Relation of the Church to Non-Christian Religions, Nostra Aetate, which declared that Jews were not rejected or accursed by God. Twelve years later, Rabbi Balfour Brickner, then director of the UAHC Department of Interreligious Affairs, attended a meeting with members of the Vatican's Commission for Religious Relations with the Jews, where Catholicism's understanding of its mission was presented as precluding proselytism. It was rather to be understood as a mission "not *to* the Jews, but *with* the Jewish people *to* the world."[51] On the Protestant side, the prominent theologian Reinhold Niebuhr in 1958 had urged fellow Christians not to seek the conversion of positively identifying Jews. Evangelical Christendom, however, was moving in the opposite direction. It launched a broadly based drive devoted to calling our continent to Christ with the stated intent of bringing new converts into its churches. A list composed by the Task Force on Missionary Activity of the Jewish Community Relations Council of New York and titled "Fighting the Missionary Groups" listed sixty-two organizations devoted wholly or in part to the conversion of the Jews.[52]

Among Jews, some feared that undertaking an active program of proselytization would estrange those Christians whose leadership had recently moved away from their own proselytizing efforts and at the same time would provide justification for other Christian groups that were reinforcing their own missionizing efforts toward the Jews. Moreover, it would look a bit like the cults, and especially the ashrams, that were succeeding in attracting younger Jews at that time. Recently, one such cult—though not attractive to Jews—had extinguished itself through mass suicide in Jonestown, Guyana. There was also the rising competitive attraction for some Jews of "Jews for Jesus" and similar groups. A few years later, such missionizing of Jews prompted the UAHC to produce a thirty-minute video documentary titled "The Target Is You."[53] In short, Jews were being dangerously seduced from different directions. Under these circumstances, the question was: Should Reform Judaism become in any sense like groups that were missionizing Reform's adherents, even as such approaches were declining among Christian liberals?

It may have been a surprise to Schindler—but if so, a most pleasant one—that his proposal received a warm reception among mainline Christians. Writing in the Jewish periodical *Commentary*, the sociologist and liberal Protestant theologian Peter L. Berger described Schindler's proposal as "a sensible and low-risk measure of Jewish demographic self-defense"; like Schindler, he was persuaded that "you will not be able to keep your own unless you are prepared to persuade others."[54] For Berger, contestation among the faiths was not a concern; within contemporary society, the real problem was "the historic battle against the inroads of modern secularism."[55] His view was not an isolated instance. When Rabbi Brickner sent Schindler's proposal to prominent Protestant and Roman Catholic churchmen asking for their response, they expressed some misgivings but basically supported Schindler's plan, seeing it as a sign of American Jewish vitality. They did not believe it would bolster attempts to proselytize Jews to Christianity. Among those who replied positively were, on the Protestant side: Krister Stendahl, dean of the Harvard Divinity School;[56] Harvey Cox, a professor at that school; and the Methodist theologian A. Roy Eckhardt; on the Catholic side: John Pawlikowski, a theologian at the Catholic Theological Union in Chicago, and Eugene Fisher of the United States Catholic Conference.[57] Fisher concluded his response by asserting that "an active Judaism which vigorously proclaims its message to the world and openly invites all interested in experiencing the richness and depth of its religious tradition is something to be welcomed in a pluralistic society."[58]

Among most traditional Jews, Schindler's proselytization proposal was viewed more critically than among liberal Christians. Within a few days of his 1978 address, both Rabbi Saul Teplitz, president of the Conservative Rabbinical Assembly, and Rabbi Bernard Rosensweig, president of the Orthodox Rabbinical Council of America, expressed their opposition.

According to Teplitz, the Jewish task was rather "to convert Jews to Judaism."[59] Similarly, Rosensweig held that the drive should be for the "unsynagogued" and not for the "unchurched."[60] Rabbi Wolfe Kelman, executive vice president of the Conservative Movement's Rabbinical Assembly, argued against Schindler's plan in the name of religious pluralism: "Reverence for diversity should become our religious charter. We must learn to accept the potential for holiness in those who seek to quench their thirst for the words of the Lord from different wells and springs."[61] Even Rabbi Harold M. Schulweis, a good friend of Schindler and fundamentally in agreement, expressed caution, lest Christian missionaries regard his words as offering them legitimacy.[62]

Although the Reform rabbinate was, in general, favorably inclined toward a renewal of Jewish proselytizing,[63] one leading figure in Reform Judaism almost immediately expressed opposition to Schindler's effort. Even as he opposed patrilineal descent, so did Rabbi David Polish express doubt about proselytism—not because it was intrinsically wrong, but because he believed it was not the best means for strengthening the Jewish community. He maintained that the focus should rather be on helping unmarried Jewish women find Jewish mates, increasing the number of Jewish births, and offering free Jewish schooling to the children of the Jewish poor.[64]

Yet Schindler could derive satisfaction from at least a few voices outside Reform's official ranks that did not hesitate to express a more favorable view of his proposal. The outspoken Jewish author, editor, and feminist Trude Weiss-Rosmarin was unconditional in her approval: "Jews who are convinced that their way is right have the obligation to invite others to join them. Conviction and the urge to convert are inseparable."[65] Rabbi Schulweis argued that it was possible to develop "a Jewish ethics of proselytizing sensitive to the pluralistic rights of other faiths" and that interpreting Judaism to the world could gain for Jews "a new self-awareness, self-esteem and articulateness."[66] Milton Himmelfarb, a widely read Jewish intellectual and officer of the American Jewish Committee, began his positive response with a verse from the prophet Isaiah (55:1): "Ho, everyone athirst, come for water."[67] More remarkable were the words of two Orthodox leaders. Rabbi Irving Greenberg on the left, as we have seen, opposed patrilineality, but he called the proposal for proselytization bold and imaginative. To be sure, the conversion process would need to be respected and recognized by all, but he concluded, "More and more, the people who are Jews will be those who want to be Jews. Some will be Jews by birth, but all will be Jews by choice."[68] Most remarkably, the foremost leader of mainstream Orthodoxy, Rabbi Joseph (Dov) Soloveitchik, seems also to have favored Schindler's proposal. In a Hebrew interview that he gave to the Orthodox scholar and columnist Rabbi Pinchas Pelli in 1985, he said that he approved of the Reform method of welcoming potential converts. "The correct way is specifically the way of the Reform," he told his interviewer, "(and I am sure that many of my Orthodox friends will stone me on account of what I am saying)—of course, with Orthodox content."[69] Soloveitchik did not advocate for a program of missionizing beyond the Jewish community, but he did clearly favor urging non-Jewish spouses to convert, and it must be remembered that non-Jewish spouses were also Schindler's principal target for conversion.

After the initial contestations, the debate over proselytism ebbed for a few years until the fall of 1993, when it resurged no less virulently. The Union's Outreach Commission had initially been active on the other forms of outreach, preferring to move proselytizing gentiles with no connection to Judaism "to the back burner." It had centered its efforts on non-Jews who were already bound to the Jewish community by marriage.[70] Now Schindler decided to bring proselytism to the fore. He set out a dramatic suggestion to create a $5 million fund for "making the glories of Judaism available to non-Jews."[71] It was his opinion that "the time is ripe to move forward with the wider mission." The UAHC Biennial Assembly thereupon adopted the proposal unanimously; $100,000 was quickly in hand and close to half a million pledged.[72]

As a result of this new effort to bring potential converts from outside the Jewish community into Judaism, leading Conservative Jews became Schindler's critics. Rabbi Ismar Schorsch, chancellor of the Jewish Theological Seminary, found the proposal to divert contributions to proselytization "incredulous" while Gerald Zelizer, president of the Rabbinical Assembly, thought that Reform was, sadly, forgetting more important priorities.[73] In a widely circulated article titled "Proselytizing Is Bad for the Jews," Jack Wertheimer, professor of Jewish history at the Seminary, offended Schindler by suggesting that Reform conversions to

Judaism were not serious: "We should not encourage individuals to treat religion as yet another replaceable *shmatte*, a cheap suit, try it on for size and then dispose of it when the fashion passes," he wrote. Moreover, proselytizing could lead to Christian missionary groups unleashing "their full arsenal of weapons against American Jews."[74] Schindler replied no less forcefully, accusing Wertheimer of placing himself among those "who are ashamed of the notion of an assertive Judaism." Further, his critic's words manifested "an unreasoned hatred of Reform." Wertheimer should consider that fully 50 percent of individuals raised as Conservative Jews were currently marrying non-Jews—hence the need to replace those lost with fresh influx from outside the community, with an emphasis on Jews' non-Jewish spouses.[75]

The new impetus likewise provoked dispute within Reform Judaism, not only over the principle but also the financial priority of the project. Rabbi Joseph Glaser, the executive vice president of the CCAR, feared that outreach was "taking on a life of its own."[76] Rabbi Richard Hirsch condemned the new proposal outright. Not only was it "most deleterious to the essence of Reform Judaism," it would also be a movement toward sectarianism, widening the gap between American Jewry, Reform Jews elsewhere, and the State of Israel.[77] In addition, he believed it would draw funds away from other UAHC activities. The latter was an assertion that Schindler vigorously denied, and he assured Hirsch that such a diminution would not occur. In the last eighteen months, he had raised in excess of $20 million for the Endowment and Trust Fund of the UAHC, more than doubling its previous amount.[78]

Reform laypersons, too, requested justification. One asked whether it would not be better to focus on remedying the lack of outreach to "our very own Jews."[79] Taken aback, Schindler retreated. He wrote to Raquel Newman, "The truth of the matter is that I wanted to evoke a discussion. I want people to think about their Judaism and how much they value it, and whether they value it sufficiently to offer it to others in the market place of ideas."[80] Moreover, proselytism was not at the center of UAHC activities: "The bulk of the money of the Union goes to camping programs, [the] education program, youth programs."[81] Only the interest from the projected $5 million dollar fund would be used for proselytism, perhaps an annual amount of $250,000 out of the total $27 million UAHC budget.[82]

Nonetheless, Reform rabbi Daniel Schiff in Pittsburgh put his objection tersely: "We do not need new Jews . . . we urgently need renewed Jews."[83] Schindler's response to Schiff was similar to what he wrote to Newman: "I want to evoke debate because when you feed people pablum, they yawn and go to sleep."[84] Schiff's letter had angered Schindler. He was not, as Schiff claimed, exercising "leadership by sensational headlines rather than through the creation of a truly thoughtful democratic solution for the Jewish future."[85] That was simply not the case, Schindler insisted. He may have propounded his ideas vigorously before his constituency, but it was not true that they were "announced to the media by UAHC leaders, then sold to the lay leadership and finally discussed and debated and hastily approved by the rabbinate."[86] Quite to the contrary: beginning in 1978, rabbinate and laity had been given their share in this discussion before implementation was undertaken.[87]

By the time of this second round of controversy, the Union, under Schindler's direction, had succeeded in establishing an institutional structure for outreach. It focused on bringing non-Jews with Jewish family connections fully into the community and providing an attractive path for conversion to Judaism for people who chose to cast their lot entirely with the Jewish people—whether they came from within or without the extended Jewish community.

Schindler followed up his dramatic 1978 speech with the appointment of a twenty-six-member UAHC/CCAR Task Force on Reform Jewish Outreach. It was enthusiastically chaired during its first decade by a financially successful, politically conservative layman, David W. Belin of Des Moines, Iowa, who had previously served as counsel for the Warren Commission investigating the Kennedy assassination.[88] The co-chair was Max Shapiro of Minneapolis, a rabbi known for playing a large role in Jewish-Christian relations. The Union supplied a full-time staff member, Rabbi Sanford Seltzer, as its director of research; Schindler chose not to be a member of the Task Force himself. Its report, issued in August 1981, recommended the development of programs and educational materials that would help couples in an interfaith marriage "enhance the Jewish content of their family life and create a warm and supportive climate that will encourage them to raise their children as Jews and [the non-Jewish partners] to choose Judaism as their own personal faith."[89] In particular, the Task Force urged the strengthening and improvement of "Introduction to Judaism" classes with the clear aim to create a more structured and attractive path to conversion. The message of Judaism was to be communicated with dignity both to unaffiliated Jews and to non-Jews lacking any religious preference, but not to active adherents of other religions. The initiative would have the collateral benefit of strengthening the religious identity of people born Jewish. The report concluded by expressing indebtedness to Rabbi Alexander Schindler "for his visionary genius in calling for the organization of our Task Force."[90] Grandiosely, the members declared that their study could result "in one of the great milestones in American Jewish history—and, indeed, in world Jewish history."[91] They were clearly aiming very high.

Schindler explained that the program advocated by the Task Force was the best answer to "the problems presented to us by the dramatic and continuing rise in the rate of Jewish intermarriage."[92] He had concluded that interfaith marriage could not be stopped, only "retarded" by raising Jewish consciousness in a variety of ways. He listed his specific objectives in order of priority: removing the "not welcome" signs from Reform congregations; improving education of prospective Jews-by-choice; working with interfaith married couples both within and outside the synagogue; providing children of interfaith marriages with Jewish education; and, finally, reaching out to "seekers after truth," who might be interested in Judaism.[93] He was pleased that a preliminary investigation revealed that 10 percent of those converting to Judaism did so for reasons other than wanting to marry a Jew.[94]

In response to Schindler's persistent urgings, an elaborate framework to implement his ideas came into existence. For those congregants whose partners had converted to Judaism but felt uncomfortable in their synagogues, the Union held retreats intended to make them feel less alien. At the heart of its program were the Introduction to Judaism courses, some conducted by the Reform, some independently by the Conservative Movement. Participation, it was soon recognized, differed by gender and origin. A survey indicated that nearly 75 percent of those enrolled in the programs were women, and that more Roman Catholics than Protestants participated. Nearly all participants intended to raise their children as

Lydia Kukoff, the head of Reform Judaism's Outreach Program, in 1982. *The Oregonian*, October 30, 1982. Photo by Tom E. Treick.

Jews.[95] Schindler clearly recognized the need to carefully monitor the program in order to determine its effectiveness. "We cannot be content to proceed without some objective data," he noted. "We cannot always fly by the seat of our pants."[96]

In 1981 the Union published a highly successful volume titled *Choosing Judaism*.[97] The slim paperback volume remained in print for over twenty years, serving as a guide for all who were entering Judaism from the outside. Its author, Lydia Kukoff, headed the Union's Outreach Program for its first thirteen years as it gradually expanded.[98] From her own experience as a person who converted to Judaism, she was able skillfully to present her own story along with suggestions for others seeking to convert to Judaism or recently having done so. By 1984, the Commission on Reform Jewish Outreach had become a full department of the Union with a serious budget of $300,000, of which a portion was to be used for part-time coordinators in each of the Union's regions. Soon several hundred Reform congregations had functioning outreach committees. By 1986, with UAHC-sponsored classes for prospective converts widespread throughout the country, Schindler could boast, "We have taken the discussion of intermarriage out of the house of mourning and into the house of study—indeed into the sanctuary itself. Without condoning intermarriage, we have recognized its reality and have begun to grapple with it. *Hob nit kayn moire wen du host nit kayn andere breyre*—holds the Yiddish proverb—'Don't be afraid when you have no other choice.' Thus we have counseled, and the Jewish community listened."[99] Still, Schindler was well aware of the doubts held by many, and felt compelled to tell his Board that no more than 5 percent of the Union's budget was devoted to outreach: "'Inreach' is by far our *raison d'etre* as an organization. Outreach may be making headlines, but inreach is writing volumes, inscribing a Jewish identity in the hearts of thousands of Jewish children."[100] Schindler did not want his much-publicized outreach campaign to overshadow the commitment to the religious education of Jewish young people, whom he had served earlier as the director of the Union's Department of Jewish Education. Nonetheless, as his career came to an end, he took most pride in the Union's Outreach Program, which he had conceived and which by 1995 had an annual budget that had grown to nearly $600,000—a higher rate of growth than any other Union department. He had come to see it as "a form of Jewish self-defense" and "a tool of Jewish survival."[101] Frequently during his last years, Schindler expressed his wish that he be remembered, above all, for this program.[102]

CHAPTER 6
Issues and Actions

ALTHOUGH chairing the Presidents' Conference dominated Schindler's attention for more than two years and outreach remained a recurrent interest through the end of Schindler's term as UAHC president in December 1995, being the head of Reform Judaism's congregational union for close to a quarter of a century simultaneously and more fundamentally involved unavoidable administrative tasks as well as exercise of leadership within the Reform community on issues of political and moral concern.

At the start of Schindler's tenure as president, the Union of American Hebrew Congregations—which had expanded rapidly in the early years of Maurice Eisendrath's presidency—was in a "decade-long decline and stagnation in membership growth."[1] But it then resumed expansion, if not immediately and consistently, during Schindler's two decades. When he assumed office in 1973, the Union numbered slightly more than 700 congregations; at the end of his tenure it could boast above 850 congregations, with a total membership of at least a million individuals. Given that this growth was impressive in relation to Orthodox and Conservative Judaism, Schindler felt justified to boast in 1982, "The future clearly belongs to us."[2]

But Schindler was forced to note that the ranks of the unaffiliated were expanding at an even more impressive rate. During his initial years as president, a national economic recession reduced UAHC income to the point that he was, unhappily, forced to propose a deficit budget—the first, he claimed, in the recent history of the Union.[3] Nonetheless, Reform Judaism continued to strengthen, especially in the suburbs, though some urban areas marked declines in membership, especially in Brooklyn and the Bronx, largely on account of out-migration. The Union had two major sources of income: the annual Maintenance of Union Membership assessment (familiarly known as MUM), which in 1978 required payment of 12 percent of congregational dues and constituted 84.6 percent of the Union budget, and the individual contributions raised by the Reform

Jewish Appeal (RJA), which made up an additional 10.4 percent. The two—even after funds were shared with the Hebrew Union College–Jewish Institute of Religion—were sufficient to allow for an extensive and variegated program. However, Schindler thought that the Union would be able to accomplish even more if Reform Jews gave philanthropic priority to their synagogues over their local federations.[4] Whereas MUM involved no fundraising activity, the RJA did—and Schindler was expected to play a large role in expanding RJA income. Yet according to more than one member of his staff, fundraising was not a task that Schindler performed well. He was able to establish friendly relationships with wealthy prospective donors, but he was not a capable "closer"; it was simply not in his character to press individuals for major contributions. Moreover, raising funds for what was essentially an umbrella organization was necessarily difficult. Toward the end of Schindler's tenure, the Union's financial situation again became precarious. An increasing number of congregations, under their own financial constraints, were cutting back on their MUM dues payments. In response, the congregational MUM assessment was lowered from 12 percent to 11 percent and Union expenses were reduced. The list of suspended congregations, especially in the West (where many congregations had only a brief history as members of the UAHC), was growing longer. Schindler tried to ignore this situation, but could not avoid being reminded of it.[5] Nonetheless, considering his nature and realizing the necessity of displaying optimism, Schindler continued proclaiming only a bright future for the Reform Movement, at least in public.[6]

Although not an effective fundraiser, Schindler may have been an efficient administrator (views among his associates are divided on that issue). On administrative issues he could always turn to the chair of the Board of Trustees, who served as the Union's official CEO and had the final word on major decisions.[7] In day-to-day practice, however, Schindler was clearly in charge. Board chairs devoted varying amounts of time to their offices; some became Schindler's close friends. In contrast to Eisendrath and upon David Saperstein's suggestion, Schindler involved the UAHC Board of Trustees actively in the decision-making process. He was fortunate to have a capable senior staff headed by his senior vice president Albert Vorspan, a talented layman who directed the Union's Social Action Commission and was his closest confidant; Vorspan would regularly advise Schindler, especially with regard to social issues. Also working closely with Schindler was Rabbi David Saperstein, the energetic director of the Union's Religious Action Center in Washington, who was able to give the Union some weight in political decisions affecting moral issues on which the Union (and Schindler personally) had taken a stand. Once the Reform Movement formally associated itself with the Zionist movement, the third of Schindler's "lieutenants"—the intellectually inclined Rabbi Eric Yoffie, whom Schindler had known from Worcester—took over directorship of its Zionist subsidiary, the Association of Reform Zionists of America (ARZA). The Union's senior staff also included, at different times, Rabbi Daniel Syme, who oversaw multiple programmatic areas of Union activity, and the strong civil rights advocate Rabbi Balfour Brickner, who for a time headed the Union's Department of Interreligious Affairs. According to Yoffie, Schindler was not a micromanager. As long as he was informed and was not given ultimata, he was willing to let members of the staff embark on their own initiatives. He listened to criticism from his staff, even if he did not encourage it.

In addition to the UAHC staff centered in the New York area, there were fourteen regional offices spread out across the United States and Canada, each headed by a centrally appointed rabbi, and on which the Union expended between one-third to one-half of its budget. Other staff were employed as directors of the nine UAHC camp institutes, which flourished during the Schindler years, or in publishing the Union's quarterly magazine, *Reform Judaism*, sent without charge to members of UAHC congregations and capably edited by Aron Hirt-Manheimer. Yet other staff were responsible for the Union's extensive list of textbooks and curricula for religious schools and adult education. Although the president could occasionally rebuke members of his staff for acting too independently of his authority,[8] he was lenient in making appointments and was surprisingly willing to employ rabbis on the Union staff who had been fired by congregations for sexual misconduct.[9] Schindler was a great believer in the power of repentance (*t'shuvah*) and in giving transgressors a second chance.

Schindler's proclivity to be forgiving was put to the test when Jonathan Pollard, convicted of having sold closely guarded American state secrets to Israel and sentenced to life in prison, appealed to him in 1992 for assistance

Rabbi David Saperstein, Senator Edward Kennedy, and Rabbi Schindler.
Courtesy of American Jewish Archives, Cincinnati, Ohio.

in gaining commutation of his sentence. When Pollard's sister, Carol, was then invited to present her brother's case before the UAHC Commission on Social Action, Schindler received a lengthy handwritten letter from Pollard thanking him for the intervention. However, following Carol's appearance, the Commission voted 26–4 against seeking commutation. That decision resulted in a second letter from Pollard, this one very brief and nasty. "In light of your belief that G-d doesn't want us to stand by in the face of injustice, will the UAHC be making any statement on my behalf? I didn't think so. I guess my sentence isn't covered by your organization's definition of justice."[10] Despite the insulting note, Schindler nonetheless decided to act against the decision of the Commission. Eschewing UAHC stationery, he wrote a personal letter regarding Pollard to President Clinton: "He has been paying a rather high penalty for his acknowledged wrong-doing and I believe it is time to offer him forgiveness and a new beginning. I am writing as a private citizen and on a personal level to urge that his sentence be commuted to time already served." Schindler insisted that his letter not be released to the public lest he "get into a confrontational position with my leadership." Shortly thereafter, the 1993 UAHC Biennial Assembly overwhelming passed a resolution urging commutation, thus eliminating the gap between Schindler and his lay leadership.

Schindler again wrote to Clinton, this time on official stationery, but the president once more and in explicit language turned down his request.[11]

During Schindler's tenure as president there were no women in UAHC senior staff positions. However, as early as his initial year in the UAHC presidency in 1973, Schindler could point to the first woman officer of the Union, Norma Levitt, who had just been elected one of its vice chairs. And, as mentioned earlier, Schindler was greatly dependent upon and gave considerable authority to his assistant, Edith (Edie) J. Miller, who joined Schindler's staff in 1976 and played a central role in administering the Union through the end of his term. Without her work, Schindler would arguably not have been able to function. Though in a subordinate position, she was nonetheless able to play an active role in the decision-making process.[12] According to interviews with members of the staff, a large percentage of the letters sent out over Schindler's signature were in fact written, or at least formulated, by Edie Miller.

In preparing his major addresses, especially those he delivered to the biennially held Union assemblies—which toward the end of his term drew close to five thousand attendees—Schindler would exchange ideas with his senior staff, sorting out those he thought were important and could be presented effectively.[13] To Saperstein, who on one occasion had given him multiple suggestions, he wrote, "If I developed each and every point—and what with all the other issues I want to or am pressed to cover—I'd speak longer than all of the prior S[tate] of the [Reform] U[nion] messages, MNE's[14] included."[15] For his most important addresses Schindler, at Union expense, engaged a talented speechwriter—or perhaps better called a "speechwriting assistant"—named Lawrence Bush, whose Jewishly committed religious atheism was not, in Schindler's view, a disqualification. During his thirteen years with Schindler, from 1984 to 1996, Bush did not actually compose the speeches from start to finish. Rather, as he recalled, "What Alex sought from me was poetic metaphors that could uplift listeners, and the expression of progressive political perspectives through religious language. We just naturally shared a poetic/inspirational/philosophical bent."[16] Despite his speechwriting assistant's denial of God and his more radical politics, the two men developed what Bush called "a real heart connection."[17]

As head of its congregational union, Schindler was the American Reform Movement's unchallenged principal leader. At an earlier time, the president of the Hebrew Union College had played that role, even as the chancellor of the Jewish Theological Seminary of America enjoyed the distinction for Conservative Judaism. But for American Reform Judaism, ever since Maurice Eisendrath assumed the Union's presidency, the voice of Reform Judaism had emanated from 838 Fifth Avenue in New York, the home of the UAHC. Ideas originated there. When they had political implications, they were transformed into action by its Religious Action Center in Washington. Schindler, who greatly enjoyed making public statements, would therefore frequently express a viewpoint or take action on behalf of Reform Judaism. His views were of sufficient influence to be reported with some frequency in the Jewish—and even in the general—press. Among the domestic issues on which Schindler spoke out were equal rights for women and gay and lesbian individuals, abortion, race relations, and the Christian Right.

The issue of whether women should be allowed to become rabbis had been settled in the Reform Movement before Schindler became the Union's president; the first female rabbi in America, Sally Priesand, was ordained in Cincinnati in 1972. In 1995, Schindler would happily install one of his daughters, Judith, in her first pulpit. Yet like many other male rabbis (and laymen), Schindler found the shift to egalitarianism a bit unnerving; unlike most, he was willing to admit to that fact. "To be sure, there are times when I feel disoriented by all these transformations," he noted. "After all, I was born of a different age, and so there are times when the unfamiliar land of the feminist community bewilders me and I inadvertently stumble back into more habitual tracks of thought and speech."[18] It may well have been his assistant Edie Miller, or perhaps his wife Rhea or his daughters, who brought him around to advocating for fully equal roles for women in Reform Judaism.

Although on January 22, 1973, the Supreme Court had declared abortion a constitutional right in the case of *Roe v. Wade*, the issue remained controversial and hence alive. In 1981, on the date of the eighth anniversary of the decision, advocates of free choice and abortion rights called upon Schindler to provide it with a religious justification. Speaking for the interdenominational Religious Coalition for Abortion Rights, he explained that in rabbinic law the fetus is not a juridical personality and that it becomes a *nefesh*, a living soul, only when it leaves the womb. To this legal explanation for the Jewish position, Schindler added a more personally motivated argument: "It is precisely because we value life that we are opposed to accidental and indiscriminate reproduction in a world which is already overpopulated and underfed. The cries of emerging life *are* a delight. But we must also hear the silent crying of parents who see the bloated bellies of their starving infants and are helpless to give them surcease."[19] When later that year Schindler testified on abortion before the United States Senate's Judiciary Subcommittee on the Separation of Powers, he cited the resolution passed by the 1975 UAHC Biennial Assembly supporting the constitutional right of a woman to obtain a legal abortion. He then proceeded to a much more extensive explanation of Talmudic law and rabbinic responsa on the subject. Schindler concluded that the restrictive legislation as it lay before the committee was at variance with long-standing Jewish religious tradition. Declaring a fetus a human being, as a proposed amendment would have it, ran counter to Jewish law. As Schindler put it tersely, in Judaism "feticide is not regarded as homicide."[20]

The issue of "homosexuals" (the term then in use) arose for the Union in connection with the question of whether a congregation composed mainly of such individuals should be admitted to membership in the Union.[21] The Union's Pacific Southwest regional director, Rabbi Erwin Herman, had provided encouragement to the founders of the first Jewish gay and lesbian congregation in America, Beth Chayim Chadashim in Los Angeles. Herman acted in consultation with Schindler, who gave him his personal support. Not surprisingly, this produced a quick negative reaction, expressed by both Reform rabbis and laity. To one rabbi who inquired about the Union's stance, Schindler replied that criteria for congregational membership were nowhere stated in the Union's constitution. He then went on to make a further argument for providing Union assistance:

> I certainly had no *moral* grounds to refuse such aid. On the contrary, the moral imperative of the situation dictates that aid be given here. If we accept the orthodox psychological judgment that homosexuality is an illness, these people deserve compassionate understanding and not rejection, much in the manner say in which we help congregations for

the deaf. And if we accept the minority view among psychiatrists that homosexuality is a state of being, not an illness, why then these people certainly have the right to be who they were born to be. As a matter of general principle, I would prefer if homosexuals were to be integrated as individuals into existing congregations. At the same time, I recognize that they are not always made to feel comfortable in the heterosexual, family environment of the average congregation and hence the legitimacy of their desire for separate groupings ought to be respected.[22]

However, Schindler was not yet fully convinced that it was a good idea to establish such congregations, as opposed to encouraging individual memberships in preexisting congregations. He penned a confidential letter to twenty-three Reform rabbis asking for their opinions: Should the Union accept such congregations into membership? And how would the rabbis respond to requests that they bless a same-sex relationship? He concluded by noting that a Union board member had already introduced a resolution insisting that the "Union refrain from having anything to do with Sodomites."[23] Prominent among those who responded negatively to Schindler's letter was Rabbi Eugene Borowitz, a professor at the New York campus of HUC-JIR and a noted theologian. According to his view of the covenant between God and Israel, "homosexuality cannot be considered, for Jews, a sexual option of equal status to heterosexuality. Or more directly, I do not see how Judaism, understood as life under the Covenant, can welcome, encourage or honor homosexuality in the Jewish community."[24] Hence Borowitz was strongly opposed to admitting such a congregation to the Union and likewise to rabbis officiating at homosexual marriage ceremonies. The highly respected Rabbi Solomon Freehof of Pittsburgh, who believed that homosexual activity was a sin, wrote similarly: "To isolate them into a separate congregation and thus increase their mutual availability is certainly wrong. It is hardly worth mentioning that to officiate at a so-called 'marriage' of two homosexuals and to describe their mode of life as Kiddushin (i.e., Sacred in Judaism) is a contravention of all that is respected in Jewish life."[25] In answering Freehof, Schindler gave his own views on the questions he had asked, namely his agreement with Freehof that "homosexual congregations are not to be encouraged and that every effort should be made to integrate homosexuals as individuals in existing congregations." He was willing for the Union to offer aid to gay and lesbian congregations but not to recognize them; he believed such recognition would "sanction a lifestyle which is totally at variance with our traditional conception of the family and the community. Obviously, I am opposed to all 'marriage' ceremonies of this sort, for that would be a mockery of what the word marriage means in Judaism."[26] Clearly, at this stage, Schindler was still vacillating in his attitude.

Nonetheless, Beth Chayim Chadashim of Los Angeles was accepted as a member congregation of the Union not long after Schindler's confidential letter to the rabbis. He justified the decision by noting that the congregation, as opposed to another one recently established in New York, was open to anyone and not solely reserved for Jews who were gay.[27] Still, opposition to its inclusion did not immediately die out. David Belin, the Union's most enthusiastic supporter of its Outreach Program, continued to suggest, as late as 1986, the possibility that homosexuality was a medical problem that required medical attention. He objected to the Union's failure to inform Jewish young people through its *Keeping Posted* youth periodical that some psychiatrists continued to believe that homosexuality can and should be treated.[28] At about the same time, Rabbi Jakob Petuchowski, a well-known professor on the Cincinnati campus, in a *CCAR Journal* satire, went so far as to compare the Los Angeles gay congregation to a "synagogue of thieves."[29] To that sarcasm, Schindler angrily replied, "Petuchowski's bigotry has no place in a publication that bears the name of our community."[30]

By the time Petuchowski wrote his sharp rejection of the Los Angeles congregation, the chief issue in the gay community had become the plague of AIDS. What was of particular concern to Schindler about this devastating disease, beyond the dreadful effect on its victims, was what he called the "secondary scourge," a phenomenon "as deadly as the primary affliction: a wave of hysteria in a public which does not truly understand the disease and is therefore blinded by fear and prejudice."[31] Reflecting his own shift in attitude, Schindler believed that only showing compassion for AIDS victims was an insufficient reaction; beyond compassion lay the more adequate act of "identification." Addressing a Jewish Community Service in Support of People with AIDS, Schindler brought the subject into the realm both of Jewish history and of his own biography: "We who were Marranos in Madrid, who clung to the closet of assimilation and conversion in order to live without molestation, we cannot deny the demand for gay and lesbian visibility."[32] He admitted that resolving the issue for himself had not been easy. He had had "to wrestle with demons in the depths of my own being, demons I never thought were there."[33] However, he explained that he now felt able to fully identify with AIDS victims, not least because he too had been stricken with the fear of death. In his youth, he noted, he had been a refugee from Hitler's Germany and more recently a heart patient "looking on death's face."[34] He was proud that the Union had acted in response to the AIDS crisis. It created a national committee to deal with the issue and distributed a packet of educational materials to combat misinformation for rabbis and laypersons in UAHC congregations. Schindler claimed that the Union was the only national Jewish organization that was addressing the issue.[35] Speaking to his colleagues at the centennial celebration of the Central Conference of American Rabbis, he challenged them—and himself—to "once and for all declare ourselves rabbis for *all* Jews, at every moment of life, not only the heterosexual Jews—or for gay Jews, only at their funerals when they die of AIDS."[36]

When the Jewish War Veterans of the USA, acting in accord with widespread public opinion, adopted as its policy support of the official—if not fully observed—ban on homosexuals serving in the United States armed forces, Schindler pulled out his own record of military service as refutation: "I spent four years in the United States Army," he wrote to the associate editor of the organization's periodical, "was a volunteer in the Ski Troops, fought in three campaigns, was wounded in action, and I have a bronze star for bravery. And I can tell you that the only moral problems we ever encountered were from our heterosexual comrades in arms."[37]

There was a remaining question: Should gay and lesbian individuals be allowed to be ordained as rabbis? There were distinguished rabbis, such as Solomon Freehof, who wrote in opposition and also Union leaders who were opposed; as one of them put it, "Being a Rabbi is something different and very special, for the Rabbi serves as a Judaic role model."[38] However, it is not surprising that on this issue, as well, Schindler reached an unorthodox position. He noted that numerous gay and lesbian rabbis, who had been forced to hide their sexual identity, were already serving with honor and without "even the slightest hint or suspicion that the fact they were homosexuals impaired their functioning as exemplary role models."[39]

Acting on his conviction, Schindler installed Rabbi Sharon Kleinbaum, a lesbian, as spiritual leader of the twelve-hundred-member Beit Simchat Torah synagogue in New York on September 11, 1992.[40] Thus although he had been initially reluctant to press for full gender equality, Schindler gradually moved to a position of assertive advocacy, and members of the gay and lesbian community came to regard him with admiration and gratitude. Schindler himself was deeply proud of his position.

A commitment to social justice had been Maurice Eisendrath's first priority, and the establishment of the Religious Action Center (RAC) in Washington, DC, his outstanding achievement. During Schindler's term of office, the RAC's activities were effectively carried out by the highly active Rabbi David Saperstein. Schindler took pride in Saperstein's accomplishments, but with his own office in New York, he was less directly involved in the RAC's activities. Still, social justice concerns appeared regularly in Schindler's speeches to the Union's biennial assemblies and to meetings of its Board of Trustees. Since the Board regularly included Republicans as well as Democrats—supporters of recently elected Ronald Reagan in 1980 as well as liberals—Schindler had to maintain an equilibrium. To placate those who did not share his political views, he chose on one occasion to become self-critical. "We liberals are often too sanctimonious, entirely too aggrandizing in our self-perception," he admitted. "We think that we hold a patent on decency. We do not."[41]

Unlike his predecessor, Schindler was not one to participate regularly in public demonstrations, a task he left to other rabbis and to the RAC. Nonetheless, he came under criticism for giving social justice issues too much attention in his speeches and too high an allocation in the Union budget. In a lengthy letter during Schindler's last years in office, directed to the then chairman of the Union's Board of Trustees but copied to Schindler, David Belin castigated the Union for being stuck in the ways of the 1970s and 1980s.[42] Social justice may have deserved priority in those decades, he argued, but now the community was more focused on issues of spirituality. Why did Schindler's addresses not give more attention to that subject? Some of its adherents were warning that Reform was "in grave danger of having social action become the golden calf of liberal Judaism."[43] And why did it ignore antisemitism in the Black community?

Then, plunging in the dagger, Belin dared to suggest, "The ultimate irony of the UAHC emphasis on social action is that contrary to the perception given to our Trustees and the delegates at Biennials, those who truly know the ways of Washington recognize that resolutions passed by the UAHC have minimal significance in the ultimate decisions made by Congress and by the President."[44] Belin wanted to turn the Union toward Judaism's existential concerns. Yet in Schindler's eyes, taking responsibility for the society in which Jews lived was a legitimate extension of the religious spirit—no matter how limited the effect. Or, as Schindler put it in a sermon a few months later, "There is no not-holy. There is only that which has not been hallowed. The so called 'political' and 'economic' matters are religious in their essence—and in their solution."[45]

Among the social issues to which Schindler directed attention were the proliferation of guns and protection of the environment. When yet another "plague of violence" broke out in 1977, Schindler wrote to President Carter urging him to go beyond his promise simply to reduce the number of weapons available to criminals and the mentally ill. Speaking for the UAHC, he called for legislation "to eliminate the manufacture, importation, transportation, advertising and sale, transfer and possession of handguns except for limited instances, such as the military, police, security guards and licensed and regulated pistol clubs."[46] Needless to say, this was a wholly unrealistic demand within American society, even under a Democratic president. Schindler apparently wanted to express a personal ideal, rather than urge an achievable course of action.

Schindler was also committed to environmental activism. Shortly after the interdenominational Coalition on the Environment and Jewish Life was established in 1993, he agreed to serve as a member of its Board of Advisers. Whereas the organization planned for the Jewish Theological Seminary to focus on conceptual issues, it tasked the UAHC's Religious Action Center with national and local political action, as well as broadbased congregational education.[47]

Schindler believed that race relations was another one of the dominant social issues on which a religious body was required to take a stand. This focus was strongly supported by Kivie Kaplan, a wealthy Jewish businessman and philanthropist who had been a member of the UAHC Board of Trustees as well as president of the National Association for the

Advancement of Colored People from 1966 until his death in 1975. Kaplan was the principal layperson behind the contentious establishment of the Religious Action Center and one of numerous Jews who played leading roles in the American Civil Rights movement. However, by the time Schindler assumed presidency of the Union, the militant Black Power movement was acting to exclude non-Blacks from the ranks of civil rights leadership.[48] Relations between Jews and African Americans were deteriorating, as differences arose regarding their respective roles both in the civil rights movement and within the Jewish community.[49] Conservatively inclined Jews opposed affirmative action in college admissions policy, whereas liberal Jews, including many within the UAHC, supported the Black community in seeking it.

During Schindler's tenure, two Black leaders caused major controversy: Andrew Young and Jesse Jackson. Despite the Jewish community's differences of opinion about the two men, Schindler—if hesitatingly—voiced his support for both. In March 1977, Jimmy Carter had named Young, a close confidant of Dr. Martin Luther King, Jr., to be the first Black United States ambassador to the United Nations. As mentioned earlier, Schindler had welcomed that appointment on behalf of the Presidents' Conference. However, two years later, in his diplomatic capacity, Young met with the UN representative of the Palestine Liberation Organization, and news of the meeting became public when it was leaked by Israel. Young's act caused a stir among American Jews, since the United States had promised Israel there would be no direct meeting with the PLO until that organization recognized Israel's right to exist—a policy with which Schindler fully agreed. He therefore found himself caught between his support for Andrew Young as a civil rights leader and his support for America's official policy. When a reporter called him in the middle of the night and asked, "Don't you think that Young should be fired?" Schindler later claimed that he had known better than to say yes.[50] When Carter shortly thereafter did call for Young's resignation, it was widely assumed that the Jewish community was behind the action. Soon, Young added to the tension between himself and the Jewish community when he publicly stated that Israel was "stubborn and intransigent."[51] As Schindler had sought to bridge the gulf between American Jewry and Menachem Begin, here again he sought to prevent division, in this case between a Black civil rights leader whose

Rabbi Schindler with Andrew Young. *Courtesy of American Jewish Archives, Cincinnati, Ohio.*

intentions he supported and a Jewish community concerned, as he was, with the security of Israel. He came up with an answer that vindicated Young while averring the correctness of not recognizing the PLO. Neither American Jewry nor Israel had called for Young's ouster, he pointed out; guilt for the break between American Blacks and Jews lay with a third party. Andrew Young, Schindler suggested, had been "a steadfast friend of Jewish causes from his earliest days in the Civil Rights movement."[52] He deserved no blame for what had occurred; rather, the responsible party for the tension was the State Department, whose policy sought "to cosmetize the PLO and transform this terrorist gang into a fit negotiating partner in the Middle-East peace talks."[53] Forces within the State Department had brought about Young's meeting with the PLO, he maintained. How Schindler came to that conclusion is not clear, but it provided him with an answer that could absolve both sides of the dispute.[54] Not long thereafter, he came up with a second equally undocumented, explanation: It was none other than Jimmy Carter who, as he was then running for reelection, kept suspiciously silent on the matter of Young's dismissal in order to deflect Black anger at the dismissal away from himself and onto the Jews.[55] Why had the president not said, as Schindler believed he should have, that he had not yielded to any Jewish pressure nor even felt it?[56]

Even more problematic for Schindler than the "Andy Young Affair" was a series of comments by Jesse Jackson. Jackson—at the time the ambitious president of the tactically assertive Operation PUSH (People United to Serve Humanity)—charged Menachem Begin with pursuing a deleterious "no-talk" policy, prompting Schindler once again to come to his Israeli friend's defense. Begin had been willing to surrender the whole of Sinai, while the PLO offered no olive branch in response, he countered. In a less than friendly note to Jackson, Schindler nevertheless concluded with reconciliation: "Our two communities share many common goals. Let us end the demagoguery and get back to work."[57] He denied that Jackson had become pro-Arab; his Middle East views were prompted by his fundamental commitment to the civil rights cause. In a letter to the son of a rabbinical colleague, Schindler cited from a Jackson speech to the effect that "unless the oil-rich Arabs come up with some dollars for American civil rights use, three letters will drop out of the black alphabet—PLO."[58] In other words, the Black leadership was not fundamentally pro-Arab, but primarily concerned with the welfare of its own movement. Of course, Schindler could scarcely rejoice over Jackson's calling Begin "a terrorist," his infamous reference to New York City as "Hymietown," or his failure to denounce the antisemitic Louis Farrakhan. But in later years Jackson sought to mend his relationship with the Jewish community, an effort very much in keeping with Schindler's hopes for restoring the close relationship between Black and Jewish leadership. In introducing Jackson at a conference sponsored by the World Jewish Congress in Brussels in 1992, Schindler could speak of commonalities that far exceeded differences and of the shared vision held by Blacks and Jews.[59] Assured by Jackson's insistence upon "secure borders" for Israel, his enthusiastic support of the Camp David Accords, his efforts to gain freedom for Syrian Jews, his on-camera confrontation with Mikhail Gorbachev over Soviet Jewry, and his remarks on the unique meaning of the Holocaust, Schindler invited Jackson to address the UAHC Board. It was time, Schindler believed, "to look beyond the hurts and grievances of the past."[60] In the area of race relations, too, Schindler was ready to forgive if he believed that such forgiveness would help to secure the future.

Meanwhile, a new crisis between Blacks and Jews had arisen. In August of 1983, there was to be a planned march on Washington marking the twentieth anniversary of Martin Luther King, Jr.'s famous speech. At issue was UAHC's participation, given that anti-Israel organizations would be taking part and might use the occasion to attack the Jewish state. Moreover, the march would occur on the Jewish Sabbath. Most Jewish organizations decided not to participate. Schindler, too, did not want to be part of a demonstration whose speakers turned to anti-Israel diatribes, nor did he want to violate a religious observance for the sake of a political cause. On the other hand, Jews had played a role in the original march and their refusal to participate this time would be understood as Jewish rejection of Black civil rights. Schindler therefore undertook to set aside these two obstacles. Leaders of the UAHC, including Schindler, met with Black leaders Coretta King, Walter Fauntroy, and others to express their concerns and "make it clear that if those concerns are not addressed, we will quietly disengage."[61] They also sought to influence the choice of speakers and extend the event to the entire weekend, so that it would not take place solely on Saturday.[62] With regard to his first objective, Schindler's efforts were apparently successful and he received the assurances that the UAHC was seeking: In a joint letter, Fauntroy, the national director of the event, and Coretta King, one of its co-chairs, expressed their intention to stress the goal of international peace without articulating a specific strategy for achieving it. In addition, they gave assurances that marshals would not allow placards or banners that were not in keeping with the theme of jobs, peace, and freedom. Should an anti-Israel statement issue nonetheless from one of the speakers, the co-chairs would publicly disavow such a statement as "inconsistent with the spirit of the March and coalition."[63] Given these assurances, Schindler and the members of the UAHC Board believed that Jewish interests were best served by staying in the event's planning coalition.[64] As it turned out, the understandings were fully respected. In their speeches, Senator Abourezk did not attack Israel, and Jesse Jackson did not refer to the Middle East at all.[65] Schindler had found a way to retain a positive relationship with the Black and Hispanic communities, which, as he noted to the Israeli ambassador in Washington, was very much in Israel's interest.[66] With obstacles thus cleared out of the way, Schindler agreed to deliver the closing benediction. He uttered it "as the Sabbath sun was dropping low behind the Lincoln Memorial."[67]

These are his eloquent concluding words, styled in a poetic fashion, as was Schindler's frequent custom:

> If we say we believe in equal opportunity,
> > give us the determination to make a full and creative life possible
> > for all people.
>
> If we say we believe in peace,
> > give us the courage to take those risks required for its attainment.
>
> If we say we believe in liberty, then give us the strength
> > to loosen the fetters,
> > to break the bonds,
> > to shatter the chains,
> > until the freedom of all is secured.[68]

Later that year yet another race-related issue came to the fore, one that had been undermining Jewish-Black relations for some time: What position should the Union take with regard to apartheid in South Africa? The Black community in America called for strong condemnation of the racist state, while the State of Israel was selling it arms and maintaining vibrant economic relations with it. In December 1984, Schindler—who, as we noted, seldom took part in public demonstrations—had joined a long list of activist Blacks in protesting at the South African embassy. According to the *Chicago Tribune*, Schindler was briefly arrested for his participation, together with four other Jewish leaders including Theodore Mann, his successor as chair of the Presidents' Conference.[69] The following year, the Union's General Assembly adopted a resolution that reaffirmed condemnation of apartheid, called for the release of Nelson Mandela, and demanded the institution of various economic sanctions.[70] Even as Maurice Eisendrath had virulently opposed United States participation in the war in Vietnam despite Israel's support of it, here Schindler similarly felt that he was morally compelled to denounce South Africa's racist policy even though Israel, for political reasons, needed to maintain its relationship with that country. The tension was relieved in 1990 when Nelson Mandela was released from prison. At that time, Schindler wrote an emotional letter of appreciation to President De Klerk: "Like so many others active in the world-wide pursuit of social justice, seeing the freed Nelson Mandela brought tears to my eyes. Your courage was historic."[71] Yet, Schindler was not entirely happy with the new situation in South Africa. The courageous Mandela was not a friend of Israel, as evidenced by his commending Yasser Arafat for "fighting against a unique form of colonialism."[72] In response, Schindler's deputy, Albert Vorspan, assumed a Zionist stance and suggested to Mandela that "it might be more appropriate to equate the dream of your people to Zionism, the liberation movement of the Jewish people, which resulted in the establishment of the democratic state of Israel nearly 42 years ago."[73] For Schindler, the situation required that he continue holding together his vision of a fully emancipated South Africa, even if it did not yet fully appreciate the values it shared with American Jewry and with a democratic, racially tolerant Israel. In the 1980s and thereafter, he could not ignore that the ties were continuing to fray.

Even as the Black Power movement distanced liberal Jews from its cause, so too did a burgeoning movement within Christianity drive away American Jews. Judaism and Christianity had forged important connections following Vatican II, when Roman Catholicism began to emphasize dialogue and religious commonalities. Howver, in the 1980s, as liberal trends in American Protestantism further weakened, a growing fundamentalism—whose political views were regarded unfavorably by most Jews—came to the fore. On September 14, 1980, the president of the Southern Baptist Convention, Rev. Bailey Smith, declared at a large evangelical meeting in Dallas that "God almighty does not hear the prayer of a Jew" because Jews do not accept Jesus as the Messiah.[74] In a sermon delivered a month later, he followed up with demeaning remarks that can only be considered antisemitic: "I think they [the Jews] got funny noses, myself. I don't know why He chose the Jews. That's God's business. Amen."[75] Not long thereafter, Schindler addressed this troubling trend toward intolerance. Speaking in San Francisco to the Union Board, he linked Evangelicals with antisemitism and called upon American Jews to reach out to moderate Christians and Black groups in order to form "coalitions of decency against the chilling power of the radical right."[76] In his remarks, he referred not only to Bailey Smith but also to the head of the recently formed Moral Majority, Jerry Falwell, who was calling for a "Christian Bill of Rights."

What especially disturbed Schindler was the fact that certain Jewish groups were "flirting with this new force on the American scene."[77] Why had the right-wing Zionist Jabotinsky Foundation presented Falwell an award, and the Anti-Defamation League offered its national platform to TV evangelist Pat Robertson of the Christian Broadcasting Network? The reason, of course, was their support for Israel. But for Schindler, that support was insufficient cause for honoring them when they encouraged antisemitism, albeit indirectly. At the same time, connecting closely with liberal Christianity was not an option for liberal Jews who were committed Zionists, since the National Council of Churches had issued a statement in support of the PLO. With pressure from both the right and the left, Schindler concluded that the UAHC should neither identify with nor cut itself off fully from either the Christian Left or the Christian Right. Instead, he believed the Union should seek coalitions with regard to those issues on which they agreed: with liberal Christianity on such matters as abortion; with the Christian Right on support for the security of Israel.[78] Following the election of Ronald Reagan, Schindler feared that the rightward pull within Christianity would only become stronger as it reflected the changing political atmosphere. With typical Schindler hyperbole, he wrote of "evangelical ayatollahs" and termed the movement "McCarthyism reborn and wearing clerical robes."[79]

Schindler's position drew criticism from both Christians and Jews. Jerry Falwell called his charge that religious fundamentalism fosters antisemitism "false and absolutely without foundation."[80] The popular Christian leader asserted that he had been not only an advocate of Israel but also a friend of the Jewish people in America and around the world. A more aggressive response came from Rabbi Abraham Hecht, president of the [Orthodox] Rabbinical Alliance of America, who called Schindler's accusation against Falwell "both scurrilous and inane."[81] Hecht had met and cooperated with the Moral Majority and could therefore state that the ominous threats Schindler had laid out were a totally unfounded fantasy.[82] More friendly but likewise critical was the reaction of the politically conservative Reform rabbi Joshua O. Haberman of the influential Washington Hebrew Congregation. He disagreed with the Moral Majority on abortion and prayer in public schools, but objected to Schindler's demonizing the group; he thought there were areas in which the Union could and should cooperate with it.[83]

But was the Moral Majority at least good when it came to Israel? It did indeed support the state with donations and propaganda, but as Schindler noted, in a more significant way it was actually undermining it. In a letter to the director of the Prime Minister's Office, he pointed out that the Moral Majority worked to defeat the American senators who were the staunchest supporters of Israel, on account of their views on domestic issues—including Frank Church of Idaho, Howard Metzenbaum of Ohio, Edward Kennedy of Massachusetts, and Henry Jackson of Washington. Schindler wanted Prime Minister Begin to realize the damage that the Christian Right was doing to Israel "by going to bed with the political assassins of some of our best friends over the decades."[84] However, the following month Schindler received a message from his friend Menachem Begin, indicating that he "wants me to meet with Jerry Falwell."[85] Meanwhile, Falwell had apparently become aware of Schindler's views and decided to correct what he believed to be false conclusions. He decided that the most effective way to do that would be to send every rabbi and Jewish leader in the country the book *Jerry Falwell and the Jews*, written by Merrill Simon, "a devoted Jew and ardent Zionist." He also wrote Schindler a letter debunking the notion that he believed the State of Israel to be the fulfillment of the Armageddon prophecy; on the contrary, he believed in the Abrahamic covenant promising the Land of Israel to the Jewish people forever. Moreover, he had visited Israel fourteen times. Domestically, the only religious issue he wanted to bring before the American Supreme Court was the issue of right-to-life. Schindler should read the proffered book, and it would disabuse him of his mistaken views and show him that evangelical Christians and Jews shared more moral values than did the Jewish people with the liberal National Council of Churches.[86]

Either at that time or a few years later, Schindler did come into closer contact with Jerry Falwell. What we know is that in response to an article by conservative intellectual William F. Buckley, Jr. sarcastically attacking Schindler for linking Falwell to a rise in antisemitism, Schindler noted, "I have invited Jerry Falwell to address the UAHC's fifth biennial Consultation on Conscience, Sunday, April 14, 1985, at 8:00 p.m. in Washington, D.C. and he has accepted. He and I will speak on the same topic: 'The Role of Religion in Politics.'"[87] The event was scheduled to take place at Haberman's congregation.

As it turned out, Falwell fell ill and could not appear at the event. In his place came the highly popular religious broadcaster and spokesman of the Religious Right, Pat Robertson. Welcoming Robertson, who spoke first, Schindler began his own speech with an analogy scarcely favorable to Falwell. He described the substitution of Robertson for Falwell as like at the opera: When Pavarotti has a cold you end up with Plácido Domingo, and while one might be flashier, the other has the more solid voice. Robertson, in explaining his agreement to be the substitute, had said he did not want a debate and that he would eschew harsh rhetoric; and in fact he spoke in terms of rapprochement rather than antagonism. Not so, however, the second speaker. "I never speak dispassionately," Schindler confessed at the very start of his response. And he did not do so. Instead, after giving the Moral Majority credit for focusing attention on such matters as deterioration of the family, the debasement of sex, and the indiscriminate permissiveness in our society (which the Jewish community had failed to do), he proceeded to delineate differences between Reform Judaism and the Religious Right. These included the Christian Right's opposition to the Genocide Convention and its leaving up to God such matters as toxic waste dumps, rent gouging, and unequal pay for women. Contrary to the Jewish interest, it favored prayer in public education, thereby chipping away at the separation between church and state. Using his often colorful language, Schindler explained Jewish opposition to such infringement as the result of its "allowing the separating wall to crumble into a moat where the sharks of religious hatred thrash about and sharpen their teeth for victims."[88] He then cited a statement Robertson had recently made during one of his 700 Club broadcasts: "The Constitution of the United States is a marvelous instrument for self-government by Christian people. But the minute you turn it into the hands of non-Christian people, and atheistic people, they can use it to destroy the very foundations of our society. And that is what's been happening."[89] One can imagine how that quote must have shaken up the Jewish audience that had crowded into the expansive synagogue. Schindler then raised a fundamental question intended to undermine the theological certainty with which the Christian Right preached its message: "Can we really know God's will on all the issues facing our nation?"[90] That expression of theological modesty, however, was a two-edged sword, for did not Schindler and the Union's Religious Action Center also hold that their ethically grounded political positions were in some sense the will of God, even if they did not say so explicitly?[91]

In a later speech, Schindler sought to distinguish the two relationships to divinity as clearly as possible: "We uphold the right of fundamentalist preachers to speak out on public policy. We do not see the First Amendment as precluding a political involvement by the religious community.... If Schindler can hold forth on nuclear disarmament and economic justice, why then Pat Robertson has every right to take the stump for prayer in the public schools even as Cardinal O'Connor has the right to inveigh against abortion."[92] The distinction between the Religious Right's political advocacy and Reform Judaism's social justice program lay not in the religious obligation to speak out on issues in the public square, but rather in the manner and certainty of expression. Whereas the Religious Right cast everything in apocalyptic terms, "as a struggle between good and evil, between God and Satan, between the forces of light and of darkness," Judaism did not claim such knowledge.[93] As Schindler put it, "Can we really know God's will on all the issues facing our nation? Can any being of flesh and blood know with a certainty what God Almighty wills on a particular policy matter? Surely that is a knowledge which neither Christian nor Jew, however learned or pious, has the right to claim!"[94] To confidently proclaim God's will on a specific issue was, in Schindler's view, nothing less than "blasphemy."[95] But how then separate a Jewish religious pursuit of social justice from one instituted by a secular organization? Schindler does not deal with that issue. One can only suppose that, along with the Religious Right, he believed that God demanded a moral society; whereas with the secularists, he was reluctant to apply God's will to the position taken on this or that particular issue.[96] Schindler sought somehow to combine divine commandment with human fallibility.

During the same years that the Protestant Religious Right came into conflict with the Jewish community, tension also arose in relations between Jews and Catholics. The immediate cause was Pope John Paul II inviting Kurt Waldheim, who had been accused of Nazi war crimes, for an official visit to the Vatican in the summer of 1987. Shortly thereafter, Schindler himself participated in a Jewish delegation that met with Vatican officials and the Pope. In the confidential report that Schindler rendered to his Board of Trustees following the trip, he made reference to some of the divisive issues aside from the Waldheim visit. These included the beatification of the Christian convert from Judaism Edith Stein, the current rise of antisemitism in the Christian countries of France and Austria, papal homilies that Schindler judged to be throwbacks to pre–Vatican II theology (a subject that Schindler had researched and on which he spoke to the delegation), and the failure to establish full diplomatic ties with Israel. To his pleasant surprise, Schindler found the church leaders sufficiently responsive for him to return from Rome believing that Jewish-Catholic dialogue, "far from being ruptured, was considerably advanced."[97]

Although Schindler's international influence declined following the end of his term as chair of the Presidents' Conference, he continued to be involved in the affairs of the Jewish people worldwide—an involvement that remained until the end of his life. Participating in international organizations that often involved travel to interesting places was a principal joy. Some of his connections with international Jewish organizations date back to his earliest years with the UAHC while others came only later; they brought him into close contact with the leading figures in world Jewry. As early as 1975, Schindler was playing a large role in the Memorial Foundation for Jewish Culture, which, founded by Nahum Goldmann in 1965 with German reparation funds, was devoted to subsidizing younger scholars as well as various activities that might serve to fill the cultural gap left by the Holocaust. It was no doubt Schindler's background as a refugee from Nazi Germany, as well as his position as the head of a major Jewish organization, that prompted the Foundation's chairman Jerry Hochbaum to appoint Schindler as chair of its Commission on the Holocaust, whose members included leading experts in that field. The commission's special tasks, as Schindler outlined them, were to evaluate programs of financial support for burgeoning scholars of the subject and to recommend projects that the Foundation would consider worthy of support.[98] During Schindler's tenure, the commission urged the advancement of a major undertaking: publication of a series of volumes ultimately titled *Pinkasei HaK'hilot, Encyclopedia of Jewish Communities from Their Foundation till after the Holocaust*.[99] After his retirement from the UAHC presidency and throughout the last years of his life, Schindler served as the Memorial Foundation's president, along with the chairman of the Foundation's Executive, Israeli politician Yosef Burg.[100]

Though a German Jew, Schindler expressed interest in the Memorial Foundation's Eastern European endeavors, perhaps in recollection of the rich religious and cultural life in which his own ancestors had played a role. Shortly after his election to the Foundation's presidency, he arranged for an inventory of Jewish cultural assets, artifacts, ritual objects, and libraries in Eastern Europe. The Foundation's activities there, he believed, "afford us a sense of optimism and lead us to the belief that the struggle to revive and restore a flourishing cultural life where half a century ago there were only ashes will indeed be won."[101] Concerned to reestablish Jewish continuity in Eastern Europe, Schindler pointed to the example of the Bratzlaver Hasidim who had managed for two centuries to continue their tradition even without their revered leader; perhaps the Foundation could learn from them.[102] Summing up, Schindler declared the activity of the Memorial Foundation to be "holy work."[103]

Schindler wanted the UAHC also to play a role in the cultural and spiritual revival of Russian Jewry, preferably in the direction of Reform Judaism. Early in his presidency, he set up the Task Force on Soviet Jewry that was chaired for many years by Betty Golomb of Port Washington, New York, one of the most active women in the Union's inner circle of lay leadership. In the late 1970s, the Task Force prepared a Russian-language Sabbath evening service and a Russian issue of *Keeping Posted* dealing with Reform Judaism. The publications were intended equally for Russian Jewish immigrants to the United States, those remaining in Russia, and immigrants in Israel.[104] In 1987, Schindler traveled to Moscow to participate in the eighth congress of the International Physicians for the Prevention of Nuclear War. While there, he visited Refuseniks, attended religious services in Moscow and Leningrad, and had what he called "a fruitful exchange" with Georgi Arbatov, a Jewish political scientist who served as adviser to secretaries of the Communist Party.[105] Schindler believed that during his visit he was "even able to plant some seedlings towards the development of Reform Judaism there."[106]

As the Soviet Union continued to oppress its Jewish population, Schindler made the astonishing suggestion that perhaps the United States was partially at fault: "So long as the US continues to follow a double standard [with regard to racial equality], its protestations on human rights will be ignored—particularly in the Soviet Union."[107] That point of analysis drew an angry response from Elliott Abrams, head of the Bureau of Human Rights and Humanitarian Affairs in the new Ronald Reagan administration. He wrote to Schindler, "I submit that your efforts to blame the Reagan administration for the plight of Soviet Jews not only fail, but are damaging to the cause of Soviet Jewry."[108] In this instance, at least in Abrams's view, one of Schindler's domestic concerns had gotten in the way of an international objective.

When the World Jewish Congress met in Vienna in 1985, Schindler was asked to deliver a principal address that was devoted mostly to the Soviet Union and its Jews. Rejecting Ronald Reagan's "evil empire" characterization, he instead described his critique of the USSR as a protest of conscience against its various assaults upon the Jewish people: its failure to commemorate the Jews whom the Nazis destroyed on its territory, its trampling on Jewish culture, its suppression of Jewish organizations, its limitation of Jewish emigration, its denigration of Zionism and finally, its declaring Jewish dissenters to be suffering from a psychiatric disorder. To the demand "Let my people go," Schindler proposed adding the demand for Russian Jews who remained, "Let my people stay a people—with a national organization, with full human rights, and with a full encouragement of the Jewish tradition."[109]

The Jewish exodus from the Soviet Union presented Schindler with a quandary that set a moral concern for non-Jews against an obligation to fellow Jews. The Jewish refugees were not the only ones who sought a safe haven in America; there were also Vietnamese boat people, Chinese political refugees, and El Salvadorans fleeing death squads. The United States had set a refugee ceiling of fifty thousand immigrants per year, which in 1989 was about to be reached. Should the UAHC press for an increase in the number of Jewish refugees admitted to America, even if it meant reducing the admissions for individuals who were in greater need and who did not have the Jewish alternative of settling in Israel? Schindler concluded that he had an obligation to press for a dramatic increase in the overall refugee ceiling: "In a world awash with fourteen million refugees, we dare not declare this Ark America to be chiefly ours."[110]

Schindler's interest in Russian Jewry was paralleled by concern for the Jews of Poland. As early as January 1976, the American Federation of Polish Jews selected Schindler to preside over its organization.[111] The following month, he and Yehuda Hellman traveled to Poland, stopping in Warsaw, Cracow, and Auschwitz. He met with local Jews and returned convinced that much could be done for the religious and cultural life of Polish Jewry. A principal concern was the neglect of Jewish graves in Poland, an issue that Schindler raised with the Polish government and thereafter became the subject of a conference in Borough Park, Brooklyn, in which Schindler participated. In this setting he worked with Orthodox Jews, some of whom had labeled the Reform rabbi as "wicked," but who were nonetheless prepared to cooperate with him in a common cause.[112] When in 1981 the Polish military regime arrested Marek Edelman—a leader of the Warsaw Ghetto uprising—on account of his continuing support of the independent labor movement called Solidarity, Schindler cabled General Wojciech Jaruzelski claiming antisemitism was behind the arrest and calling for Edelman's release.[113] Edelman was released, perhaps influenced at least in part by Schindler's action.

An assistant to Rabbi Schindler, Rabbi Philip Hiat, led the Union's project to recover Polish Judaica and present a sampling to Americans who were interested in the subject. With funding from Armand Hammer, chairman of the Board of Occidental Petroleum, and the National Endowment for the Humanities, as well as with assistance from the Polish government, the Union was able to display 104 examples of Jewish art and artifacts, most of them never seen outside Poland, in an exhibition titled "Fragments of Greatness Rediscovered: The Recovery of Polish Judaica."[114] The exhibition traveled to Harvard's Widener Library, to New York City, and elsewhere in the United States. Schindler took great pride in this accomplishment, which he believed enabled the viewer to look beyond the Holocaust and "never forget the Golden Age of our People, our history as a people in Poland."[115]

More controversial and with more direct involvement by Schindler was the UAHC's participation in the commemoration of the fortieth anniversary of the Warsaw Ghetto uprising, held in the Polish capital during April 1983. Despite his misgivings regarding Poland's military government and possible exploitation of the occasion for its own propaganda purposes, Schindler decided to accept the invitations of both the Polish Jewish community and the Polish government to lead a twenty-four-member UAHC delegation to Poland. A large Israeli delegation participated as well. In response to critics, Schindler told a reporter, "It seems to me that the blood-soaked fields of Poland are a far more appropriate place to say kaddish than a suburban temple in America."[116] He added that at the ceremony he wore a yarmulke, which he did not normally do, because he wanted to ensure that the Polish people knew he was there as a Jew.[117]

During his tenure as head of the Presidents' Conference, Schindler also addressed the issue of Jews in Romania. The United States had granted Romania "favored nation status," which imposed the obligation to allow free emigration—a requirement that was not being met. Schindler traveled to Romania at the invitation of the Romanian government, where he met with President Nicolae Ceausescu. Shortly thereafter, he testified before the Senate Committee on Finance, where he endorsed a qualified one-year extension of Romania's special status, since it had pursued a foreign policy independent of the USSR and was allowing at least a few Jews to leave.[118] A few months later, when reporting on the same trip to Prime Minister Rabin in Jerusalem, Schindler confessed that there was little hope of gaining permission for Romanian Jews to immigrate to Israel in larger numbers. Ceausescu had given him the excuse that only a few of them desired to leave his country—an assertion that Schindler refuted, claiming that no fewer than ten thousand Jews wanted to go to Israel. Schindler also reported that Romanian chief rabbi Moses Rosen enjoyed his sense of power and was not encouraging *aliyah*, though he was providing support for local Jewish institutions.[119]

A decade later, Schindler's attention turned, at least for a few weeks, to the land of his birth. In commemoration of the end of World War II in Europe, President Ronald Reagan had accepted German chancellor Helmut Kohl's invitation to lay a wreath at the German military cemetery near Bitburg in May of 1985. The purpose of the ceremony was to dramatize the reconciliation between Germany and the United States. When it was discovered that among the graves were those of forty-nine members of the Waffen-SS, controversy arose: Should Reagan therefore cancel the planned trip? As a palliative, it was decided that he would visit the Bergen-Belsen concentration camp on his way to Bitburg. Although he was pleased at Reagan's decision to visit a camp, Schindler was among those who spoke out repeatedly against the planned ceremony at Bitburg.[120] In a private letter following the ceremony, he expanded upon his reaction, which combined revulsion at Reagan's act with a more positive note:

> The head of the SS cabled Chancellor Kohl and President Reagan to thank them both for their "exceedingly generous gesture to the SS," and immediately after the cameras left the Bitburg cemetery, giant wreaths from the SS were placed alongside those placed by President Reagan. If nothing else, this proves the moral misjudgment which our President made....
>
> I have absolutely no animosity toward the people of Germany. They have a right to lead their lives. I don't believe in collective guilt and no reasonable person can.... Why did the President not go to a Tomb of the Unknown Soldier, which abound in Germany, or he could have made a visit to Adenauer's grave[121] the central piece of his reconciliation visit instead of making it an afterthought, which no one noticed. Adenauer is the true symbol of the newer Germany and not the SS.[122]

Schindler was likewise troubled by the increased awareness of the United States' role in protecting leading Nazis following the war. When it became known that Klaus Barbie, the "Butcher of Lyon," had been employed by United States intelligence services and was helped to escape to Bolivia, Schindler demanded an official inquiry. His request was apparently heeded, as Senator Daniel Patrick Moynihan, vice chairman of the Senate Select Committee on Intelligence, informed Schindler shortly thereafter that such an investigation had been launched on March 15, 1983, and would be concluded within a few months.[123]

When Germany was in the process of reunifying a few years later, in 1990, a reporter from *Le Monde* called Schindler from Paris and asked him how American Jews felt about that historic development, which would result in a larger and stronger German state. He answered that the response was mixed, almost generational in its nature. Then, in a Rosh HaShanah sermon that year, Schindler provided personal evidence for his opinion:

> My mother, who lived through two world wars in her lifetime, is certain that history is about to repeat itself, that a reunited and economically powerful Germany poses a threat to world peace. My children, on the other hand, were struck by the wonder of it all, relieved by the realization that the tearing down of the walls spelt an end to the hazardous superpower confrontation. I found myself, and still do, somewhere in the middle between these two views, even as I am of the middle generation. Intellectually, I am able to accept the inevitability of German

unification, but emotionally I shuddered when I watched TV as the Berlin wall was torn down and I saw the German Parliamentarians in Bonn rising to a man to sing their national anthem with zeal and zest. The words were new, but the melody was old and I remembered the earlier version.... It is the singing of this song that made me shiver.[124]

Yet another organization in which Schindler played a leadership role was the United Nations Association of the United States of America, which he served as a "governor" for at least fifteen years—a period extending longer than the usual two five-year terms.[125] With regard to the United Nations, two matters seem to have been of principal interest for Schindler: Kurt Waldheim and nuclear disarmament. It was during Waldheim's tenure as secretary general that the United Nations General Assembly invited Yasser Arafat to speak from its rostrum in 1974, and a year later passed the resolution declaring Zionism "a form of racism." Both aroused Schindler's protests. In 1977, when Waldheim was planning to resume the 1973 Geneva Peace Conference on the Middle East, Schindler told him that he feared it would not serve Israel's interests, and soon thereafter received a written justification.[126] Later, in 1986, when Waldheim was campaigning to become the president of Austria and suspicions arose regarding his activities during the Nazi era, Schindler urged Edwin Meese, the American attorney general, to determine the truth of the allegations by instituting a search of relevant archives.[127] As Schindler saw it, the UN's anti-Israel actions could be linked, at least in part, to lingering animosity rooted in Waldheim's past.

In the spring of 1979, discussions began that would yield in November a new strategic arms limitation treaty between the United States and the Soviet Union (SALT II), and President Carter wrote to Schindler requesting his personal views on the subject.[128] Schindler's reply—if there was one—is not extant, but his views are clear from his speeches and writings, albeit only from the period after Reagan had replaced Carter. He spoke of "the folly of nuclear deterrence" and urged a "clamor for the universal abolition of nuclear arms."[129] Not surprisingly, he opposed the so-called balance of terror, whose most frightening consequence was the escalation of the nuclear race by word and deed. Ronald Reagan had blithely stated on at least two occasions that the use of nuclear weapons in the field would not necessarily lead to an all-out nuclear war. Talk about a neutron bomb that doesn't destroy tanks or buildings, but just kills people, evoked a bitter sarcasm, unusual for Schindler: "How reassuring to know that our telescreens and Gucci loafers will survive us," he said.[130] Speaking at a Center for Defense Information Forum in 1982, he concluded, "What Vietnam represented to the public conscience in the 60's, the nuclear race will represent in the 80's and 90's. As religious leaders we must resolve to lead this moral enterprise *now* as we led it successfully then."[131] Schindler's views on nuclear disarmament were reflected in a Nuclear Handbook produced by the UAHC's Religious Action Center and in his speeches to the biennial assemblies of the Union, where they led to resolutions titled "Control of Nuclear Arms" (1981) and in "Preventing Nuclear Holocaust" (1983).[132] To assist Senator Kennedy in his efforts on behalf of a nuclear freeze in October 1983, Schindler—together with Bishop James Armstrong, president of the National Council of Churches, and Bishop Thomas J. Gumbleton, president of Pax Christi U.S.A.—signed a joint statement declaring that a nuclear weapons freeze and reduction initiative was "not only a political issue; it is a profound moral issue which reflects the imperative of human survival in the nuclear age."[133]

When Schindler then went to Moscow in 1987 for the conference of physicians opposed to nuclear war, his speech turned to a Jewish perspective. Nuclear warfare, he said, is something different from other forms of warfare: "It is the Shoah, the holocaust. It is the shattering of the covenant, the rending of the fabric of creation. It is the grossest version of human sacrifice—the rejection of which marked Judaism, from its beginnings, as a religious advance."[134] Schindler had long been on the advisory council of the Shalom Center, located in a suburb of Philadelphia and directed by the controversial Arthur Waskow. In 1988, Waskow invited Schindler to accept its Brit HaDorot Award for his "extraordinary work toward preventing nuclear holocaust and toward ending the nuclear arms race."[135] Schindler was at first hesitant to accept, feeling used and angry when he realized—what he should have known—that such events are used to raise funds from acquaintances and associates of the honoree. However, he acquiesced and used the occasion of the New York dinner in his honor to speak of specific steps that might be taken to diminish the nuclear danger. In general terms, he spoke of a "window of opportunity" that was afforded by what he believed was a new hopeful era in US-Soviet relations. That window needed to be wedged open ever wider in a new age in which the force of life, rather than "the mushroom-shaped, skull-shaped shadow of death becomes the driving power of our unification."[136]

Of all the issues beyond the American scene that occupied Schindler in the years following his tenure as chairman of the Presidents' Conference, none was of greater significance than his relationship to the State of Israel, both in general terms and in terms of Reform Judaism's position within the state. As he had done when he represented American Jewry as a whole, Schindler briefly continued to support the Israeli government's right to build settlements in the West Bank for purposes of Israel's security. The claim to sovereignty there was "at least as good as anyone else's," he said.[137] He also continued to see the Palestine Liberation Organization as the chief obstacle to peace and increasingly found Jimmy Carter to be a grave disappointment.

However, by the early 1980s Schindler was becoming ever more critical of Israeli policies. On a trip to Israel in February 1980, he scored the government for diverting virtually all of its settlement funds across the "green line," to the disadvantage of the Galilee and especially the Aravah in the south, where the Reform Movement was establishing its two kibbutzim. The Israeli Left enthused over Schindler's critique: "This is the first time that a Jewish leader of the stature and status of Rabbi Schindler publicly and with sharp words attacks the policy of the government of Israel."[138] Although he did not envisage a fully independent Palestinian state, Schindler began to express sympathy for the Palestinian people. In an interview with *Time* magazine he said, "I feel almost a kinship with the Palestinians. The role they are playing in the Arab world is not unlike the role of the Jews in the world: rootless wanderers."[139] The reporter regarded it "a rarity" that an America Jewish leader should openly profess compassion for the Palestinian people and recognize the need for co-existence and mutual trust. A few months later, Schindler signed on to a statement initiated by prominent Israelis and endorsed by fifty-six American Jewish leaders, titled "Our Way Is Not Theirs," accusing the government of extremism, chauvinism, and the distortion of Zionism.[140] Schindler's views made him a black sheep in right-wing Zionist circles; his invitation to speak at an Israel Independence Day celebration in Australia was peremptorily withdrawn.[141]

Then, in June 1982, Israel invaded Lebanon, hoping thereby to protect Jewish settlements in the Galilee from persistent shelling. Initially intended as a limited operation to remove the danger posed by the PLO operating there, the war dragged on for many months. Schindler believed that the incursion by the Israeli army was justified by the events preceding it, but he could not ignore the human tragedy, the immense loss of life on both sides, and of course, the massacres perpetrated by Christian Phalangists in the refugee camps of Sabra and Shatila. The Israeli forces might have prevented them but chose to stand aside. Schindler urged Prime Minister Begin to speedily launch a Commission of Inquiry and, speaking on Israeli television, said he should fire his defense minister, Ariel Sharon, who was responsible for the inaction. It was at this point that Schindler conclusively came to the view that the vital stake American Jews had in Israel required them to voice their honest opinions not only in private to Israelis but in public as well. To his Board of Trustees he said:

> Over the years, the Jewish community has reached a theoretical consensus on this score: full and free debate of any and all issues *within* the community, coupled with the obligation that we communicate our views to the Israelis through every channel at our command—from Prime Minister on down. Strictures were applied only to *public* dissent. This was discouraged lest it provide wood for the axes of our enemies and dilute our effectiveness in Washington. The assumption was that a united front adds weight to the political effort. Unfortunately, this public reticence does not always work out well in practice, particularly when it comes to letting the Israelis know precisely how we feel. In our personal conversations we are honest with them, yet how can we expect them to believe what we say in private when we say such very different things in public? Inevitably, our private protestations are overwhelmed by our public proclamations of unqualified support.[142]

Schindler then went on to express his own passionate commitment to Israel, which he believed gave him the right and responsibility to express what he—and many Israelis—believed best served its interests. He imagined bringing to life a "Parliament for the Jewish People" that would be broadly representative, but he never explained how that idea could be brought to fruition.

Israeli reaction was the opposite of what might have been expected. Prominent leaders of the Labor Party, though in agreement with

Schindler's views on the West Bank, allegedly told him, "We may agree with you but you have no business telling us what to do since you live in the safety of America." It did not help that Schindler singled out for severe criticism Israel's minister of defense, Yitzhak Rabin, who had set forth a policy of the "iron fist," which meant dealing harshly with recalcitrant West Bank Palestinians. Menachem Begin, however, was not averse to Schindler's criticism. Unlike the Labor Party's representatives, he was "most understanding" of Schindler's opinions and said to him, "Our friendship is really not touched by differences in view."[143]

After Begin resigned from office as prime minister in October 1983, Schindler lost the extraordinary access to Israeli political authority that he had enjoyed earlier. He did not get on well with Begin's successor, Yitzhak Shamir; he did, though, admire the new Israel ambassador to the United Nations, Benjamin Netanyahu, whom he called "an exemplar of the best which the Israeli Foreign Service has to offer."[144] With Shamir and Rabin in office, Schindler had no partner for communication in the highest ranks of Israeli government, so instead he chose to express his anger and sorrow at indiscriminate beatings of Palestinians during the riots of the First Intifada in a cable to Israel's president, Chaim Herzog, with whom he did have a friendly relationship. In an almost immediate and lengthy response, Herzog claimed there could be no negotiations without the prerequisite of restored law and order. Moreover, Jewish ethics were clear regarding the duty to defend oneself if in mortal danger. Herzog concluded that he had responded seriously and frankly to Schindler's cable because he believed that involvement of American Jews in Israel's problems and dilemmas "are a priceless source of strength to our nation."[145] The correspondence ended with Schindler urging Herzog that Israel undertake a persistent initiative for peace, "constantly pursuing all avenues that will lead to it."[146] Such efforts would in fact move forward with the Oslo Accords in 1993, only to be eventually squelched following Yitzhak Rabin's murder two years later and finally by the Second Intifada of 2000 to 2005.

Schindler's cable and Herzog's response were widely reported in both the Israeli and the American press. When the correspondence came to the attention of the Israeli literary community, four of its leading members—the poet Yehuda Amichai, the journalist Amos Elon, and the writers Amos Oz and A. B. Yehoshua—joined in a letter "To the Editor" of *The New York*

Times asking American Jews to speak up: "We cannot believe they are indifferent to whether Israel will remain a democracy. By their very silence, they are massively intervening in Israeli politics and silently but effectively supporting one side in the debate, the tragically wrong side. We implore them to speak up."[147]

The exchange with Herzog also led to an unusual letter to Schindler from his cousin Ruben Schindler in Israel, who had not communicated with him in thirty years. An Orthodox Jew and a dean at Bar Ilan University whose sons served in the Israeli army, Ruben expressed agreement with President Herzog and went beyond it. Unlike Herzog, he thought that Diaspora Jews had no right to castigate Israel, but only to support it. Living outside of Israel, they should seek to understand "the complexity of our destiny" rather than deplore our actions.[148] His cousin responded with a letter pointing out that restoration of order was indeed desirable, but not random violence "such as soldiers going into houses in the middle of the night, smashing furniture, pulling out all males and breaking their bones.... May I remind you that I served in WW II... that we, too, were called upon to occupy hostile villages and had we committed any of these things, we would have been charged with war crimes."[149]

Despite his ever more severe critique of Israeli policies, Schindler's admiration for Menachem Begin continued unabated. When Begin died in 1992 and the Presidents' Conference asked Schindler to present a eulogy, he said of Begin that "history will rank him among our generation's foremost leaders."[150] His positive feelings for his friend, he noted, had been fully compensated. He recalled a conversation when the Lebanon War had just taken a disastrous turn: "We argued violently one night, till the early hours of the morning. But before we parted we still embraced, and he generously said [to me]: 'All this has nothing to do with our more personal relationship... it is on a different, deeper plane, where soul touches soul.'"[151]

The enduring close relationship of these two men requires a word of explanation. Despite their political differences, Begin and Schindler were very similar in their background and the nature of their Jewish identity. Both men were Holocaust refugees, and both had roots in Eastern Europe and in the depth of its *Yiddishkeit*. Schindler's father had been a Yiddish poet, and Schindler, though born in Germany, always stressed his Eastern

European roots. Each man regarded himself as a non-Orthodox religious Jew who had high regard for Jewish tradition without being scrupulously observant.[152] Each was motivated by feelings no less than by reason. Just as Schindler saw himself as a Jew more fundamentally than as an American, so did Begin regard himself as a Jew more fundamentally than as an Israeli. For both men, "Jew" was the noun while "American" or "Israeli" was the adjective. It is therefore not surprising that Schindler remained closer to Begin than to any other Israeli prime minister.[153]

For the remainder of his tenure as UAHC president, Schindler combined appreciation for Israel as "a democratic oasis in a harsh landscape of dictatorships and fundamentalism" with a perceived "devaluation of values among Israelis, more materialistic, more like the values of the rest of the world."[154] The reality of conquest had functioned like "a chronic disease draining vital resources—most especially the precious resource of morale."[155] He continued to sympathize with the Palestinians in the territories, whose situation he described as "miserable."[156] In a university lecture, before an almost entirely non-Jewish audience, he deplored Yitzhak Shamir's expression of a wish to crush the Palestinian rioters "like grasshoppers" and listed some of the disabilities of Palestinians in the conquered territories: "They lack political dignity; they can't vote, they can't get elected; they are shoved around by the bureaucrats and the soldiers; they don't have passports; they don't have flags—and dignity is more important in the Arab culture than is economy."[157] But he also pointed the students to the PLO covenant that called for the total extermination of Israel and he deplored the intransigence of the Arab nations.[158] Moreover, at no point did Schindler suggest to Jewish audiences that they should distance themselves from the Jewish homeland. On his trips to Israel, he continued to be received by high officials and he served on the Board of Governors of the Jewish Agency. To the end of his life he continued to be an American Jew who was influential beyond America. A reporter for the Israeli newspaper *Haaretz* even claimed—to be sure, from his limited perspective—that "next to Eli Wiesel, Alexander Schindler is thought to be the best known and most famous American Jew."[159]

In 1992, Yitzhak Rabin became prime minister and shortly thereafter the First Intifada came to an end. With the negotiations in Oslo, a new hopefulness arose that the Israeli-Palestinian conflict would finally draw to a close. The Labor-led government included as minister of education Shulamit Aloni, a champion of internal pluralism and Palestinian self-determination whom Schindler greatly admired.[160] He wrote that he would have preferred Peres as prime minister over Rabin, but he was willing to concede that "perhaps the years have mellowed him."[161] On October 4, 1994 Israel and Jordan signed a peace treaty on a piece of land once contested by both states. Schindler and his wife Rhea were both present, a glorious moment that they felt "privileged to witness."[162] Most important, Rabin was actively pushing forward a process that had a chance of bringing about peace with the Palestinians. Like Jews everywhere, Schindler was distressed at Rabin's assassination on November 4, 1995, which suddenly dashed the hopes that had been raised so high. But in typical fashion, he tried to remain optimistic. "The momentum for peace is irreversible," he said in his last address to a Union General Assembly.[163] Fifty-eight countries had established renewed relations with Israel since the Oslo Agreement was signed. He defined his position as "a prophetic Zionism" that looked toward a better future, a "joint enterprise" of Jews in Israel and the Diaspora.[164]

During these same years, much of Schindler's Israel concern was directed toward the advancement of Israeli Reform Judaism. The persistent point of conflict between the Reform Movement and the Israeli government in this regard was the principle of Reform's religious legitimacy. It manifested itself through various issues, including subsidy of Reform institutions on an equal basis with allocations for their Orthodox equivalents, state recognition of weddings performed by Israeli Reform rabbis, and giving proper legal status to immigrants who had been converted by Reform rabbis abroad. Of these issues, the one that Schindler most frequently addressed was the last, although the others were of broader significance. In 1950 Israel had adopted a Law of Return, which gave individuals with one or more Jewish grandparents and their spouses the right to immigrate to Israel and acquire Israeli citizenship. Orthodox parties in the government and their right-wing coalition partners urged that, insofar as a convert was involved, that individual did not qualify unless the conversion process was conducted by an approved Orthodox rabbi. Repeatedly, efforts were made to bring about an amendment of the law.

As noted earlier, Schindler claimed that during his chairmanship of the Presidents' Conference he had used his influence to persuade Begin's governing coalition to oppose the attempt. But the agitation to bring about an amendment refused to die out, and Schindler repeatedly did his best to undermine each attempt. In a cable to Begin in 1981, he used language intended to prey upon the prime minister's sensitivities. "How can any Jewish leader after Auschwitz permit the setting up of a selection process at Jerusalem's gates?" he asked.[165] To galvanize support against the amendment, Rabbi Eric Yoffie—then executive director of the Association of Reform Zionists of America—compiled a statement on the Law of Return, which was signed by Schindler as well as other leaders of both American Reform and Conservative Judaism. It noted as particularly objectionable that even conversions performed entirely according to Jewish law were judged to be unacceptable when they were not performed by an Orthodox rabbi.[166] Shortly thereafter, Schindler wrote on the same subject to Yitzhak Shamir, who was about to become prime minister, and held up to him the example of his predecessor, Menachem Begin. Schindler remarked that Begin, "while personally sympathetic to a more traditional point of view, nonetheless always understood that the passage of such a law would plunge the Jewish world into a Kulturkampf whose only result would be national suicide. As a consequence, he always insisted that this matter never be subject to party discipline, and as a consequence the effort was always abortive."[167]

However, the battle over the Law of Return proved to be unending. Again and again an amendment was brought up in the Knesset and repeatedly defeated. Individual members of Shamir's coalition either absented themselves during the vote or abstained.[168] And again and again Schindler wrote to Shamir. In 1987, he argued that such an amendment "would fracture the unity of the Jewish people beyond repair."[169] The opposition proved strong enough that even the attempt to define a conversion as acceptable only when it was conducted "according to Jewish law" remained unsuccessful. It is hard to say how much of the credit for that success should go to Schindler, but surely his efforts played a role.

There were other Israeli issues during the 1980s on which Schindler felt obligated to voice an opinion—including one of significance that did not directly touch Reform Jews, although it affected their sense of moral responsibility. The Israeli Orthodox rabbinate regarded Ethiopian Jews the way they regarded converted Reform Jews—as less than fully Jewish. Jews making *aliyah* from Ethiopia believed themselves to be observant, entirely legitimate members of the Jewish people, but the Israeli Chief Rabbinate did not agree. Even before Ethiopian Jews were able to reach Israel, while they were suffering famine and illness in Ethiopian refugee camps, the UAHC's Religious Action Center took steps to assist them. It started a financial assistance program to raise money for food relief. Through its Project REAP (Reform Movement's Ethiopian Jewry Assistance Program), it arranged for physicians to travel to Ethiopia, where they would provide medical care and distribute medical equipment in Gondor, where most Ethiopian Jews lived.[170] An advertisement appearing in *The New York Times* promoting this effort urged that contributions be sent to the Union's president; Schindler expressed his satisfaction that the ad produced "a superb response."[171] Still, he worried that these suffering individuals, who regarded themselves as fully Jewish, would be considered less than completely Jewish and that they would be required to undergo conversion if they were fortunate enough to reach Israel. Not surprisingly, he believed that "such demands are both offensive and humiliating to a Jewish community that has guarded its Jewish identity for some 2,000 years in the face of persecution, poverty and isolation from the rest of the Jewish world."[172] The issue was finally resolved, not to Schindler's satisfaction, when rabbinic authorities eliminated a re-circumcision requirement but maintained that of ritual immersion.

Other issues, like the Law of Return, had more direct consequence to the slowly growing Israeli Reform Movement. In cooperation with representatives of the kibbutz movement, the Israel Movement for Progressive Judaism (the name for Reform Judaism in Israel) had succeeded in establishing two collective agricultural settlements of its own in the Israeli Aravah desert—Yahel in 1977 and Lotan in 1983—and a communal settlement in the Galilee, Har Halutz, in 1985. It was hoped that these settlements, redolent with the spirit of Israel's pioneers, would make Israeli Reform Judaism seem more at home in the Israeli environment. A photograph of the dedication ceremony at Yahel shows Alexander Schindler wearing kippah and tallit, proudly carrying a Torah scroll under a sun-shielding canopy.[173] Although Schindler visited these

Reform-initiated settlements infrequently, as head of the UAHC he had an obligation to provide for their welfare. In that regard, he appears to have had some, if limited, success. For Lotan he was able to secure from Ben-Gurion University in Beersheba rights to the cultivation of certain houseplants that Lotan hoped to develop for the European market.[174] In 1985 he sought funds to pave a road to Har Halutz and three years later tried to secure a large allocation from the World Zionist Organization's Settlement Department. But despite his willingness to use the influence of his office and his position within the Jewish Agency to urge financial commitments, it is not clear how many of his efforts came to fruition, and some of the young settlers felt that he could have displayed greater interest in their ventures.

One minimal intervention clearly did not yield results. In 1994 Schindler wrote to the prime minister's legal adviser to express "the commitment of Reform Judaism to the right of women to gather at the Kotel (the ancient Jerusalem wall), adorned by tallitot if they so choose, and with Torah in hand in order to pray and study together as a community of Jews."[175] He wanted this government official to know that not only Israeli Progressive Jews but also American Reform Jews were deeply committed to religious pluralism as well as to the rights of women.[176] That objective, however, remained beyond reach—even long after Schindler had passed from the scene.

One issue of the Israeli Reform Movement absorbed and agitated Schindler far more than any other: Reform Judaism's physical presence in Jerusalem. This issue agitated the long-standing rivalry between Schindler and Rabbi Richard Hirsch, which, as we previously explored, had its origins during Schindler's first years as UAHC president. In 1973 Hirsch, a fervent Zionist, had assumed the executive directorship of Reform Judaism's international body, the World Union for Progressive Judaism, and thereupon moved its headquarters from the United States to Israel. Compared with the American Union, the World Union was a poor cousin, with a budget of less than $75,000—a tiny fraction of what the UAHC spent every year.[177] Hirsch intended to turn the World Union into a well-funded and effective organization, which required more financial support from the UAHC than Schindler and his board were willing to supply. Ongoing tensions soon arose between the two men. Hirsch said they consisted of ideological, institutional, and personality differences.[178] Unlike Schindler, he had dreams of matching the centrality of Jerusalem for world Jewry with centrality, as well, for the Reform Movement. Hirsch believed that it was the responsibility of the Union to provide a large portion of the funding that would advance this goal. Schindler was surely a Zionist, but he felt a principal responsibility to the Reform Movement in America and its multiple projects, including the development of American congregations, the Religious Action Center, the Outreach movement, and summer youth camps. He felt he could not give as much funding as Hirsch desired for the World Education Center that he was proposing be created in conjunction with the HUC-JIR campus on King David Street in Jerusalem. The UAHC was initially called upon to pay $250,000 of the costs.[179] That center was to be anchored in a youth hostel bearing the name Beit Shmuel, which would serve Reform young people visiting the country and act as a venue for Jewish cultural activities. Hirsch believed, as he wrote in an autobiography, that "if we, as a progressive movement, wanted to attract Israelis, the probability is that we would be able to attract them not to our religious services or to ritual observance, but to educational and cultural experiences that would enrich their life experience."[180] Although on one level the two men remained friends, their dispute became acrimonious at times and was unpleasant for each of them. According to Hirsch, Schindler failed to realize that he benefited from the close identification of the UAHC with the World Union, which made him the leader of a world movement rather than just of an American one.

The controversy between the two men was never resolved. Hirsch continued to blame Schindler for slow progress, since he believed the UAHC president had far better access to funds than he did but failed to share them sufficiently. For his part, Schindler had long claimed that programming was more important than grandiose buildings. When a delegation of the UAHC Board traveled to Jerusalem and toured the site for Beit Shmuel, they supposedly reported, "Hirsch is building a Taj Mahal." Justifying his reluctance to spend huge sums on the building, Schindler told Alfred Gottschalk that he had committed to taking over the hostel project provided that it could be built for $3 million.[181] He also claimed, with justification, that the UAHC had expressed its commitment to Israeli Reform Judaism in other ways. It had a paid staff in Israel devoted to bringing youngsters from the National Federation of Temple Youth to Israel, where they could come into contact with their Israeli counterparts. That investment, he believed, was more effective than a hostel in Jerusalem. The UAHC, Schindler wrote further, spent over half a million dollars on Reform projects in Israel that he regarded as an important stimulus to Reform Judaism there. Hence he was reluctant to attempt raising additional funds for Beit Shmuel, which originally was to cost $4.7 million but whose allocation soon grew until it required close to double that amount. When Schindler visited the new complex in 1986, he heard complaints from the Israeli Reform rabbis, who felt alienated from Hirsch since the World Union paid them only "a pittance for a living" and yet had enough "to squander millions on buildings." He was told that the World Union's building activity had led to severe indebtedness to its creditors.[182]

Further controversy arose with regard to establishing in Israel an equivalent to the Union's Religious Action Center in Washington. The UAHC Board wanted to make it an American-linked project led by ARZA. Hirsch objected, indicating that he was adamantly opposed in principle to Americans presuming to speak and act in Israel, independent of the World and Israeli movements. This was a debate that Hirsch clearly won. When the institution came into being in 1987, it was locally run and not called the ARZA Religious Action Center, but rather the Israel Religious Action Center (IRAC).[183]

Yet however virulent their dispute became at times, each man nonetheless remained respectful of the other's work. When Hirsch in 1992 undertook an unsuccessful campaign to unseat the incumbent chairman of the World Zionist Organization, Simcha Dinitz, Alexander Schindler arose and spoke on behalf of Hirsch's candidacy.[184] That same year he paid tribute to Rabbi Hirsch, whom he called "a friend and colleague since our days as students at the Cincinnati campus of HUC-JIR."[185] Their careers had taken parallel paths: both had chosen to carry out their rabbinates beyond the bounds of an individual synagogue, and the growth of Reform Judaism in Israel gave both men "a renewed sense of pride and achievement."[186] Their lively ambitions and the respective positions they held necessarily placed them in competitive, sometimes militant confrontations. But, in the end, the friendship sustained by earlier years of comraderie and common religious values and goals bound them together.

Alexander Schindler was never satisfied simply being the president of the Union of American Hebrew Congregations. He wanted to be more: a leader of American and world Jewry whose views would be influential on a broad range of issues—both those that were specifically Jewish and those of significance beyond the Jewish community. Again and again, he raised his voice: sometimes in vain, sometimes with significant effect. He was not easily restrained. As with his Outreach Program to non-Jews, so too he reached out to confront issues domestic and foreign, Jewish and non-Jewish. However, especially toward the end of his career—as we shall now see—he frequently also looked inward, assessing the limits of Reform Judaism and reflecting on the religious source of his own inner strength.

CHAPTER 7
Reaching In

EVEN AS MUCH of Alexander Schindler's attention during his UAHC presidency was turned outward—to bringing non-Jews into Judaism, to addressing issues of social justice, and to connecting to world Jewry—he could not neglect matters of consequence within the Jewish community, such as defining the relation of Reform Judaism to more traditional forms of Jewish expression and determining the role of non-Jews and non-believers within the Reform synagogue. These matters gained increasing significance during the last years of his presidency.

Alexander Schindler did not feel alien in an Orthodox or even a Hasidic setting. A video shows him, kippah on head and paper cup of wine in hand, joyfully singing along with a lively Hasidic melody led by Lubavitch rabbi Menachem Mendel Schneerson and echoed by his black-hatted throng.[1] Although there was little possibility for finding common ground between Reform Judaism and ultra-Orthodoxy, Schindler did hope to find some commonality with Orthodox Jews of a less extreme variety. He was distressed at the claim that, especially on account of his affirmation of patrilineal descent, he was undermining Jewish unity. Within modern Orthodoxy, as previously noted, the leading proponent of dialogue among Jewish religious denominations was Rabbi Irving (Yitz) Greenberg. Schindler also favored such dialogues, but found them fruitless since the Orthodox representatives expected all concessions in matters of religious practice to come from the Reform side and refused to recognize the authenticity of Reform Judaism. Yet, Schindler's commitment to "retaining that unity which is essential to our continuance as a people" kept him from closing off interaction.[2] He did not want Reform Judaism to be dubbed a sect on account of greater than necessary separation from the other iterations of religious Judaism.

Therefore, Schindler participated in interdenominational exchanges, but found that none of the religious leadership—including Rabbi Greenberg, Rabbi Alexander Shapiro (the president of the Conservative rabbinical body), and even Schindler himself—were ready to give ground. Greenberg held non-Orthodox leadership responsible for the deplorable division arising within American Judaism. When Shapiro called upon Reform Judaism to reverse its acceptance of patrilineal descent, Schindler retorted sarcastically that "it would be better for Rabbi Shapiro to lead his movement into the future than ours into the past."[3] He predicted that Conservative Judaism would follow Reform in but another decade: "It usually takes them about 10 years—like on the women's issue."[4] Schindler was prepared for a genuine dialogue in which each side was ready to make concessions, but, as Greenberg wrote to him, "Right now, I cannot deliver the Orthodox establishment to any serious dialogue that would involve give and take."[5] Regarding his own modern Orthodoxy, Greenberg had to admit that "the moderates among the Orthodox are now terrorized, and reluctant to take any chances."[6]

When addressing fellow Reform Jews, Schindler pulled no punches. Speaking to the Union's Biennial Assembly in Los Angeles in November 1985, he denounced Orthodox leaders who "presume to know just which rites and prayers are and are not acceptable to the Almighty."[7] He lashed out especially against an advertisement in the Jewish press telling Orthodox Jews they should rather stay home during the High Holy Days than hear the blast of the shofar in a Conservative or Reform synagogue.[8] Speaking to Reform rabbis at a CCAR convention marking its centennial, he set himself sharply apart from those who were ready to make Reform Judaism more traditional, relying upon the quixotic hope of thereby gaining broader acceptance. Employing a favorite image, he noted once again that "our forebears did not forge Reform Judaism to have us trade it in for a tinsel imitation of Orthodoxy."[9] He believed that some Reform rabbis had descended into a romanticization of Orthodoxy, which did not reflect contemporary reality; he pointed out that where Orthodoxy held sway virtually undisputed, as it did in Israel, the result was a fanatical repression of alternative religious interpretations.

When Greenberg finally managed to pull together a broadly representative dialogue of Jewish leaders in Princeton, New Jersey, during March 1986, Schindler once again unhesitatingly defended patrilineal descent, though he apologized for the tone of some of his earlier statements regarding Orthodoxy and was eager to stress common interests, such as the safety of the State of Israel. To the other rabbinical participants—liberal Orthodox Yitz Greenberg, Reconstructionist Ira Silverman, Conservative Gerson Cohen, and mainstream Orthodox Norman Lamm—Schindler recited his favorite Yiddish phrase as an expression of fundamental unity: *Vos mir zaynen zaynen mir—ober Yiden zaynen mir!* ("What we are, we are—but we are Jews!")[10] He also suggested to the unusually broad combination of participants what, he admitted, seemed "chutzpadik"—that there be a path toward some measure of convergence between traditional and progressive Judaism:

> I do devoutly wish that the *poskim* of our times, the Orthodox decisors of the Law, were just a little bit more daring in halachic creativity, more responsive to human needs of men and women—Jews living in a changing world. Maybe then, Reform would not have to be quite so daring and innovative in *its* decisions. The two movements would be infinitely more congruent.[11]

By the end of the decade, Schindler turned more conciliatory toward Orthodoxy. He had always possessed an emotional attachment to tradition, rooted in his family background; now he wanted to stress that he admired and greatly respected the tradition. He simply wanted the same respect in return, rather than a religious triumphalism that denigrated Reform. In fact, he favored the reintroduction of traditional practices that Reform Judaism had abandoned and that it had begun to recover. He was not a "classical" Reform Jew of the earlier anti-traditional sort that had taken pride in abandoning traditions judged incompatible with modern aesthetics or rational precepts. He fully agreed that Orthodoxy was an authentic form of Judaism; he only wanted the Orthodox not to exclude Reform Judaism from that distinction.[12]

Within Reform Judaism, Schindler was assessing an increasingly urgent question: Did the Movement possess any boundaries regarding non-Jews gaining synagogue membership or even holding congregational office? Should non-Jews be allowed to play a role in leading religious services? And should there be any objection to the UAHC admitting synagogues founded on the principle of denying belief in God?

Even traditional Judaism allowed gentiles to be present as guests in the synagogue during worship,[13] but what if they wanted to be more than merely guests? As interfaith marriages continued to increase, a far larger number of non-Jews joined their Jewish partners at religious services, in some cases with great regularity and enthusiasm. They did not regard themselves as mere observers from the outside; they wanted to be recognized as being fully within the community. Usually, they became members of a congregation through a Jewish partner. When such interfaith couples joined a synagogue, they generally raised their children as Jews, sending them to religious school and celebrating their bar or bat mitzvah.[14] Increasingly, the non-Jewish partners wanted their commitment to be reflected in the ritual life of the synagogue. The issue of non-Jews taking on a leadership role in the liturgy first arose well before Schindler's time, with regard to the temple choir. In both small towns and large cities, Reform congregations, finding a lack of suitably talented Jews, recruited Christians to be among the singers. In those days few Reform congregations possessed a cantor. Not comfortable with this situation, Schindler expressed his hope that the Movement's training of *chazanim* (cantors) was diminishing the need to employ non-Jewish choristers.[15]

By the 1990s, the increasing number of non-Jews active in various aspects of Reform synagogue life had become a prominent issue of lively debate within the Movement.[16] The widespread concern it produced was given clear-cut expression by Joseph Glaser, the executive vice president of the CCAR. He claimed that outreach had "taken on a life of its own."[17] Reform was splitting between a core and a periphery. "What then, is to be looked upon as the critical mass in Reform Jewish life?" Glaser asked. "Born and converted Jews, or that clientele resulting from intermarriage? . . . On which constituency do we build our programs, allocate our resources, assert our values, invest our interests?"[18] In order not to offend interfaith couples, Glaser noted, rabbis could now encourage in-marriage only at their own peril. Like non-Reform critics, he held that outreach was diluting Jewishness. Most tellingly, if there were no boundaries between Jew and non-Jew in the synagogue, "what is the point of conversion to Judaism?"[19]

Schindler was aware of the problem and frequently stressed that outreach meant only acknowledging the reality of intermarriage, not sanctioning it. During his last years in office, he continued to maintain, "We must lose no opportunity to persuade our children either to marry Jews or to urge their non-Jewish partners to opt for Judaism."[20] With regard to non-Jews who associated themselves with a Reform synagogue, he believed that they should be encouraged to convert: "Why don't we ask? Why are we so hesitant? Are we ashamed? Must one really be a madman to choose Judaism? Let us shuffle off our insecurities! Let us recapture our self-esteem! Let us demonstrate our confidence in those values which our faith enshrines."[21] For Schindler, outreach was always a conversionary movement; increasingly, however, it had become a conversionary movement that fell short of conversion. Setting boundaries therefore became crucial. Using a biblical allusion, Schindler held that before a non-Jew was given full privileges in a Reform congregation, "Abram must become Abraham and Sarai become Sarah."[22] In other words, they must, through conversion, accept the covenant that binds Jews to God.

Although Schindler remained eager that non-Jewish partners feel welcome within the Reform synagogue, he saw the necessity of setting limits to their participation. He pointed out that some interfaith couples were themselves uncomfortable when boundaries were absent, ambiguous, or unstated.[23] Like Glaser, Schindler recognized that there was an important difference between a person who was not Jewish and a person who converted to Judaism, and he believed that the difference should somehow be marked. But how? With regard to synagogue membership, he affirmed the already common practice of family memberships that embraced both the Jewish and the non-Jewish partner, with voting rights consisting of only one vote accorded each family unit.[24] However, he went further and favored membership for the non-Jewish widow or widower of a Jew and even for the non-Jew who had no personal Jewish connection.[25]

When it came to governance of the congregation, however, Schindler recognized the need for boundaries. He believed that denying a board position to a non-Jew who desired to serve did not have to result in feelings of rejection. "The non-Jew will accept it," he insisted. "He just wants to know what are the rules of the game. If it's communicated, not just coldly, but with understanding and with 'menchlikeit,' I think they'll accept it."[26] Some congregations distinguished between serving on certain committees and not on others, but Schindler rejected that distinction. He opposed all synagogue governance by non-Jews—whether as congregational officers, committee chairpersons, or even committee members. In this regard he was far stricter than most, and he refused to make a distinction between some congregational committees and others, expressing the view that "all of our synagogue committees are sacred. Is it not a fundament of Reform to affirm that the decisions of the social-action committee about *tikkun olam* are as intrinsic a part of Judaism as the decisions of the ritual committee regarding *tefilah*? Is a budget committee, for that matter, any less laden with a potential for holiness than teaching the *alef-bet* to children?"[27] Another reason for rejecting non-Jews in leadership roles was "because in Reform Judaism, certainly in all of Judaism, the leaders of the congregation are teachers. And we, in Reform Judaism, above other streams of Judaism, teach less by precept and more by example.... Leaders are the examples."[28] Similarly, Schindler would not have non-Jewish teachers in the religious school "because we're not just trying to transmit facts. We're trying to nurture, implant and nurture, certain passions, certain commitments, and that can best be done through a person—a leader—who is committed."[29] On account of this view of Jewish education as being more than just the transmission of information, Schindler welcomed the controversial resolution passed by the 1995 UAHC Biennial Assembly expressing unwillingness for Reform religious schools to admit children who simultaneously received formal training in another religion.[30] Some Reform Jews, however, regarded that resolution as contrary to Reform's declared policy of openness. When it passed, one of Reform Judaism's most prominent supporters, former senator Howard Metzenbaum, resigned from the UAHC in protest.[31]

The most controversial and incendiary issue was non-Jews participating in religious ritual. There was no objection to non-Jews reading and singing the liturgy with the congregation, but leading the ritual was another matter. And what if they wanted to introduce content that was not simply neutral, but explicitly Christian? Wouldn't that lead to transforming Reform Judaism into a non-Jewish sect or a syncretistic faith that was no longer wholly Jewish?[32]

With regard to prominent ritual participation by non-Jews, Schindler was among the liberals. This manifested itself in the area that evoked the most attention: the role of a non-Jewish parent in the ceremony of their child's bar or bat mitzvah. Here Schindler's desire to maintain a boundary between Jew and non-Jew collided with his characteristic concern for the feelings of those involved. Could a non-Jewish parent who had raised a child as a Jew be excluded from the ceremony in which that child confirmed personal Jewishness? The ritual passing of the Torah through the generations down to the bar or bat mitzvah child had become an integral part of the service, raising the question of whether a non-Jewish parent should be included. Schindler pointed out that the objection to a non-Jew coming into physical contact with the Torah had no basis in Jewish law since a Torah scroll could not be rendered impure. Prohibiting a non-Jew from touching it, he believed, was nothing more than "a very strong taboo."[33] He did, however, recognize that some might think it inappropriate to consider the non-Jewish parent a link in the chain of Jewish transmission. Hence his conclusion that "non-Jewish parents or partners should be allowed to participate in a manner virtually identical to that of Jews."[34] *Virtually* identical, but not identical. For the passing of the Torah, it could mean that non-Jewish partners stand alongside their Jewish spouse but not physically pass the scroll. However, it seems likely that were Schindler a congregational rabbi, he would have allowed a non-Jewish parent who had participated in the child's Jewish education and encouraged the child's Jewish identity no less than did the Jewish parent to pass the Torah on to the child. For Schindler, there was one underlying and fundamental consideration: He did not want anything done that would in any sense damage the self-image of the child who was being reared in Judaism and would encourage the notion that somehow the child was not quite fully a Jew.

Two other public leadership roles were under debate: the non-Jewish mother of the bar or bat mitzvah lighting the Shabbat candles in the synagogue, and non-Jewish parents being called up to the bimah to recite the blessings before and after the reading of the Torah. Schindler pointed out that lighting Shabbat and festival candles for the congregation within the temple was a Reform innovation; hence, there was no long-standing halachic discussion of the topic. To justify its performance by a non-Jew, Schindler referred to the innovation of non-Jews singing in the choir, as mentioned earlier. That still left the problem of the blessing's text, which, in the case of candlelighting in the Reform prayer book *Gates of Prayer*, included the words "who has sanctified us by His commandments and commanded us." For a non-Jew to speak those words produced an internal contradiction. Aware of this problem more than a decade before it rose to public discussion, Schindler proposed alternative language for non-Jews:

"who glorifies the Sabbath (festival) with the blessing of the Sabbath (festival) lights."[35] (He did not suggest what the Hebrew text might be.) The same issue arose when non-Jewish parents desired to participate in the blessings before and after the reading of the Torah. The words in *Gates of Prayer*, "who has chosen us from all peoples and given us His Torah," obviously made no sense when spoken by a non-Jew. In some congregations, alternate texts were being introduced in Schindler's time, but there is no apparent evidence that he composed an alternate version of the blessing. As for religious services in general, whether or not a bar or bat mitzvah was involved, Schindler was of the opinion that casting non-Jews in the role of a *sh'liach tzibur* (service leader) was "unquestionably inappropriate."[36] If they desired to play a role of leadership in a service, they should do no more than read a psalm or recite a prayer that had no specifically Christian content.

The question of boundaries also arose with regard to born or converted Jews in the synagogue, when their beliefs (or non-beliefs) were out of line with Reform Judaism as it had been conceived from its beginnings in Europe nearly two hundred years earlier. Sects that claimed to be Jewish but believed in the salvific role of Jesus were clearly beyond the boundary of Reform Judaism. Likewise was any congregation that rejected full gender equality once women were being ordained as rabbis. But what of a congregation that explicitly denied belief in God, had its own humanistic liturgy that excluded all prayers referencing God, and nonetheless applied for admission to the Union of American Hebrew Congregations? That possibility prompted Schindler to ask, "Is there *any* ideology that is beyond the pale of Reform? Just what *is* essential to a Reform outlook, what is optional—and what, if anything, is forbidden?"[37] Increasingly, he had come to see the downside of an unfettered openness to all. In his State of the Union Message in November 1991, he said:

> Reform recasts tradition, deliberately and openly. We conceive of Judaism as a dynamic and not a static faith, one that is never in a state of "being" but is always in a state of "becoming," a relentless flowing on. We insist that religious law is not frozen like ice but is a soluble substance to be mixed with human tears. . . . This very flexibility, however, directs our attention to another problem confronting Reform . . . the need to achieve ideological coherence. The elasticity of our Judaism has

produced the elasticity of our numbers, but stretched too far it can rip us apart. Reform allows for a wide spectrum of belief, a ranging gamut of theological stances. Nonetheless, some common understanding is necessary to give us the kind of ideological cohesion a religious movement, or any movement for that matter, requires to retain its distinctiveness and assure its continuity.[38]

The issue of a non-believing synagogue arose in 1990 when a decade-old "humanistic" congregation in Cincinnati calling itself Beth Adam ("the house of man")—as opposed to the frequent Beth Elohim ("the house of God")—applied for admission to the Union of American Hebrew Congregations. By this time, outreach—though still central to Schindler's concern—had been argued over without end, had been organizationally incorporated, and as a principle could no longer arouse emotions within Reform Judaism. Always eager to stir up his constituency, Schindler jumped on this new issue to reenergize internal debate. "This is a fascinating subject," he wrote to one of his regional directors. He called for an intensive study of theological limits within Reform Judaism, beginning with a review of responsa and continuing with a personal inquiry that Schindler sent to seven leading Reform rabbis seeking to ascertain their views on the subject.[39] Among the respondents to Schindler's questions was Rabbi Solomon Freehof, the chief halachic authority of the Movement. His answer was unambiguous: "We are not a secular state but a *religious* organization and certainly the word 'religious' cannot be stretched to include atheism."[40] Freehof was firmly and unconditionally against granting membership to Beth Adam. So was Rabbi David Polish of Chicago, an influential past president of the CCAR, who wrote that admission of the humanistic congregation "contradicts everything in Jewish life that I stand for."[41] However, Rabbi Eugene Mihaly, professor of rabbinic literature and homiletics at Hebrew Union College in Cincinnati, made it his personal mission to bring support for the admission of Beth Adam from rabbinic and contemporary Reform sources.[42] Initially, Schindler's characteristic desire for inclusiveness inclined him to write to the lay leader in charge of the first stage of the admission process: "I tend to agree with Gene Mihaly."[43] He believed that Mihaly's defense of the Beth Adam request was "very thoughtful and informed,"[44] but he was not fully convinced.

Slowly the Beth Adam application made its way through the stages of the UAHC admission process, from the local to the national. Debated vigorously on both levels, the question arose as to why the congregation was so eager to join the Union. Apparently, the motive was not so much to make a theological point as it was to gain the tangible benefits of increasing visibility within the Cincinnati community, to gain admission for their young people to the successful and prestigious local Reform Community High School, and possibly also to allow their youth to participate in the camping activities of the North American Federation of Temple Youth (NFTY). In addition, membership would enable employment of Reform ordinees.[45] Whatever the fundamental motivation may have been, the local Reform congregational rabbis had declared that Beth Adam's vision was not in consonance with Reform Judaism and unanimously expressed opposition.[46]

As the application process moved forward, Schindler remained silent, though he now privately told Eugene Mihaly, Beth Adam's rabbi Robert Barr, and two of its lay leaders that he had decided to oppose the congregation's admission to the Union and believed that the Reform Movement, in general, was likewise opposed.[47] Glad that the issue had stirred lively debate, Schindler held back public announcement of his own opinion, "for I have learned that when I state my own views too soon, the debate is usually foreclosed."[48]

On June 11, 1994, at the end of a long process, the Beth Adam issue came before the UAHC Board of Trustees. At that meeting Schindler at last made his own negative view publicly explicit. One cannot know to what extent his words influenced the outcome of the vote, but it was exceedingly lopsided: of nearly two hundred Board members present, only thirteen voted in favor of admission.[49] According to Schindler's notes for his unpublished speech to the Board, he used the occasion not only to address the practical matter of Beth Adam, but to give the Union's inner circle insight into what their leader, as a religious Jew, believed was the religious essence of Reform Judaism. His message included the religious principles to which he personally subscribed:

> I believe ... that the concept of God is an *ikar*, the core, the essence, the very foundation of Judaism. The quest for God, the wrestling with God, defines us as a people. It is our mission, our historic calling. ... It is the

duty that defines us as a covenant people, and as Reform Jews we see ourselves as sons and daughters of the Covenant. Yes, God is a symbol, a vessel if you will, into which we pour divergent theological conceptions, but when that vessel is not there, such a pouring is foreclosed... an outpouring of the heart and soul, of silent prayer if you will, of a motionless clinging to God. Whoever has a symbol has thereby the beginning of a spiritual idea; absent a symbol, spiritual ideas are stifled and die aborning; symbol and reality together furnish the whole.[50]

It was not, however, the lack of belief in God—even in the symbolic form to which Schindler himself adhered—that set him against welcoming Beth Adam into the Union. It was rather that congregation's failure to recognize liturgical elements that were defining for the Jewish people and rooted in its history:

I am particularly troubled by the deletion of the *sh'ma* and kaddish from the liturgy of Beth Adam for I consider these erasures not just a severing of our ideological roots but also of our historic roots as a people. If Judaism has any overarching affirmation of faith, it is the *sh'ma*, the assertion of God's unity. That is the ultimate ground of our collective being.... It was the prayer which our people sang throughout their millennial martyrology.[51]

A refugee from the Holocaust, Schindler was unwilling to excise an expression of faith in God from the liturgy, however far removed he was from subscribing to its traditional understanding. Jewish martyrs had clung to it through the centuries: "Even when they were at the center of a whirlwind of destruction which we now call the *Shoah* did our people recite the *sh'ma*.... Even there, in the innermost circle of hell, did our people voice that prayer and they sang: *Ani Ma'amin*, I believe in redemption."[52] Schindler fully recognized that without liturgical links to the Jewish past, the Reform Movement would be cut off, and like a flowering plant severed from its roots, it would swiftly wilt and die. Above all, it was this concern for historical continuity that induced Schindler to set a boundary that excluded Beth Adam, not from the Jewish people, but from the Jewish faith as represented by Reform Judaism.

In all the years of his organizational activity, the rabbi within Alexander Schindler was seldom absent. He valued that title more than any other.[53] It came to expression in writings, speeches addressed to fellow rabbis, and especially in the sermons that he delivered in synagogues all over the country. When a new Reform prayer book was published in 2007, a reflection on prayer by Rabbi Schindler was included in two places: after the silent prayer on Shabbat morning and in the evening service for festivals. It speaks of prayer's universality in the cosmos and within the human mind and heart, "the wordless outpouring of boundless longing for God."[54] Schindler had little patience for a Jewish identity in which religion was not essential, and hence he rejected the broader civilizational approach to Judaism of Mordecai Kaplan's Reconstructionist Judaism and the cultural Judaism that excluded or sidelined faith. In the *CCAR Journal* he wrote that without theological concepts like God, Torah, Israel, mitzvah, and covenant, Judaism was "reduced to a mere practice of folkways and a vague nostalgia for ethnic identification."[55] He favored a Reform Judaism that inclined toward the acceptance of traditional practices, provided that they continued to be of inherent religious value, that they continued to inspire. Thus, in speaking at the UAHC national assembly in 1979 he told his large audience, "I myself respect *massorah* [tradition] as you know, and I incline to the emotive. I specifically favor *milah* [ritual circumcision] and *tevilah* [ritual immersion before conversion]; but I favor them for their intrinsic worth as initiatory rites, and not because their observance might or might not make us more acceptable to others. Adaptive change is alien to the spirit of Reform. It substitutes political for religious judgments and thus does violence to our essential nature."[56]

Schindler was painfully aware of the charge that Reform Judaism was nothing more than "a religion of convenience." Like other Reform rabbis, he complained that Reform failed to make ritual demands on its adherents. Committed to autonomy in making personal decisions regarding religious practice, Reform Judaism lacked a necessary coherence; as such, it could not be taken seriously. In making their religious choices, Reform Jews often chose merely to render financial support or to do nothing at all.[57] In his major addresses at biennial assemblies, Schindler repeatedly insisted that, as he put it in 1985, "when the concept of individual autonomy is allowed to become the central exclusive concept of liberal Judaism, Judaism is destroyed."[58] Two years later he spoke of Reform Judaism making demands on its adherents that led to "a life built on the performance of *mitzvot.*"[59] Having opened up Reform Judaism so that it could reach out to those on its periphery, he was now increasingly concerned with strengthening the commitment of those within it. For Schindler, outreach and inreach were related to one other. He argued that they were not incompatible. Rather, "they stand in symbiotic relationship, the one reinforcing the other, thereby the whole gaining in strength."[60]

Schindler often spoke of the need to cultivate a sense of the sacred within Reform Judaism. In 1984 he joined the newly formed UAHC-CCAR Task Force on Religious Commitment, which intended to consider actions that would enshrine a sense of the sacred within the institutions of the Reform Movement.[61] Speaking to individual congregations, Schindler sought to do his part. To the members of Temple Emanuel in Wichita, Kansas, he sounded Hasidic notes and used language that recalled the theology of Rabbi Abraham Joshua Heschel. Specifically, he spoke again of "*kavonoh* [devotion in prayer] leading to *devekus* [clinging to God][62]. . . a sense of reverence which flames into a commitment, into a full-hearted response to the divine command."[63] Like Heschel, he regarded "wonderment" at the essential mystery of life as a path to belief in God.[64] In a commencement address at the University of South Carolina, later excerpted in *Readers Digest*, Schindler recalled how, emerging into the sun from the hospital where he had been confined after his first heart attack, he became aware of how, beset as he was by his many tasks, he had been oblivious to the wonder and awe of life. Awareness of that wonderment and the reverence that it produced were fundamental elements of Schindler's Judaism.[65] He did not, however, seek to define its source. Frequently, he cited Rabbi Leo Baeck, who had taught at the Hebrew Union College during Schindler's student years and with whom he may have studied.[66] Baeck held that although God's moral commandment was knowable and required human response in personal behavior and in social action for the common good, God's essence was not knowable; it remained a mystery, beyond human cognition. Perhaps it was Schindler's ongoing awareness of the Holocaust that inclined him to refrain from explaining or justifying divine providence.

Schindler's belief in life after death drew upon a phrase from the philosopher George Santayana. Immortality was neither a certain affirmation nor a certain denial, but rather, in Santayana's words, an "invincible surmise" or an "intimation," the product of momentary insight at crucial points of human life. In a Yom Kippur sermon Schindler confessed, "In my case, the assumption of a life hereafter took many years to gain the force of 'invincibility.'"[67] In the end, it was recollecting his war experience and the sight of lifeless bodies that led him to believe with a more certain faith that death was "a gateway and not an abyss into nothingness."[68] But to focus exceedingly upon the afterlife was to neglect this life. Stating it frankly and directly in his most explicit reflection on the subject, he wrote: "Let's stick with one world at a time and conduct ourselves in *this* world in such a way that if there is an afterlife with God, we will be worthy of it."[69]

Along with Jewish faith, Schindler also addressed Jewish ritual observance. He believed that Reform Jews were insufficiently disciplined in incorporating ritual into their lives. They recognized the importance of mitzvot in general, only to neglect their particular fulfillment. He was especially concerned about the Sabbath and castigated his Movement's laity for their failure to honor it:

> Walk into the typical Reform synagogue on a Sabbath when there is no bar or bat mitzvah, and how many people will you find? Will there be more than a corporal's guard of worshippers in attendance? Walk into the typical Reform Jewish home on the Sabbath and what do you find there? The candles, well yes, maybe. The kiddush, rarely. And where are the books? Where is the discourse on themes other than the everyday? How *do* we use the Sabbath to sanctify our space and time? And how in heaven's name will the Sabbath preserve us if we do not find even a single way to preserve the Sabbath?...
>
> To be a Jew in one's heart or mind is simply not enough. The pure idea can serve only a few rare individuals, theologians, philosophers, if you will. The truth—to be felt by most of us—must put on a garb. There must be rite, legend, ceremony ... visible form.[70]

Reform had long called itself "Prophetic Judaism" and it continued to emphasize the ethical mitzvot, as Schindler himself did. But he noted that the prophets—although they stressed the preeminence of the ethical life—by no means negated the significance of ritual. Late in his career, Schindler toyed with the idea of a Reform synod composed of both rabbis and laypeople that would render answers to questions of religious practice for the Reform Movement. If successfully brought into existence, it would have been as grand a project as outreach. However, neither the laity nor the rabbinate supported this idea. The laity saw autonomy as Reform's

Rabbi Schindler passing the Torah to his successor, Rabbi Eric Yoffie, on July 1, 1996. *Courtesy of American Jewish Archives, Cincinnati, Ohio.*

hallmark and therefore rejected any authoritative guide to religious practice, and the Reform rabbinate, which had issued a guide for Jewish practice as early as 1977,[71] did not welcome a body that would include laity in the decision-making process.[72] Seeing that a synod would not come into being, Schindler shifted the focus to education and suggested adult study *kallot* (gatherings)—which, in due course, did come into existence.

In 1995, Alexander Schindler announced his retirement from the presidency of the UAHC. Although he was now ready to give up the most significant source of his prestige and authority, continuing leadership roles in other Jewish organizations would easily keep him busy and satisfy his long-standing desire for broad recognition and service to the Jewish people. During his last years in office he had already begun to let go, giving more authority to his senior staff and relying more on his lay leadership. Additionally, he could no longer assume that his views would necessarily be adopted. In 1994, Schindler supported an attempt to change the name of the Union of American Hebrew Congregations to include the term "Reform," but the proposal failed at the Union Biennial Assembly.[73] The new name, Union for Reform Judaism, would not be adopted until years later.

Schindler had served the Union in ascending capacities for thirty-five years. The time had come to find a suitable successor. A list of possible successors, dated July 28, 1994, contains fourteen names. The search committee's early poll revealed that three leading candidates had received an identical number of votes, well ahead of the remainder. They were Rabbi Lawrence Hoffman, a professor at the New York campus of HUC-JIR, who withdrew before a final vote; Rabbi Daniel Syme, senior vice president of the Union; and Rabbi Eric Yoffie, vice president of the Union and director of its Commission on Social Action.[74] Since Syme held the senior position, he expected to become Schindler's successor, but the decision of the UAHC Board, made in May 1995 with a unanimous vote of the 175 Board members present, went instead to the forty-seven-year-old Yoffie. Although there is no written evidence for the assumption, it is widely believed that Yoffie—the more intellectual of the two, the possessor of a larger measure of gravitas, and the one with broader leadership experience—was Schindler's preferred choice.[75] Unlike many retiring rabbis, Schindler did not interfere with the work of his successor. "Don't bother me," he told Yoffie. If you like, "change everything."[76]

When his term of service to Reform Judaism came to an end, Schindler could point to significant successes. As director of the Union's Department of Education, he had promoted more intensive Jewish education through the creation of Reform Jewish day schools. The Religious Action Center, begun by Eisendrath, had expanded its horizons. His years chairing the Conference of Presidents of Major American Jewish Organizations had raised the profile of Reform Judaism within American and world Jewry. Within the UAHC his leadership had brought about a sharper focus on Israel, supportive but also critical; the Association of Reform Zionists of America had been created on his watch. He could feel special pride at having played a role in the publication of the Reform Movement's first Torah commentary. The Reform Outreach Program was bringing non-Jews and their children closer to Judaism. His efforts had helped to persuade the Reform rabbinate to adopt patrilineal descent as a mark of Jewish identity. Within the Union itself, he expanded its New York staff, enhanced an effective UAHC regional structure to work directly with Reform congregations, and founded a national periodical titled, appropriately, *Reform Judaism*.[77] Despite ups and downs, the budget of the Union had been able to grow along with expansion of the Union's member congregations, from approximately 700 when Schindler became UAHC president in 1973 to above 850 upon his retirement in 1995. A national survey indicated that in the late 1980s more American Jews identified with Reform Judaism than any other Jewish religious denomination.[78] In 1991, attendance at the Union General Assembly reached five thousand.[79] An insider judgment concluded that about a million North American Jews now belonged to a Reform congregation.[80]

In Atlanta, Georgia, on December 2, 1995, Schindler addressed a General Assembly of the Union of American Hebrew Congregations for the last time.[81] He chose to render his speech in the traditional Jewish form of an ethical will. It begins with a representation and evaluation of self, followed by hopes for the future of Reform Judaism following his retirement.

Schindler's underlying conviction, as he himself understood it, was neither an intellectual nor a theological principle, but rather his belief that emotion lay deeper than cognition. "My core conviction, the mainspring of all my actions, the driving power of my life," he told the leaders of American Reform Jewry, "is *ahavat yisrael*, a love of my fellow Jews which knows no limits." He then went on to enumerate the different aspects of his personality—what he called his multi-colored coat of Jewish identity—that combined to shape the character of his Judaism: child of a Yiddish poet, German Jewish boy, refugee from Nazi terrorism, American soldier fighting to demolish the Third Reich, a rabbi "offering words of prayer, encouragement, and comfort to everyday people," a spokesman who offered "words of challenge and support to leaders of nations." Finally, he saw himself as "an American Jew, fully committed to nurturing our culture, our scholarship, our civilization in this golden land," but also "a frequent flier to Israel" and a lover of that land. He wanted to be remembered not as a Reform Jew, but simply as a Jew. For him, as for Rabbi Leo Baeck, the noun "Judaism" mattered more than any adjective placed before it. Once again, he recited his favorite Yiddish phrase, which he here translated as "Whatever we may be, we may be, but this above all, we are Jews."

Only then did Schindler proceed to enumerate his accomplishments. Outreach, he claimed, was his own principal expression of *ahavat Yisrael*. For that, especially, he wanted to be remembered. He now preferred it no longer be called "outreach," but rather "ingathering," a concept that suggests embrace: "We 'outreach' beyond our bounds; we 'ingather' to a rightful home." Schindler was honest enough to admit that the Union's Outreach Program had not been nearly as successful as he hoped, but it had made a difference for those who were touched by its various activities. It had projected a Judaism that was open rather than closed, not rejecting but all-embracing and compassionate.

From the particular concern of expanding conversion to Reform Judaism, Schindler went on to the broader cause of peace for the State of Israel. He had been severely shocked by the assassination of Prime Minister Yitzhak Rabin only a few weeks earlier on November 4, 1995, which undercut the hopes for peace between Jews and Palestinians that had been raised by the Oslo Accords. He called for active support of those in the Diaspora and Israel "who opt for life over land." He deemed his own brand of support for Israel "a prophetic Zionism"—a Zionism tempered by prophetic morality. In words derived from the secular cultural Zionist Ahad Ha'am but given a religious thrust—words that regrettably would seem ever more unrealistic during the remaining years of his life—he expressed an aspiration: "We must help make Israel a model, a miniature that reflects the ideal society that God wants us to fashion on this earth." Despite Rabin's assassination, Schindler remained enough of an optimist to believe that "the momentum for peace is irreversible."

Schindler's "valedictory," as he himself called it, continued with specifically religious issues in their relation to Reform Judaism. To his mind, not only was Reform no less authentically Jewish than contemporary Orthodoxy, it was more so. Reform did not neglect halachah, but understood it as only one factor in its religious decision-making process. The task of Reform was to "defrost" halachah "until it is once again soluble in human tears, human blood, human reality." But reform, in the sense of adaptation to reality, was not the essence. Instead, the essence was religiously motivated social action together with a measure of religious practice, regarding which Schindler preached, "We Reform Jews are entirely too lax." No less central was more intensive Jewish education with, at least for a Reform elite, day schools providing encounter with Jewish texts, Reform *kallot* (gatherings) for adult education (the first held at Brown University in 1989), and summer camps with an educational component to strengthen Jewish identity.

Schindler understood the ultimate source of all Jewish activity as, borrowing a phrase from Abraham Joshua Heschel, "the terrible relevance of God"—no less relevant after "Auschwitz and the killing fields of Cambodia, Rwanda, and Bosnia make for a substantial border between our will-to-believe and what-to-believe in." Schindler often felt himself "confronted by that border, by the enormous gap between our God and our modern world." When his faith faltered, he derived comfort from a story told of the Hasidic master Levi Yitzhak of Berditchev, who, observing the life of his shtetl's marketplace from a rooftop, shouted from the top of his lungs: "*Yiden*, Jews, do not forget that God exists, and God is of this world, of this world, too!" Schindler concluded that he, too, believed that God was of this world, discerned in precious moments of remembrance, of beholding the grandeur of nature; periods of prayer, study, and ritual; and of renewed recognition of the "true goodness that springs from the human heart."

Alexander Moshe Schindler died during the night at his home in Westport, Connecticut, on November 15, 2000. He was seventy-five years old when his third, and this time fatal, heart attack brought his life to an end. The UAHC had raised funds to establish the five-hundred-thousand-tree Alexander Schindler Forest near Safed in northern Israel to enshrine his memory.[82] Only five days earlier he had delivered his last address in Baltimore, Maryland. Calling attention to the millennial year 2000, he remained typically optimistic. To be sure, during the twentieth century the Jewish future had been eviscerated by the Holocaust, but Israel had ingathered many of the survivors; the Jewish people had survived in human history while other peoples had disappeared. The Jewish spark within could not be snuffed out. American Jewry had attained undreamed of influence. It had been able to move from the fringes to the center without abandoning Judaism. Schindler's last address was entirely without critique. In celebration, it looked toward a brighter future for American Judaism.[83]

Funeral and burial followed two days later at Temple Israel in Westport and the Temple Israel cemetery in Norwalk, Connecticut. Rabbi Robert Orkand conducted the funeral. Eulogies were delivered by his closest friend and associate, Albert Vorspan, and members of his family. Among the numerous attendees from various Jewish denominations was Rabbi

Avi Weiss, a prominent leader of modern Orthodoxy.[84] In memorial tribute, Vorspan chose to quote a Schindler reflection, written in the poetic style that he often favored:

> Our lives are a wilderness,
> uncharted and unpredictable—
> untimely deaths, unexpected blows,
> unsuitable matches, unfulfilled dreams.
> And yet, by gathering our heartaches into a house of worship,
> we find something transformative happening—
> our sorrows become windows of compassion.
> Paths through the wilderness,
> hewed and marked by past generations,
> give us our bearings.
> Patterns of meaning and significance emerge.
> We are moved from self-pity to love.
> Our individual heartbeats merge with the pulse of all humankind.
> Suddenly we no longer tremble
> like an uprooted reed.[85]

On his tombstone, shaped in the form of an open book, Alexander M. Schindler is described on its left side as "Beloved Rabbi, Husband, Father and Grandfather" while the inscription on the right side consists of a slightly modified saying from the midrash: "No Monuments Need To Be Put Up For The Righteous. Their Words Are Their Monuments."[86]

CHAPTER 8
The Private Life

ALEXANDER SCHINDLER spent long hours in the office of his lovely Westport, Connecticut, home.¹ The large room was elegantly wood-paneled, with windows that overlooked the lawn, the trees, and the Saugatuck River. It was neatly organized with generous shelving along the walls bearing Judaica texts and classical literature. There he prepared his countless speeches and sermons. On his desk lay a frequently used volume titled *The Word Finder*, which helped him in locating appropriate synonyms. English, after all, was his second language, and he was a stickler about formulating his ideas just as precisely as possible. Schindler cared a great deal about his mode of expression. With typical exaggeration he used to say that he would labor hours over a single word. He felt that a well-reasoned and polished presentation demanded a lavish investment of time. "I don't like to speak extemporaneously," he confessed. "I don't even like to listen to extemporaneous talks."² Albert Vorspan noted that Schindler's oratory was less stern and prophetic than that of his predecessor Maurice Eisendrath; it was more poetic and anecdotal. Eric Yoffie observed that whereas both men possessed charisma, the difference between their public personalities could be described as that between dignity and charm. The foreign-born Schindler, unlike his predecessor, also possessed a slight accent that lent him an old-world aura. It made him seem "especially worldly, wise and intellectual."³ Whereas Eisendrath had kept his distance, Schindler was gregarious, a "people person," and ever ready to give a hug even to people he scarcely knew. At meetings, he would pat this one on the shoulder, embrace that one, say a word of acknowledgment to another. Everyone felt affirmed and recommitted to the task at hand.

Coming into New York from Connecticut involved a long commute. His daughter Judith recalls that he drove ten minutes to the train station, had a seventy-five-minute ride to New York's Grand Central Station, and from there traveled on to UAHC headquarters at 838 Fifth Avenue. He would leave early in the morning and return home well after the family dinner. Following a quick meal, he went to his home office for more work as well as frequent calls from Jewish leaders and sometimes journalists. Occasionally, he also helped one or another of his five children with their homework. When invited out for dinner, he could sometimes be seen wearing an apron, helping to do the dishes.

Alex adored his wife Rhea, who was no shrinking violet, but rather his frequently assertive and much appreciated critic. The two of them loved to poke fun at each other. One evening when she could not fall asleep, Rhea impishly suggested to her husband that he read to her from his sermons. She greatly enjoyed the privileges that came with being the wife of a renowned leader: traveling around the world, often first-class; staying in lovely hotels; meeting famous people. Like other spouses of that era, she was fiercely protective of her husband. According to the rabbi of their congregation, Robert Orkand, Alex "played the game of putting Rhea in her place, [but] it was clear that she was the boss of the family." Although she initially had only the most limited knowledge of Judaism, in 1990 at Congregation Har-El in Jerusalem, she was able to celebrate an adult bat mitzvah.

The Schindlers had five children—three girls and two boys, including a pair of boy-girl fraternal twins. Their father felt guilty that he could not spend more time with them. Day-to-day care was in Rhea's hands and in those of a nanny who assisted her. According to Vorspan, Schindler felt so much regret at being away from home that he gave Rhea a yearly Father's Day gift! Raising five children imposed a severe financial burden, to say nothing of a regular, if pleasant, disruption of the work he did at home. "Too many children underfoot," he wrote to a friend, "but it really is a pleasure."[4] The children all went to public school and to their temple's Hebrew and religious school; all five celebrated their *b'nei mitzvah*. As noted in a previous chapter, one of Schindler's daughters married a non-Jew in a ceremony that their father did not conduct. When the spouse eventually converted, he officiated at their Jewish wedding ceremony. Another of the daughters, Judith, followed in her father's footsteps and became a Reform rabbi.

Schindler's closest friend was Albert Vorspan, who had preceded him in working for the Union and was only a few months older. With Al Vorspan,

Schindler could let his hair down, exchange jokes, some even raunchy, and dispute freely with his friend's leftist politics and more critical view of Israel. Schindler had been a fancier of jokes and pranks ever since his days as a student at Hebrew Union College. One of the best known of his pranks occurred when a nosy fellow passenger on an airplane inquired from him what he did for a living. He answered, "I am a *charoset* maker." "Oh, how lovely," she exclaimed. Whereupon Schindler responded, "Yes it certainly is, but it's so seasonal!"[5] In another famous anecdote, Schindler stars as the butt of his own story. One version tells how he was once praying at the plaza opposite the Western Wall in Jerusalem, his head uncovered. When an Orthodox boy accosted him for this offense, he responded, quick as a wink and apparently in Hebrew, "But the *kippat shamayim* [the dome of heaven] is my *kippah*." No less quickly the lad replied, "Such a large heavenly *kippah* and such a small head!"

Despite Schindler's enormously busy schedule, there was always time for a family vacation, be it winter skiing trips to Stratton in Vermont or summer trips to Martha's Vineyard. In addition to all his other interests, Schindler was an avid athlete. Tennis and squash were his games. Vorspan relates that it was the latter that brought on his first heart attack: Schindler had just defeated Vorspan 15–0, when he keeled over and was taken to a hospital. That setback, however, did not discourage further athletic activity. (I remember playing tennis with Alex and Rhea. She ran speedily around the backcourt; he was deadly at the net.) Years later—this time during a 1986 Board mission trip to Israel visiting the ruins of the synagogue at Masada in the Israeli Aravah desert—Schindler suffered a second, this time massive, heart attack. (Vorspan, who was again present, said he must be "a jinx.") The patient was forced to spend some weeks in the Siroka Medical Center in Beersheba, where he was visited by, among others, the president of Israel, Chaim Herzog. For a time after this heart attack, leadership of the Union was largely in the hands of its Board chair, until Schindler could fully recover.

Schindler loved theater and opera. He recognized that a preacher, like an actor on the stage, needed a dramatic touch to be most effective. He also greatly enjoyed going to the movies; his favorite was *Casablanca*. But even more than theater or movies, Schindler felt a deep love of music. To the president of the American Conference of Cantors, who wanted to make him an honorary member, he wrote, "I am a 'closet-conductor.' Come to think of it, I have come out of the closet because every time I attend a symphony I conduct in my seat and every time I go to the opera, I sing all of the roles, in their original language, even the soprano roles, never mind that I am in the baritone range and have a mediocre voice to boot."[6] As a rabbi, Schindler had a deep appreciation for the role of music in prayer. He called it "a bridge to the sacred" and suggested that "it cleanses the soul from the dust of everyday life. It can carry us to spheres to which the spoken word, rooted as it is to the earth, cannot aspire."[7]

Schindler also loved thrills. When he was young, that meant speeding around in his top-down convertible. Unfortunately, he also loved the thrill of gambling. His game was often poker, which he played with an overestimated judgment of his skill. His poker playing began at least as early as his student days in Cincinnati, and he started the habit of stopping in Las Vegas on trips to California. During his commutes into the city, his regular card game was gin rummy. Although he earned a salary commensurate with his position, he was excessive in his expenditures, and there was a time when his gambling and other debts were so oppressive that it took eight years for him to pay back what he owed to the Union, which had agreed to bail him out. Early during his UAHC presidency, Schindler recommended that synagogues establish Jewish Gamblers Anonymous societies, but there is no evidence that he ever joined one himself.[8] In 1996 Schindler chose to invest a considerable portion of his retirement savings with Bernard Madoff, who offered attractive returns. Regrettably, a few years after Schindler's death, it was revealed that Madoff had conducted a sophisticated Ponzi scheme and all the money was lost. Upon his retirement from the presidency of the Union, Schindler had been presented with an ornate silver Torah crown and a two-hundred-year-old silver Torah pointer. Now Rhea was forced to sell their house and auction off the valuable ritual objects. The congregation served by Rabbi Judith Schindler in Charlotte wanted to obtain the crown but was outbid. It went instead to the Jewish Museum in Berlin, the pointer to a private collector.

Within the demands of his many responsibilities, focused on moral and political issues vital for the Reform Movement, for Judaism, and for the Jewish people, Schindler sought to live a personally fulfilling, Jewishly

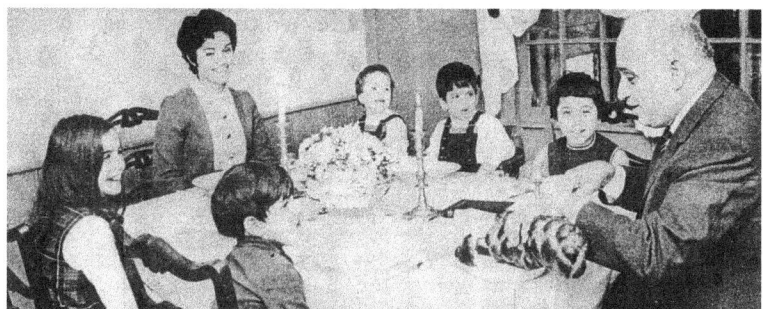

The Schindler family at the Shabbat table. *Courtesy of American Jewish Archives, Cincinnati, Ohio.*

observant life. When he was not away marking an anniversary for a Union congregation somewhere in the country, Schindler celebrated the entry of Shabbat with traditional ceremony: Rhea lighting the candles, Alex blessing the children, reciting *Eishet Chayil* in praise of Rhea, singing *Kiddush* over the wine and *Motzi* for the challah, and ending with *Birkat HaMazon*, the blessing after the meal. There were Shabbat songs, some from the Reform youth movement's summer camps, some reflecting Schindler's Yiddish background. The Schindlers did not eat pork, but they were less scrupulous about shellfish. They did not recite the *Havdalah* prayers to mark the end of the Sabbath on Saturday evening, but they did regularly build a beautiful sukkah in their garden. For Pesach, Schindler usually conducted a seder for some twenty to thirty guests. He did not regularly put on *t'fillin*, but on one occasion while visiting the Wall in Jerusalem, Rabbi Israel Friedman, the director of the Orthodox association Mizrachi, prevailed on him to do so. Supposedly, Schindler was "deeply moved" by the experience; it linked him momentarily to his Orthodox ancestors.[9]

When Schindler was in Westport, the family attended services at Temple Israel, and he occasionally spoke there. But for the High Holy Days, the entire family piled into their Lincoln Town Car and headed for Brooklyn, where they were hosted for holiday dinners by Rabbi Stanley Dreyfus and his wife Marianne, the granddaughter of Rabbi Leo Baeck. In return, Schindler yearly gave two sermons at Rabbi Dreyfus's Union Temple, one on Rosh HaShanah, on a worldly topic of Jewish interest, and one on Yom Kippur, on a spiritual theme. Among his sermons for special occasions is one addressed to a class of rabbinical students about to be ordained at HUC-JIR, in which he urged upon them what was, in effect, a statement of his own rabbinical challenge:

> The modern mood calls for a rabbi who is also something of a rebbe, in the ideal conception of that word, not just a teacher of Judaism, but also a fervent Jew who loves his people with an abounding love and who has the conviction and the courage to be a witness to God in a secular, post-Auschwitz, post-Hiroshima world. *This* is the kind of leadership to which our people responds. *This* is the kind of leadership for which they thirst, much like parched earth thirsts for the dew of heaven.[10]

Although he spent the first dozen years of his life in Germany and never completely liberated himself from his German accent, Schindler did not identify as a German Jew. Everything associated with Germany remained distasteful to him. He was not actively involved in the work of the Leo Baeck Institute, dedicated to studying and preserving the history and culture of German Jewry. Instead, his favorite charity was the Joint Distribution Committee, which had helped to assist Jews during the Holocaust. Although he knew German, he made an apparent effort not to use the language. Like nearly all of the Reform rabbinate of his generation, he was not fluent in spoken Hebrew. He always spoke with Israelis in English, but with the help of scholarly friends, he could find his way through traditional sources. He loved Yiddish as the language of Hasidism, whose appeal to religious emotion he felt was lacking in Reform Judaism.

Schindler never hesitated to be controversial or to express opinions contrary to the majority, whether in relation to Israel or to American Jewry. At one point, his views regarding Israel resulted in serious threats to his life, apparently originating with the right-wing Jewish Defense League. For a short time, he was forced to hide in his home, which was watched over by the FBI. Members of the family recall that his name appeared on a "hit list."

Schindler described himself as an "activist," not a scholar or theologian. He wanted to bring about change that he believed was vital for American Jewry and support for a State of Israel that shared values with the Diaspora. He was fortunate to head the Reform Movement at a time of institutional growth when sufficient financial support made possible a dynamic central organization. That is no longer the situation today, when Reform Judaism must struggle with contraction. Were he alive today,

Schindler would be pleased with the inclusiveness that characterizes the Movement. As for its problems, he might again recall the story from his childhood that, as noted earlier, he had once told Begin when the negotiations with Sadat were deadlocked with little hope of progress, a time when paralyzing frustration required spiritual assertion:

> When I was a little boy, my father took my sister and me to Warsaw, where we visited the *shtiebl* of the Umaner Chassidim, the devotees of Reb Nachman, the Bratslaver Rebbe. It was a shtiebl like all the other such shtiebls, with one remarkable exception: carved into the wood of the synagogue's ark was not the usual inscription, "*da lifne mi atah omed* . . . know before whom you stand," but rather a Yiddish phrase, a sentence in the vernacular, "*Yidn, zait sich nisht misya'esh* . . . Jews, do not despair."[11]

I do not know whether this story accurately represents the reality in Warsaw. But it does represent Alexander Schindler's unflinching determination and optimism—despite any setback—to carry forward his commitments and his vision.

Afterword

Rabbi Rick Jacobs

WITH THIS IMPRESSIVE VOLUME, Michael Meyer has made an important contribution to the history of Reform Judaism by sharing Rabbi Alexander Schindler's life and legacy. It is no exaggeration to say that Rabbi Schindler reshaped contemporary Jewish life. Assuming leadership of the Movement on its one hundredth anniversary, his bold vision of an inclusive, activist, soulful, and relevant Judaism has become a foundational commitment not only for Reform Jewish life but for much of the wider Jewish community as well. Indeed, the most recent Pew surveys of North American Jewish life tell the story of almost two million people who identify themselves with the Reform Movement. Much of that surge is the result of his expansive understanding of who is included in Jewish life.

Well before the 1991 Jewish Population Study announcing the stunning uptick in the number of interfaith marriages taking place sent panic through North American Jewish life, Rabbi Alexander Schindler knew that the Jewish community had to turn from scolding to warmly embracing interfaith families. In December of 1978, Rabbi Schindler began the formal Outreach Program to turn the usual harsh judgment that interfaith marriage elicited toward an elaborate series of programs that warmly welcome interfaith families into Jewish spaces. And lest you think this shift was received with excitement and approval, the strong pushback his Outreach Program received tells a different story. There was even stronger resistance to his promotion of patrilineal descent as a definition of Jewishness, with many leaders of other streams, as well as some within the Movement, predicting that this change would move Reform Judaism into sectarian isolation from the rest of the Jewish community.

In the 1970s, Rabbi Schindler also led the fight to include LGBTQ+ Jews in Jewish life with the decision to admit the first openly LGBTQ+ congregation, Beth Chayim Chadashim in Los Angeles, into the UAHC (now known as the URJ). The pushback was fierce and immediate. Rather than dissuading Rabbi Schindler from pushing forward this key component of inclusion, it led him to double down on his commitment to inclusion. In the 1980s, he took up the fight for same-sex marriages and officiation, which coincided with the deadly AIDS epidemic that devastated the LGBTQ+ community.

Rabbi Schindler's vigorous embrace of the social justice focus of Reform Judaism, built on the model of his predecessor Rabbi Maurice Eisendrath, remained strong—even as opposition to the Movement's social action agenda stiffened during the Reagan era and political conservatives in the Jewish community organized more assertively. Schindler remained an outspoken advocate of civil rights, women's rights, and gay rights, worked against the Religious Right's political agenda, and focused on foreign policy issues ranging from the Soviet Jewry movement to the nuclear freeze campaign. His leadership kept the social justice identity of the Movement front and center. During this same era, polls were showing that social justice remained one of the most common expressions of Jewish identity of American Jews, making this another key factor in the growth of the Reform Jewish Movement. Leading these fights almost simultaneously was quite a case study in leadership, but these transformational pivots were emblematic of his fearless vision.

During Rabbi Eric Yoffie's and my own tenure at the URJ, we've extended Rabbi Schindler's "big tent" even further. At the 2013 San Diego Biennial, I publicly committed to strengthening interfaith outreach, arguing that "in North America today, being 'against' intermarriage is like being 'against' gravity; you can say it all you want, but it's a fact of life." Included in that moral call to expand our already "big tent" was the need to affirm the growing number of Jews of Color, who often are still relegated to the margins of Jewish life. In 2015 we passed a far-ranging resolution on transgender rights, one of the most expansive statements by a mainstream American religious community. These shifts, like the ones Rabbi Schindler led, have not been met with universal support, but I'm confident that over time they, too, will gain wide acceptance.

At roughly the same time that Rabbi Schindler was leading bold change within the Reform Movement, he took on the tremendously important role of chairman of the Conference of Presidents of Major American

Jewish Organizations at one of the most consequential moments in the US-Israel relationship. When Menachem Begin was elected as Israel's prime minister in 1977—a political earthquake for many Israelis and even more American Jews—the decidedly liberal American Jewish community was uncertain if they could work with such a right-wing Israeli leader. Believing that the right of democracies to elect their own leaders needed to be recognized, Rabbi Schindler reached out to Prime Minister Begin to convey the congratulations of the American Jewish community, with his pledge to work closely with him. They were a highly improbable duo, as Rabbi Schindler was quite liberal, while Prime Minister Begin was not, but they nonetheless became good friends. Their partnership was deep and warm as they together navigated a turbulent period. In contrast to the intense polarization of our time, Rabbi Schindler modeled how to work with political leaders with whom there were deep disagreements. At my first meeting with Prime Minister Netanyahu in 2012, I told him that I hoped something of the Schindler-Begin relationship might inspire us to find commonality in working together on some of the big issues facing us. For a while it did, with his support for a compromise on non-Orthodox Jews sharing the Western Wall, but political considerations of his increasingly right-wing governments led him to abandon such efforts.

Even with his close relationship with Begin, Rabbi Schindler believed that he had an obligation to publicly challenge Israeli policies that he believed were flawed: "Must I indulge in annexationist fantasies to prove that I am a passionate Jew? Must I applaud this government's every act to demonstrate my love for Israel?" (page 66). His love of Israel included a commitment to the rights of Palestinians, which set him apart from most mainstream Jewish leaders of his day. His critique of Israeli policy, as forceful as it might be, was always done with a deep love for Israel and the Jewish people. I believe this is still the most authentic and effective way to voice public disagreements with Israel and one that needs to be heard even more forcefully today than in Schindler's time.

Rabbi Schindler's efforts to expand the tent of Jewish life were not at the expense of a serious and learned Reform Movement. As much as he shared the Movement's deep commitment to social justice, he strongly believed it should not come at the expense of serious Jewish learning and commitment to particularistic Jewish identity.

So many of the issues that challenged him are still front and center for today's American Jewish community, most particularly for the Reform Movement. While some in Jewish leadership take timid stances on big issues for fear of backlash, Rabbi Alexander Schindler was willing to challenge the entire Jewish establishment on matters of principle and to stand his ground even in the face of significant resistance. He did so while concurrently finding common ground with ideological adversaries. These were not contradictions, but rather leadership skills that we desperately need today.

As a leader, he surely wasn't without flaws, but his inspiring life story and his model of courageous and bold leadership of our Reform Movement and the wider Jewish community will no doubt serve as an enduring exemplar of how to shape a vibrant, relevant Jewish future. Centuries from now, students of Jewish history will recount the deeds of this charismatic, principled, and eloquent man who refused to allow the Reform Movement and the wider Jewish community to be weakened because of entrenched and limited notions of what Jewish life should be.

> Rabbi Rick Jacobs (he/him) is president of the Union for Reform Judaism, a position he has held since 2012. A longtime and devoted creative change agent, Rabbi Jacobs spent twenty years as a visionary spiritual leader at Westchester Reform Temple in Scarsdale, New York. Before that, during his tenure as the rabbi of the Brooklyn Heights Synagogue, he created the first homeless shelter in a New York City synagogue. Rabbi Jacobs and his wife, Susan K. Freedman, have three adult children.

Notes

Foreword
1. Marc Lee Raphael, *Abba Hillel Silver: A Profile in American Judaism* (New York: Holmes & Meier, 1989).
2. Alexander M. Schindler, "Introduction," in Raphael, *Abba Hillel Silver*, xvii.
3. Schindler, "Introduction," xvii.
4. Schindler, "Introduction," xvii.
5. Schindler, "Introduction," xxi.
6. Schindler, "Introduction," xxvi.
7. Schindler, "Introduction," xxvi.
8. Schindler, "Introduction," xxvi.
9. Schindler, "Introduction," xxvii–xxviii.
10. Schindler, "Introduction," xxviii.
11. Schindler, "Introduction," xxix.
12. Schindler, "Introduction," xxx.
13. Schindler, "Introduction," xxxiii.
14. Schindler, "Introduction," xxx.
15. Schindler, "Introduction," xxxii.
16. Schindler, "Introduction," xxxii.
17. Jacque Steinberg, "Rabbi Alexander Schindler, Reform Leader and Major Jewish Voice, Dies at 75," *New York Times*, November 16, 2000.

Preface
1. Conversation with Rabbi Eric Yoffie on November 27, 2022.
2. Henry A. Kissinger, "A Tribute," in *The Jewish Condition: Essays on Contemporary Judaism Honoring Rabbi Alexander M. Schindler*, ed. Aron Hirt-Manheimer (New York: UAHC Press, 1995), ix.
3. There are, however, at the Klau Library of Hebrew Union College–Jewish Institute of Religion in Cincinnati two unpublished rabbinical theses that deal with aspects of Schindler's career: Karen Companez, "Rabbi Alexander M. Schindler: A Thematic Biography" (2002) and Lynne Goldsmith, "Bridge to the Future: Alexander Schindler and His Influence on the Development of Reform Judaism's Outreach Program" (2007).
4. Alexander Moshe Schindler Papers, Manuscript Collection 630, American Jewish Archives, Cincinnati (hereafter: AJA).
5. I would also call attention to the collection by Rabbi Judith Schindler of quo-

tations by Alexander Schindler, arranged by topic, available at https://www.judyschindler.com/about/rabbi-alexander-m-schindler-legacy-project/.

Chapter 1: Origins and Youth

1. "Address before the Rabbinical Assembly," May 18, 1966, MSS 630, 24/1, AJA.
2. Pesach Schindler, "A Jewish Child Growing Up in Nazi Germany," in *German Jews and Migration to the United States, 1933–1945*, ed. Andrea A. Sinn and Andreas Heusler (London: Lexington Books, 2022), 57.
3. A *Fehlkarte* (location card) in the Munich Municipal Archives indicates that Eliezer lived in Munich beginning June 17, 1903. I am grateful to Professor Michael Brenner for sending me this and other Munich archival documents.
4. Sarah Lichtmann, Eliezer Schindler's first wife, had lived in Munich since February 20, 1902; she fled Germany for New York in 1933.
5. See File EWK65_S170_Schindler in the Munich Municipal Archives.
6. An announcement of the wedding is in Anja Siegemund, "Familie Schindler: Kaufleute, Dichter, und Rabbiner," in *Versagte Heimat: Jüdisches Leben in Münchens Isarvorstadt 1914–1945*, ed. Douglas Bokovoy and Stefan Meining (Munich: Peter Glas, 1994), 305.
7. Interview with Alexander M. Schindler, conducted by Jaclyn Jeffrey for the USC Shoah Foundation—The Institute for Visual History and Education, September 2, 1988.
8. Sally Hammond, "Daily Closeup," *New York Post*, November 9, 1973.
9. "Terror in the Desert," *San Francisco Jewish Bulletin*, September 25, 1970, 2.
10. *Daat, rachamin, tiferet.*
11. Adina Bar-El, *Under the Little Green Trees: Yiddish and Hebrew Children's Periodicals in Poland 1918–1939* [Hebrew] (Jerusalem: Dov Sadan Institute, 2006), 37; see page 288 for a contemporary's praise of Eliezer's ability to translate and adapt folktales for the Yiddish reader.
12. Boris M. Kader, "Introduction" to Eliezer Schindler, *Yiddish un hasidish: Lieder* (New York: Schulsinger, 1950), 24.
13. Cited in Pearl Benisch, *Carry Me in Your Heart: The Life and Legacy of Sarah Schenirer, Founder and Visionary of the Bais Yaakov Movement* (Jerusalem and New York: Feldheim Publishers, 2003), 106.
14. Transcript of interview with Alexander M. Schindler by Billie Gold, conducted in June and October of 1990 and deposited at the American Jewish Historical Society. Eliezer successfully persuaded Nathan Birnbaum that proselytizing should take place among the questionably Jewish Ethiopian Beta Yisrael and the Christian descendants of the Marranos. See Jess Olson, *Nathan Birnbaum and Jewish Modernity: Architect of Zionism, Yiddishism, and Orthodoxy* (Stanford, CA: Stanford University Press, 2013), 359.
15. "High Holiday Sermon at Union Temple," probably given in 1987; MSS 630, 24/7, AJA.

16. "Why Jews Should Seek Converts," *Reform Judaism*, Spring 1994, 16.
17. "Why Jews Should Seek Converts, 16.
18. Billie Gold interview (see note 14 above).
19. In the family's possession is a German letter from Rabbi Baerwald, dated April 16, 1930, thanking Eliezer for sending a few of his writings. Baerwald indicated that he planned to use some of them in his religious school.
20. Alexander Schindler recalled that his mother was secretly drawing funds out of the business. When a Nazi controller, in a sarcastic gesture, suggested, "I guess a woman doesn't know how to run a business," Sali cleverly responded, "Yes, I guess that's my problem. I need a man." (Quoted in Billie Gold interview.)
21. Undated lecture that Eva Oles gave to a high school class in the United States, received by the author from her daughter, Miriam Oles.
22. Speech to NFTY Convention 1993, Ellis Island, NY, MSS 630, 25/5, AJA.
23. Questionnaire on file at the American Jewish Archives, n.d., SC10979.
24. For a general account of the campaign, see Peter Shelton, *Climb to Conquer: The Untold Story of World War II's 10th Mountain Division Ski Troops* (New York: Scribner, 2003).
25. Billie Gold interview.
26. "Address to Jewish War Veterans," n.d., MSS 630, 24/4, AJA.
27. "Address at the Center for Defense Information Forum on National Security and Defense," Washington, DC, February 10, 1982, MSS 630, 24/4, AJA.
28. In a generally positive review of William Shirer's immensely popular *The Rise and Fall of the Third Reich*, Schindler criticized it for failing to recognize how the Dachaus of the 1930s were laboratories for the development of techniques of subjugation later used in the death camps in the east (*Central Conference of American Rabbis Journal*, October 1961, 64–66).
29. A relation of friendship existed between Leo Baeck and the Schindler family. A letter that Baeck wrote to Alexander's parents on December 16, 1952, from Cincinnati thanks them for an invitation to spend time at their home in Lakewood. The letter mentions that Baeck had gotten to know their son, as well as other members of the family. Handwritten in German, it contains Hebrew insertions and, unusual for Baeck, also the traditional Hebrew abbreviation *bet-hei*, invoking God (*Baruch HaShem*), at the upper left. Schindler would frequently mention Baeck in sermons and speeches throughout his life. The letter is in SC-634, AJA.
30. The above is taken from Schindler's Shoah Foundation interview, available for viewing at subscribing institutions. For many years he served as head of the Memorial Foundation for Jewish Culture, an institution supported by German reparation funds and dedicated to regenerating the Jewish creativity that had been so grievously diminished.

31. Schindler to Chava and Arthur [Moshe Aharon] Oles, n.d., in possession of the family. The letter, written while he was still in the army and containing some negative reflections on its protocols, was apparently composed in German to avoid censorship or worse.
32. Based on the transcript sent to Hebrew Union College in MSS 20, J86-20, AJA. This transcript, which goes back to his earlier studies at CCNY, surprisingly indicates that he entered from R. L. Stevenson High School, not Townsend Harris or Stuyvesant.
33. Alexander M. Schindler File, MSS 20, J86-20, AJA.
34. The thesis, dated fall 1949, can be found in the Klau Library of Hebrew Union College–Jewish Institute of Religion in Cincinnati.
35. Recalling this periodical in a letter dated February 10, 1994, to Dru Greenwood, then head of the Union of American Hebrew Congregations Outreach Program, Schindler wrote, "My father was interested in *United Israel* principally because it was an outreach organization intended to bring non-Jews to Judaism and to welcome them appropriately. . . . David Horowitz, the founding guru of this organization, still keeps sending me his bulletin." MSS 630, 10/2, AJA.
36. *United Israel Bulletin*, Summer 1947.
37. Alexander Schindler, "Another Ruth in Israel: The Life Story of Nahida Ruth Remy Lazarus," *United Israel Bulletin*, November–December 1947. On her role in Reform Judaism, see Michael A. Meyer, "Women in the Thought and Practice of the European Jewish Reform Movement," in *Gender and Jewish History*, ed. Marion A. Kaplan and Deborah Dash Moore (Bloomington, IN: Indiana University Press, 2011), 147–49.
38. Billie Gold interview.
39. As early as December 15, 1947, Alexander's parents had written to Rabbi Robert L. Katz, the director of field activities at Hebrew Union College, advocating for their son's admission to the rabbinical program. The letter, probably composed by Eliezer judging by the penmanship but signed simply "Mr. & Mrs. Schindler," is in MSS 20, J86-20, AJA. When Eliezer lay deathly ill from a heart attack at the Good Samaritan Hospital in Phoenix, Arizona, Alexander's mother, Sali, wrote to Professor Jacob Rader Marcus at Hebrew Union College on March 8, 1957, that her husband would be unable to accept President Nelson Glueck's invitation to speak to the students and chose to add that he "loves H.U.C. He loves your American Jewish Archives with its tremendous cultural treasures. H.U.C. represents to him the Jewish Universal Sanctuary in the New World." The letter is in SC-10983, AJA.
40. Alexander M. Schindler File, MSS 20, J86-20, AJA.
41. Alexander M. Schindler File, MSS 20, J86-20, AJA.
42. For the character of Hebrew Union College in these years, see Michael A. Meyer, *Hebrew Union College–Jewish Institute of Religion: A Centennial History*,

1875–1975 (Cincinnati: Hebrew Union College Press, rev. ed. 1992), 171–243.
43. Special Meeting of the Executive Committee of the Faculty on Student Evaluations, May 16, 1950, HUC Faculty Minutes, AJA.
44. Billie Gold interview.
45. For the above, see the Hebrew Union College Faculty Minutes, AJA, May 16, 1950.
46. Titled "The Sermons of Solomon Plessner," completed in 1953, and refereed by Israel Bettan, Schindler's 128-page thesis is available by download from the Klau Library of the Hebrew Union College–Jewish Institute of Religion in Cincinnati, http://library.huc.edu/pdf/theses/Schindler%20Alexander%20M-CN-Rab-1953%20rdf.pdf.
47. Alexander Schindler, "The Sermons of Solomon Plessner" (rabbinical thesis, Hebrew Union College, 1953), 13.
48. Schindler, "The Sermons of Solomon Plessner," 15.
49. Schindler, "The Sermons of Solomon Plessner," 84.
50. Schindler, "The Sermons of Solomon Plessner," 126. In his report on Schindler's thesis, Bettan declared the work "a fine scholarly effort" that, with some revisions, "would make an interesting and worthwhile monograph." The report, dated April 14, 1953, is found in MSS 20, J86-20, AJA.

Chapter 2: Ascending the Ladder

1. Theodore I. Lenn and Associates, *Rabbi and Synagogue in Reform Judaism* (New York: CCAR, 1972), 38.
2. Not long after his arrival at Temple Emanuel, Schindler, who was a lover of classical music, published a free English translation of a German cantata "Bearers of Light," composed by Adler with words by Rabbi Max Gruenewald, formerly of Mannheim, Germany (Worcester, MA, 1954). In his earliest publication in the *CCAR Journal*, Schindler criticized Rabbi Beryl Cohon, author of a recently re-issued book on the Biblical prophets, for calling the use of music and dances by the pre-literary prophets an artificial stimulation to inspiration when, as Schindler believed, "music is a proper source for the religious spirit; it is itself divinely inspired" (vol. 9, no. 2 [June 1961]: 71).
3. Speech to NFTY Convention 1993, Ellis Island, NY, MSS 630, 25/5, AJA.
4. Speech to NFTY Convention 1993.
5. Harvey Rayner, "Profile: Rabbi Alexander M. Schindler, Associate Rabbi of Temple Emanuel, Is Outstanding Youth Leader, Finds Work 'Most Satisfying,'" *Worcester Sunday Telegram*, March 18, 1956, Feature Parade Section.
6. Leonard Zion, recorder, "The Pulpit as an Educational Medium," *CCAR Yearbook* 67 (1957): 117.
7. Alexander Schindler, "Militant Radicalism—Salvation or Doom for the Jew," ca. 1955/56, MSS 630, 26/4, AJA. Similar language occurs in "The One and the Many (*Mishpotim*)," n.s., MSS 630, 26/4, AJA.

8. Schindler, "Militant Radicalism."
9. Schindler, "Militant Radicalism."
10. Alexander Schindler, untitled sermon for Chanukah 1953, MSS 630, 26/4, AJA.
11. Schindler, untitled sermon for Chanukah 1953.
12. Schindler, untitled sermon for Chanukah 1953.
13. Schindler, untitled sermon for Chanukah 1953.
14. Alexander Schindler, "As Driven Sand . . . The Problem of the Arab Refugees," undated sermon, ca. 1955, MSS 630, 26/4, AJA.
15. "As Driven Sand."
16. Alexander Schindler, "Good-Bye God, I'm Going to College," undated manuscript, MSS 630, 26/4, AJA.
17. Schindler, "Good-Bye God."
18. Schindler, "Good-Bye God."
19. Alexander Schindler, "Yiskor-Shemini Atzeres 5714," MSS 630, 26/5, AJA.
20. Schindler, "Yiskor-Shemini Atzeres 5714."
21. Schindler, "Yiskor-Shemini Atzeres 5714."
22. Schindler, "Yiskor-Shemini Atzeres 5714."
23. Alexander Schindler, "The 'New Look' in Christian Theology," *National Jewish Monthly*, February 1959, 14.
24. Alexander Schindler, "Do We Seek Converts? Judaism: A Missionary Religion," n.d., MSS 630, 26/4, AJA.
25. Schindler, "Do We Seek Converts?"
26. Schindler, "Do We Seek Converts?" Schindler was not the only Reform rabbi to consider the question of proselytizing non-Jews in the 1950s. Even then it had become a controversial issue. On the positive side see, for example, Abraham Schusterman, "Some Notes on Proselytism," *CCAR Journal*, October 195, 31–33, 38, who cites both the Liberal Jewish thinker Leo Baeck and the Conservative rabbi Robert Gordis as being in favor. However, a prominent Reform rabbi, Robert I. Kahn of Houston, raised questions about the projected effort, asking, "Our God might be their God, but will our people be their people?"; letter to the editor, in *CCAR Journal*, April 1959, 72.
27. The undated and untitled manuscript (MSS 630, 26/5, AJA) originally had "conflict." But, by hand, Schindler moderated the relationship to "competition."
28. Schindler, undated manuscript.
29. Schindler, undated manuscript.
30. "Clergymen's Wives: Mrs. A. M. Schindler's Interests Range from Cookery to Crafts," *Worcester Sunday Telegram*, March 31, 1957, 6D.
31. "Clergymen's Wives."
32. Interview with Eric Yoffie, November 27, 2022.
33. "The Role of the Congregational Rabbi and the Hillel Foundations," *CCAR Yearbook* 71 (1961): 171–73.

34. "The Role of the Congregational Rabbi and the Hillel Foundations," 173.
35. Schindler to Rabbi Sheldon Zimmerman in Dallas, TX, January 4, 1995, MSS 72, D-10, AJA.
36. Schindler noted that the new curriculum for the one-day and three-day Reform religious schools, proposed during his directorship, "bore the stamp of the knowledge and talents" of his predecessor, who had left the Union to become a professor at Hebrew Union College–Jewish Institute of Religion (*An Outline of the Curriculum for the Jewish Religious School* [New York: Union of American Hebrew Congregations, 1964], v).
37. However, when Schindler organized a symposium on contemporary Jewish theology for a magazine that he briefly edited, he invited Mordecai Kaplan, along with the Orthodox rabbi Norman Lamm, the traditionalist Reform rabbi Arnold Jacob Wolf, and the Maimonidean Jewish philosopher Samuel Atlas to participate ("Editor's Page," *Dimension*, Winter 1967).
38. Alexander Schindler, "Jewish Unity and Jewish Education," remarks before the Rabbinical Assembly (Conservative), 66th Annual Convention, Toronto, Canada, May 18, 1966, MSS 630, 24/1, AJA.
39. Undated and untitled lecture, but clearly delivered to educators during the period when Schindler was head of Jewish education, MSS 630, 26/5, AJA.
40. Lecture to educators (see previous note).
41. Lecture to educators.
42. Alexander M. Schindler, "Reform Judaism and Education," in *America's Schools and Churches: Partners in Conflict*, ed. David W. Beggs III and R. Bruce McQuigg (Bloomington, IN: Indiana University Press, 1965), 116.
43. Lecture to educators (italicization added).
44. "The American Jew: Retrospect and Prospect: A New Curriculum for a New Community," ca. 1966, MSS 630, 24/1, AJA.
45. Editorial by Alexnder Schindler, "Toward a New Curriculum," *The Jewish Teacher*, November 1965, 2, 35.
46. "Educating the Post-Confirmand," *The Jewish Teacher*, April 1964, 25.
47. "The Scholar and the Community: Founders' Day Address" (Cincinnati: HUC-JIR, March 28, 1973), 9.
48. Alexander Schindler, "Jewish Scholarship and the Jewish Community: A Reform Perspective," in *From the Scholar to the Classroom: Translating Jewish Tradition into Curriculum*, ed. Seymour Fox and Geraldine Rosenfield (New York: Jewish Theological Seminary, 1977), 86–97.
49. "Reform Judaism and Jewish Education," 128.
50. "Religion and Education: A Jewish View," n.d., MSS 630, 26/4, AJA.
51. Editorial by Alexander M. Schindler, "The Assembly Speaks: Toward Standards of Reform Religious Education," *The Jewish Teacher*, February 1964, 2.
52. Schindler to Roberta Goodman, RJE, October 8, 1993, MSS 630, 8/3, AJA.
53. Schindler to Alan D. Bennett and Richard M. Morin, November 16, 1990,

MSS 630, 8/4, AJA; see also, "Keynote Address at NATE 40th Anniversary," December 24, 1994, MSS 630, 26/1, AJA. On the organization, see Alan D. Bennett, *The Vision and the Will: A History of the National Association of Temple Educators, 1954–2004* (New York: URJ Press, 2005).

54. "The American Jew: Retrospect and Prospect."
55. "The American Jew: Retrospect and Prospect."
56. "The Challenge of Protesting Youth," Banquet Address, National Association of Temple Educators, 13th Annual Convention, December 28, 1967, MSS 630, 24/1, AJA.
57. "The Challenge of Protesting Youth."
58. "2 Reform Rabbis Back Day Schools," *New York Times*, November 17, 1963. For a summary treatment of the earlier stages of the issue, see Alvin Irwin Schiff, *The Jewish Day School in America* (New York: Jewish Education Committee Press, 1966), 210–18.
59. *CCAR Yearbook* 60 (1950): 134–35. Seventeen members of the Conference participated in the discussion. Unfortunately, the texts of the speeches were not preserved.
60. "1963 Commission Report on Day Schools," MSS 630, 4/1, AJA.
61. "1963 Commission Report."
62. Sylvan D. Schwartzman, "Who Wants Reform All-Day Schools?," *CCAR Journal*, April 1964, 3–10, 13.
63. Maurice Eisendrath to Samuel Kaufman, February 27, 1964, MSS 630, 4/1, AJA. In a book that he published that same year, Eisendrath wrote, "I for one am still not convinced that parochial schools are the answer to the very real problems of the inadequacy of our religious school system nor of our public schools either"; see his *Can Faith Survive? The Thoughts and Afterthoughts of an American Rabbi*, New York: McGraw-Hill, 1964, 106.
64. Schindler to Rabbi Sanford M. Shapero in Bridgeport, CT, August 9, 1963, MSS 630, 4/1, AJA. Schindler would probably have sent his own children to a Jewish day school had they existed when the children were young. In the absence of such a school, his five children received afternoon Jewish education, as well as Jewish camp and Israel experiences, to supplement their studies in the excellent public schools of Westport, Connecticut. (Personal communication from Rabbi Judith Schindler.)
65. Minutes of the 1969 UAHC Biennial Assembly, MS 630, 4/1, AJA.
66. Minutes of the 1969 UAHC Biennial Assembly.
67. Speech delivered on December 13, 1993, MSS 630, 10/2, AJA.
68. "Consecration Address as President of the Union of American Hebrew Congregations" (New York: UAHC, November 12, 1973).
69. Schindler to Gunter Hirschberg in New York, May 16, 1973, MSS 630, 3/7, AJA.
70. "Draft of Revised Report to the Commission on Reform Jewish Day

Schools," MSS 630, 3/7, AJA. The five were located in New York, Miami, Beverly Hills, Phoenix, and Willowdale, Ontario.

71. Michael Zeldin, *The Status of a Quiet Revolution: Reform Jewish Day Schools in the 1980s* (Los Angeles: UAHC, 1985), 1.
72. "Presidential Sermon at the Union of American Hebrew Congregations 53rd Assembly," November 7, 1975, Schindler Nearprint Collection, AJA.
73. Schindler to Eleanor H. Kurz in Sands Point, NY, February 5, 1976, MSS 630, 3/7, AJA.
74. "Reform Day Schools Are Proliferating as Historic Opposition Fades Away," *Jewish Exponent*, May 20, 1988.
75. "Reform Day Schools Are Proliferating," 1988.
76. "Reform Day Schools Are Proliferating," 1988.
77. "Reform Day Schools Are Proliferating," 1988.
78. "Day Schools—A Vital Option for the Reform Jewish Community," Founding Meeting, Council of Reform Jewish Day Schools, Temple Israel, Boston, MA, March 20, 1988, MS 630, 24/8, AJA.
79. "A Reform Torah Commentary," *Reform Judaism*, November 1980, 1.
80. "A Reform Torah Commentary," 14.
81. "A Reform Torah Commentary," 1.
82. In his preface to the first edition, Gunther Plaut gives no single person credit for initiating the project but only mentions the support that Schindler gave it, along with other individuals. See Plaut's "Preface," *The Torah: A Modern Commentary* (New York: UAHC, 1981).
83. Transcript of interview by Billie Gold for the Oral History Project, UJA-Federation of Jewish Philanthropies of New York, June and October 1990, American Jewish Historical Society.
84. In a letter dated December 1, 1969, to Kivie Kaplan, a principal supporter of the UAHC, Schindler writes, "Since assuming the vice presidency, I have not been directly in touch with the Commentary project," an indication that as director of Jewish education he was centrally involved with it, MSS 26, 11/13, AJA.
85. Interview with Rabbi Eric Yoffie (November 27, 2022).
86. Interview by Billie Gold.
87. Interview by Billie Gold.
88. In his regular presidential "Dear Reader" column in *Reform Judaism* for Summer 1993, Schindler called for a more active relationship with "our sacred texts," suggesting that "encountering a text can be a religious experience."

Chapter 3: Becoming the Voice of Reform Judaism

1. On Eisendrath, see Avi M. Schulman, *Like a Raging Fire: A Biography of Maurice N. Eisendrath* (New York: UAHC Press, 1993).
2. Albert I. Gordon, *Jews in Suburbia* (Boston: Beacon Press, 1959), 231.

3. Maurice N. Eisendrath, "The Union of American Hebrew Congregations: Centennial Reflections," *American Jewish Historical Quarterly* 63.2 (December 1973): 144; Michael A. Meyer, "From Cincinnati to New York: A Symbolic Move," in *The Jewish Condition: Essays on Contemporary Judaism Honoring Alexander M. Schindler*, ed. Aron-Hirt Manheimer (New York: UAHC Press, 1995), 302–13.
4. Toward the end of his UAHC presidency, Eisendrath was willing to admit that his views had changed somewhat over the years, largely in the same direction as did Reform Judaism. See his *Can Faith Survive? The Thoughts and Afterthoughts of an American Rabbi* (New York: McGraw-Hill, 1964). But he remained out of sympathy with what he called "the present penchant to emphasize the particular over the universal. If this present posture hardens into a permanent stance, it paradoxically might be just as suicidal as an overemphasis on universalism" ("Report on UAHC," *Central Conference of American Rabbi Yearbook* 82 [1972]: 106).
5. Cited in Jonathan D. Sarna, *American Judaism: A History* (New Haven: Yale University Press, 2004), 314.
6. After Kaufman died in 1971, Schindler eulogized him as a Reform Jew for whom the noun was always more important than the adjective, an emphasis Schindler shared ("In Memoriam Rabbi Jay Kaufman," MSS 630, 23/9, AJA).
7. Memo to Rabbi Leonard Schoolman, March 19, 1970, MSS 72, D14, AJA.
8. Alexander Schindler, "Image of a Likely Tomorrow: Some Thoughts Concerning the Future of the UAHC and the Synagogue," January 25, 1971, MSS 630, 24/1, AJA.
9. Schindler, "Image of a Likely Tomorrow."
10. Schindler, "Image of a Likely Tomorrow."
11. From Psalm 90:4.
12. Schindler, "Image of a Likely Tomorrow."
13. Schindler, "Image of a Likely Tomorrow."
14. Schindler, "Image of a Likely Tomorrow."
15. Schindler, "Image of a Likely Tomorrow."
16. Schindler, "Image of a Likely Tomorrow."
17. Schindler, "Image of a Likely Tomorrow."
18. Thomas B. Morgan, "The Vanishing American Jew," *Look*, May 5, 1964, 41–46.
19. Schindler to Alfred Gottschalk, April 24, 1973, MSS 630, 5/3, AJA.
20. Schindler to Philip M. Klutznick, June 2, 1970, MSS 26, 11/13; Michael A. Meyer, *Response to Modernity: A History of the Reform Movement in Judaism* (New York: Oxford University Press, 1988), 369–70.
21. Wade Clark Roof and William McKinney, *American Mainline Religion: Its Changing Shape and Future* (New Brunswick, NJ: Rutgers University Press,

1987), 13; George Gallup, Jr. and Jim Castelli, *The People's Religion: American Faith in the 90's* (New York: Macmillan, 1989), 9–15.
22. Theodore I. Lenn, *Rabbi and Synagogue in Reform Judaism* (New York: CCAR, 1972), 75.
23. *Initial Findings of National Jewish Population Study* (New York: Council of Jewish Federations and Welfare Funds, 1972), 15.
24. Lenn, *Rabbi and Synagogue*, 128, 134.
25. Cited in Eisendrath, *Can Faith Survive*, 15.
26. Joseph Klein to Alexander Schindler, March 22, 1972, MSS 72, D-15, AJA.
27. Joseph Klein to Alexander Schindler.
28. *CCAR Yearbook* 81 (1971): 16, cited in Mark Kaiserman, "A Historical Analysis of Rabbinical Officiation at Interfaith Marriages in the American Reform Movement" (ordination thesis, HUC-JIR, Cincinnati, 1997), 46.
29. "Rabbi Officiating at a Mixed Marriage" (1982), *American Reform Responsa*, ed. Walter Jacob (New York: CCAR, 1983), 470.
30. Eisendrath, *Can Faith Survive*, 16.
31. Eugene Mihaly, *Teshuvot (Responsa) on Jewish Marriage with Special Reference to "Reform Rabbis and Mixed Marriage"* (Cincinnati: privately published, May 1985), 70.
32. See the press release of the association in MSS 72, D-10, AJA. After a relatively short time, the association faded away. Schindler was of the opinion that "it might not be wise to attack this group, lest they be enlarged." But, typical for Schindler (in this and other areas as well), he believed that the controversy the association had aroused might actually produce stimulating discussion of the issue (Schindler to Hillel Gamoran in Hoffman Estates, IL, December 10, 1974, MSS 72, D-10, AJA). Schindler also thought it important that Reform responsa shed light on the issue. See his "From the President's Desk," *Reform Judaism*, September 1975.
33. Lenn, *Rabbi and Synagogue*, 134.
34. Cited in Mark L. Winer, "Should Rabbis Perform Mixed Marriages?," *Reform Judaism*, Summer 1985, 2.
35. Committee of 100, *Reform Rabbis and Mixed Marriage* (Elkins Park, PA: privately published, November 25, 1984).
36. Schindler to Lou H. Silberman at Vanderbilt University, February 29, 1972, MSS 72, D-15, AJA.
37. Schindler to Irvin Ross in Edina, MN, July 26, 1977, MSS 72, D-15, AJA.
38. Schindler to Ross, 1977.
39. Schindler to Rheba L. Marks in North Miami, FL, June 13, 1983, MSS 630, 12/1, AJA.
40. Schindler to Rabbi Robert J. Orkand in Westport, CT, November 25, 1985, MSS 630, 11/5, AJA. Schindler was firmly opposed to weddings conducted by a rabbi together with non-Jewish clergy. To an inquiry in this regard he

responded, "I would be negating everything I stand for were I to recommend a rabbi who might perform your marriage ceremony with a Catholic priest" (Schindler to Dorothy M. Wright in Urbana IL [February 14, 1986], MSS 630, 10/10, AJA).
41. Schindler to Carla J. Fachini in Fargo, ND, March 11, 1991, MSS 630, 10/11, AJA.
42. Lenn, *Rabbi and Synagogue*, 235.
43. "A Problem of Communications," *CCAR Journal*, Winter 1973, 25.
44. "Reform Judaism: A Centenary Perspective," available online at https://www.ccarnet.org/rabbinic-voice/platforms/article-reform-judaism-centenary-perspective/.
45. For the earlier statements of 1869 and 1885, see Michael A. Meyer and W. Gunther Plaut, *The Reform Judaism Reader: North American Documents* (New York: UAHC Press, 2000), 196–99.
46. Liberal Protestant denominations, similarly troubled, also decided to conduct surveys of their membership. See Dean R. Hoge and David A. Roozen, eds., *Understanding Church Growth and Decline: 1950–1978* (New York: Pilgrim Press, 1979), 17.
47. Leonard J. Fein, et al., *Reform Is a Verb: Notes on Reform and Reforming Jews* (New York: UAHC, 1972), 34. However, a relatively larger percentage judged synagogue attendance and in-marriage, if not as essential, at least as "desirable."
48. Schindler to Gunther Lawrence, August 23, 1971, MSS 72, D-15, AJA.
49. "Protest of Youth Termed 'Religion at Its Finest'," *JTA Daily News Bulletin*, December 7, 1970.
50. "Jews Told Trend to Conservatism Alienates Young," *Jewish Exponent*, November 24, 1972, 8.
51. "Jews Told Trend," 1972.
52. "Protest of Youth," 1970.
53. "What Has the 'Death of God' Done to Religion?" Remarks by Rabbi Alexander M. Schindler to the Public Relations Society of America, November 17, 1970, MSS 630, 24/1, AJA.
54. Schindler, "What Has the 'Death of God' Done to Religion?"
55. "Rabbi Cites Mystic Need in Religion," *San Francisco Jewish Bulletin*, May 12, 1972.
56. Joseph Fletcher, *Situation Ethics: The New Morality* (Philadelphia: Westminster, 1966).
57. "Judaism and the New Morality," *CCAR Yearbook* 79 (1969): 195. The CCAR was prompted to publish a volume in which various Reform rabbis and intellectuals took on the issue of a contemporary Jewish ethics: Daniel Jeremy Silver, ed., *Judaism and Ethics* (New York: Ktav, 1970).
58. "Judaism and the New Morality," 197.

59. "Report on UAHC," 101.
60. "Report on UAHC," 101.
61. "Report on UAHC," 101.
62. Joseph R. Narot to Roland B. Gittelsohn, July 6, 1971, MSS 72, D-44, AJA.
63. Edward L. Kozberg, president of Wilshire Boulevard Temple in Los Angeles, to Mr. ____, President, sample letter, June 24, 1971, MSS 72, D-44, AJA.
64. In a personal communication to the author, Rabbi Clifford Kulwin related an oral tradition that there were also two rival candidates: Rabbi Richard Hirsch, who in 1973 moved to Israel as executive director of the World Union for Progressive Judaism, and Rabbi Erwin Herman, who was the director of the Union's Southwest Region. Eric Yoffie is of the opinion that Balfour Brickner was also a candidate.
65. Eugene B. Borowitz, "Reform Judaism's Coming Power Struggle," *Sh'ma: A Journal of Jewish Responsibility*, March 19, 1971, 75–79.
66. Borowitz, "Reform Judaism's Coming Power Struggle."
67. "The Torah Is Passed On," *Reform Judaism* 2, no. 4 (December 1973): 5.
68. Maurice N. Eisendrath, "Presidential Sermon" (New York: UAHC, 1973), 15.
69. Rabbi Alexander M. Schindler, "Consecration Address" (New York: Temple Emanu-El, November 12, 1973), 10.
70. Schindler, "Consecration Address."
71. Schindler, "Consecration Address."
72. "New York Diary: Jews of America Are Cast from One Condition into Another," *Ha-Tzofeh*, November 23, 1973. The secretary of state referred to is, of course, Henry Kissinger. The writer errs in thinking that it was the Reform rabbinical association, rather than the congregational association, to whose presidency Schindler was elected. It is possible that he was not personally present in Temple Emanu-El but received an early copy of the printed text of Schindler's address.
73. David Landau, "New Reform Head Sees Stronger Role for Presidents' Conference," *Jerusalem Post*, December 13, 1973, 3.
74. "Proceedings of the Executive Committee of the UAHC Board of Trustees," February 8, 1973, MF3663, AJA.
75. "Dear Fellow-Board Member" (personal and confidential), December 1973, MSS 26, 11/13, AJA.
76. "Dear Fellow Board Member," 1973. The World Union for Progressive Judaism had led in this regard, holding its International Convention in Israel, for the first time, just after the Six-Day War.
77. "Presidential Message," Board of Trustees Meeting, October 14, 1974, MSS, 630, 24/1, AJA.
78. "UAHC Board Mission at the K'nesset," October 20, 1974, MSS, 630, 24/1, AJA.

79. Schindler to "Fellow Board Member," December 1974, MSS 26, 11/13, AJA.
80. Herbert A. Friedman to Rabbi Alexander Schindler, April 2, 1973, MSS 630, 18/3, AJA.
81. Schindler to Richard G. Hirsch, August 6, 1973, MSS 630, 18/3, AJA.
82. Schindler to Matthew Ross in New York, September 21, 1973, MSS 630, 19/1, AJA; Schindler to Harry K. Gutmann, April 17, 1974, MS 630 18/2, AJA. Schindler to Alfred Gottschalk, October 28, 1976: "Herb is doing absolutely nothing for us and there is no justification whatsoever for continuing to bear these expenses just for the psychological reason of 'keeping the project alive'"; MSS 630, 18/3, AJA.
83. Alfred Gottschalk to Herbert A. Friedman, December 30, 1976, MSS 630, 18/2, AJA. Friedman describes his three years connected with the project as happy ones in his *Roots of the Future* (Jerusalem: Gefen, 1999), 309–11.
84. Alexander Schindler, "Report of the President to the Board of Trustees," May 30, 1975, Klau Library, HUC-JIR, Cincinnati.
85. "Union of American Hebrew Congregations News," June 1975, MSS 72, D-6, AJA.
86. "Union of American Hebrew Congregations News," 1975.
87. Letter to Robert L. Adler in Chicago, November 18, 1974, MSS 72, D-10, AJA.
88. Interview with David Saperstein, October 26, 2022.
89. Anonymous, "To Alex and Al; Personal and Confidential," June 24, 1974, MSS 72, D-22, AJA.
90. Edith J. Miller to Rabbi Joseph Glaser, September 18, 1975, MSS 72, D-11, AJA. She signed the letter: "Yours in equality."
91. George Dugan, "Group of Jewish Women Opposes Masculine Terminology in Liturgy," *New York Times*, September 13, 1976.
92. "Aide Is Appointed to Rabbi Schindler," *American Israelite*, July 1, 1976.
93. "Brown's Bomb," *Time*, November 25, 1974.
94. Schindler to President Gerald Ford, November 15, 1974, MSS 72, D17, AJA.
95. Gerald R. Ford to Rabbi Schindler, November 26, 1974, MSS 72, D17, AJA. The rebuke did not, however, eliminate further problems that Brown created for the Jewish community. Two years later Schindler considered it necessary, on behalf of the majority of the Presidents' Conference, to call on Ford to "publicly censure" General Brown for a "dangerous course of action" he was recommending with regard to America's Israel policy ("Statement of Rabbi Alexander Schindler, Chairman, Conference of Presidents of Major American Jewish Organizations" [October 19, 1976]; MSS 630, 20/8, AJA). In this instance the critique may not have reflected his personal view. See his letter to David E. Molish in Philadelphia, October 28, 1976, MSS 630, 20/8, AJA.
96. In any case, Brown continued to harbor similar views. Two years later he still declared that Israel was a burden to the Pentagon; MSS 630, 20/8, AJA.

Chapter 4: Spokesman for American Jewry

1. "Moment Interviews. Alex Schindler: By the Presidents He's a President," *Moment*, February–March 1977, 16. The Conference, in fact, came into existence over a period of time, possibly beginning as early as 1951 and formally organizing as late as 1959. It has been argued that the initial impetus came in 1953, in reaction to an Israeli reprisal attack on the Palestinian village of Qibya, which was widely condemned, including by the United States. See Doug Rossinow, "'The Edge of the Abyss': The Origins of the Israel Lobby, 1949–1954," *Modern American History* 1, no. 1 (2018): 39–41. The relevant Jewish Virtual Library website relating to the Conference of Presidents of Major American Jewish Organizations tells a yet different story. Strangely, it does not mention Maurice Eisendrath (www.jewishvirtuallibrary.org/conference-of-presidents-of-major-jewish-organizations). Regrettably, the archives of the Conference are not readily available.
2. Nahum Goldmann, *Staatsmann ohne Staat: Autobiographie* (Cologne: Kiepenhauer & Witsch, 1970), 440.
3. Maurice N. Eisendrath, "The Union of American Hebrew Congregations: Centennial Reflections," *American Jewish Historical Quarterly* 63, no. 2 (December 1973): 145.
4. Schindler to Henry J. Fensterwald, December 31, 1970, MSS 630, 17/6, AJA. Fensterwald was the president of the Baltimore Hebrew Congregation. Opposition came, as well, from Alvin E. Coleman, writing for the board of Temple Emanu-El in New York City, who argued that association should be limited to the World Union for Progressive Judaism, "whose interests have a special kinship with us" (Coleman to Maurice N. Eisendrath [March 25, 1971], MSS 630, 17/6, AJA). Klutznick, a Reform Jew, did become president of the World Jewish Congress from 1977 to 1979. Prinz had been president of the American Jewish Congress from 1958 to 1966, but he did not become president of the World Jewish Congress.
5. Jay Kaufman to Maurice N. Eisendrath and Emil N. Baar, January 16, 1963, MSS 630, 22/4, AJA. The two other founders, Goldmann and Philip Klutznick, had both served as presidents of the organization. Perhaps some thought it appropriate that the third founder should also receive that honor.
6. Jay Kaufman to Yehuda Hellman (executive vice president of the Conference), December 21, 1962, MSS 630, 23/2, AJA and November 30, 1964, MSS 630, 22/4, AJA.
7. "Some Thoughts on a Journey to Jerusalem" (1969), 4, MSS 630, 24/1, AJA.
8. Schindler to Rabbi Herschel Schacter, December 18, 1969, MSS 630, 22/4, AJA.
9. Joachim Prinz to Alexander Schindler, February 30, 1970, MSS 630 19/3, AJA.
10. David Landau, "New Reform Head Sees Stronger Role for Presidents' Con-

ference," *Jerusalem Post*, December 13, 1973, 3. Like Herschel Schacter, Israel Miller was an Orthodox rabbi.
11. Schindler to Alvin I. Schiff, June 2, 1976, MSS 630, 20/9, AJA. Cf. MS 630, 20/11, AJA. The budget of the Presidents' Conference at the time apparently amounted to only $150,000, and it could employ only one professional staff member, the very capable Yehuda Hellman (Gary S. Schiff, "American Jews and Israel: A Study in Political Conduct," *Forum on the Jewish People, Zionism, and Israel* 1 [1976]: 16). Schiff's devaluation of the role of the Presidents' Conference provoked Schindler's angry response; see Schindler to Josef Almogi in Jerusalem, August 27, 1976, MSS 630, 21/7, AJA.
12. Landau, "New Reform Head Sees Stronger Role for Presidents' Conference," 3.
13. Landau, "New Reform Head," 3.
14. Schindler to "Fellow Board Member," personal and confidential, March 12, 1974, MSS 26, 11/13, AJA.
15. Alexander Schindler, "Israel and the Diaspora: Our Responsibilities," *CCAR Yearbook* 84 (1974): 139.
16. Schindler, "Israel and the Diaspora," 139.
17. Schindler, "Israel and the Diaspora," 139.
18. Schindler, "Israel and the Diaspora," 140. Schindler's speech was reprinted in full for lay consumption in *Reform Judaism* (May 1974), and summarized in the same issue under the title "Israel Must Not Be a Surrogate Synagogue."
19. Albert Vorspan to UAHC Board of Trustees, Rabbis, Congregational Presidents, Commission on Social Action, January 21, 1976, MSS 86, 8/6, AJA.
20. Anonymous, "Jewish Power in the U.S. Today," *Haaretz*, April 30, 1976 [Hebrew], MSS 630, 21/7, AJA.
21. "Moment Interviews," 16.
22. "Schindler Vows No Whitewash of Israel," *San Francisco Jewish Bulletin*, January 23, 1976.
23. "Moment Interviews," 17; italicization added.
24. Schindler to the Honorable Henry Kissinger, Washington, DC, April 9, 1976, MSS 630, 22/11, AJA.
25. Richard Cohen, "Report on Brussels II: World Jewry United in Solidarity with the Jews of the USSR," *Congress Monthly*, March 1976, 6.
26. Cohen, "Report on Brussels II."
27. Abba Eban, "Do Not Withhold Assistance to Soviet Jewish 'Dropouts,'" *Cleveland Jewish News*, December 3, 1976, 15.
28. "Statement By Rabbi Alexander Schindler . . . Before the Senate Committee on Finance," September 8, 1976, MS 630, 22/11, AJA. Unlike both Ford and Carter, Schindler favored using the economic leverage gained by the Jackson-Vanik amendment, believing that "there is nothing morally unworthy when we relate human rights to trade" ("Jackson-Vanik Law Working, Schindler

Says," *American Israelite* [September 23, 1976]).
29. Schindler to Max M. Fisher in Detroit, MI, March 10, 1976, MSS 630, 20/2, AJA; Schindler to Philip M. Klutznick in Chicago, March 22, 1976, MSS 630, 8/2, AJA.
30. Joseph R. Biden, Jr. to Alexander Schindler, March 17, 1976, MSS 630, 21/1, AJA. Schindler had written to Biden in regard to the projected sale of six C-130 military transport aircraft to Egypt.
31. Kissinger, born in Fürth, Germany, was two years older than Schindler. Like him, he had fled to the United States in 1938. Schindler's evaluation of Kissinger is of interest: "I often sit in the State Department, knowing that Kissinger is using the U.S. Jewish leadership as a pawn to some extent. He wants us to persuade Israel to make more concessions. But I look at the pictures there of the past Secretaries and say to myself that I'd rather be dealing with this man than with any of the others. I am convinced that the time will come when Israel and U.S. Jews will be yearning for the time when they had Kissinger" (cited in Phil Bronstein, "'For Some Jews, Israel Is It': Vitality of U.S. Jewish Community is Growing," *San Francisco Jewish Bulletin*, July 9, 1976, 1). Schindler and Kissinger remained good friends for many years. When a Schindler Festschrift appeared many years later, Kissinger's tribute to Schindler opened the volume (Aron Hirt-Manheimer, ed., *The Jewish Condition: Essays on Contemporary Judaism Honoring Rabbi Alexander Schindler* [New York: UAHC Press, 1995], ix).
32. Transcript of Meeting of President Gerald R. Ford and Secretary of State Henry Kissinger with American Jewish Leaders at the White House (March 17, 1976), in Mark A. Raider and Gary Phillip Zola, eds., *New Perspectives in American Jewish History: A Documentary Tribute to Jonathan D. Sarna* (Waltham, MA: Brandeis University Press, 2021), 347–48. See also Conference of Presidents of Major American Jewish Organizations, "Report for the Year Ending March 31, 1976," 21.
33. Transcript of Meeting, 1976.
34. "Jewish Power in the U.S. Today."
35. "Jewish Power in the U.S. Today."
36. Anonymous, "Schindler: There Is No Crisis in Relations with the United States and No Reason for Panic" [Hebrew], *Haaretz*, March 29, 1976.
37. Bronstein, "For Some Jews Israel Is It"; Schindler to His Excellency, the American Ambassador William Scranton in New York, April 9, 1976, MSS 630, 23/5, AJA.
38. Personal letter from Abramov to Schindler, April 16, 1976, MS 630, 21/7, AJA.
39. Richard G. Hirsch in Jerusalem to Alexander M. Schindler, April 7, 1976, MSS 630, 18/4, AJA.
40. Hirsch to Schindler. Hirsch assumed that Schindler would not know the slang term *dugri*.

41. Rowland Evans and Robert Novak, "Crossroads for Israel?" *New York Post*, April 2, 1976.
42. Evans and Novak, "Crossroads for Israel?"
43. Schindler to Alfred Gottschalk, April 9, 1976, uncatalogued Gottschalk papers, AJA.
44. Schindler to Gottschalk.
45. Schindler to Rabbi Fabian Schonfeld, Young Israel of Kew Garden Hills, June 10, 1976, MSS 630, 21/7, AJA; Schindler to Rabbi Eugene Borowitz, June 10, 1976, MSS 630, 21/7, AJA; Press Release of the Conference of Presidents of Major American Jewish Organizations, June 17, 1976, MSS 630, 21/7, AJA.
46. "Report of the President of the Union of American Hebrew Congregations to the Board of Trustees," New York City, May 21–23, 1976, MSS 630, 24/2, AJA.
47. Robert A. Riesman, "Joining the Jackals," *Community Voice*, published by the Jewish Federation of Rhode Island, September 15, 1976, MSS 630, 21/7, AJA.
48. Breira is briefly analyzed in Edward Tivnan, *The Lobby: Jewish Political Power and American Foreign Policy* (New York: Simon and Schuster, 1987), 90–96.
49. Cited in Phil Bronstein, "Presidents' Conference Chairman Sounds Off: American Jewry Faces New Approach, New Priorities," *San Francisco Jewish Bulletin*, July 2, 1976, 1.
50. However, when Arthur Green, at the time president of the Reconstructionist Rabbinical College, dismissed the radical activist Arthur Waskow from its faculty under donor pressure, Schindler urged him to reconsider—even though he admitted to not always agreeing with Waskow on matters related to Israel (Schindler to Arthur Green in Wyncote, Pennsylvania, September 6, 1989, MSS 630, 14/1, AJA).
51. Bronstein, "Presidents' Conference Chairman Sounds Off."
52. Bronstein, "Presidents' Conference Chairman Sounds Off."
53. Cited in Bronstein, "For Some Jews, Israel Is It," 1.
54. Bronstein, "Presidents' Conference Chairman Sounds Off."
55. *San Francisco Jewish Bulletin*, July 30, 1976.
56. Schindler to Ben L. Kaufman at the *Cincinnati Enquirer*, July 29, 1976. *Messira* refers to the act of a Jew delivering sensitive information to gentile authorities, thereby creating possible disaster for an entire Jewish community if it was then held responsible for the misdeeds of an individual from its midst, as happened from time to time during the Middle Ages.
57. Mrs. Max N. Matzkin to Rabbi Alexander Schindler, August 5, 1976, MSS 630, 21/7, AJA.
58. Alexander Schindler to Mrs. Max N. Matzkin, August 11, 1976, MSS 630, 21/7, AJA.

59. Schindler to Mrs. Max N. Matzkin.
60. Malka Rabinowitz, "Israel Treating U.S. Jews Like Milk Cows," *Jerusalem Post*, September 12, 1976; *Maariv*, September 12, 1976; *JTA Daily News Bulletin*, September 14, 1976. Amended notes for the lecture are at MSS 630, 24/2, AJA.
61. Schindler to Ambassador Simcha Dinitz in Washington, October 1, 1976, MSS 630, 21/7, AJA.
62. "Our Economic Dependence on the United States Is Insulting and There is No Chance That Anyone Will Agree to Pay So That We Can Live Better: Holiday Interview with Golda Meir" [Hebrew], *Maariv*, September 24, 1976.
63. Personal, handwritten letter from Richard Hirsch to Alexander Schindler, September 14, 1976, MSS 630, 21/7, AJA.
64. Hirsch to Schindler.
65. Alexander M. Schindler, "From the President's Desk: Entebbe and Beirut," *Reform Judaism*, September 1976, 4.
66. Schindler to Mrs. David M. Levitt in Great Neck, New York, July 28, 1976, MSS 630, 9/3, AJA. Mrs. Levitt served for many years as the World Union for Progressive Judaism's representative to the United Nations.
67. Schindler, "From the President's Desk," 4. See also Schindler to Mrs. David M. Levitt, 1976.
68. Alexander M. Schindler, "The Big—and Bigger—Lie," *Keeping Posted*, March 1976, 16–17.
69. *New York Times*, Sunday, November 28, 1976, E-18. I have not found a source indicating how many readers of the *Times* responded to the advertisement, how much money was raised, or how that money might have been spent.
70. Eva K. Opton to Rabbi Alexander M. Schindler, November 28, 1976, MSS 630, 21/7, AJA.
71. Opton to Schindler, 1976.
72. At that time Kurt Waldheim's past as an intelligence officer in the Nazi Wehrmacht had not yet been revealed.
73. Schindler to Mrs. Frank G. Opton in New York, December 1, 1976, MSS 630, 21/7, AJA.
74. Schindler to Opton.
75. Schindler to the Honorable William W. Scranton, May 18, 1977, MSS 630, 15/8, AJA.
76. "Rabbi Asserts American Jews Will Spurn One-Issue Candidate," *New York Times*, November 9, 1975.
77. "Rabbi Asserts American Jews."
78. Conference of Presidents of Major American Jewish Organizations, "Report for the Year Ending March 31, 1977" (New York, 1977), 24. Schindler believed that in his high regard for Kissinger in relation to Israel, he was in the minority within the Presidents' Conference. See "Ford Requires

the Hercules [Planes] Deal to Strengthen His Position Within His Party Says Rabbi Alexander Schindler . . . in an Interview with Raphael Bashan," [Hebrew] *Yediot Aharonot*, April 2, 1976.
79. Remarks of Rabbi Alexander M. Schindler at the Tribute to Dr. Henry Kissinger by the Conference of Presidents of Major American Jewish Organizations, January 11, 1977, MSS 630, 23/1, AJA.
80. Morris J. Amitay to Alexander Schindler, February 27, 1976, MSS 630, 23/4, AJA.
81. Amitay to Schindler.
82. Schindler to "Fellow Board Member," June 3, 1976, MSS 630 20/10, AJA.
83. "Moment Interviews," 57.
84. Schindler to Nathan Greenberg in Worcester, MA, September 21, 1976, MSS 630, 20/10, AJA.
85. Schindler to Stuart E. Eizenstat in Atlanta, GA, June 10, 1976, MSS 630, 20/10, AJA.
86. Schindler to Bruce Corwin in Los Angeles, October 20, 1976 (confidential), MSS 630, 20/10, AJA.
87. "Moment Interviews," 57.
88. Conference of Presidents, "Report. . . March 31, 1977," 12–13.
89. Conference of Presidents, "Report. . . March 31, 1977."
90. Speech to the National Federation of Sisterhoods, November 9, 1976, MSS 630, 24/2, AJA.
91. Schindler mailgram to President-Elect Jimmy Carter, December 16, 1976, MSS 630, 20/10, AJA.
92. Conference of Presidents, "Report. . . March 31, 1977," 9–11.
93. Schindler to Robert Jacobs in New York, February 18, 1977, MSS 630, 23/3, AJA; Kathleen Christison, *Perceptions of Palestine: Their Influence on U.S. Middle East Policy* (Berkeley: University of California Press, 2000), 171.
94. Seth Anziska, *Preventing Palestine: A Political History from Camp David to Oslo* (Princeton, NJ: Princeton University Press, 2018), 41.
95. Memorandum from William B. Quandt to Zbigniew Brzezinski, April 5, 1977, Schindler File, Carter Library, Atlanta, GA.
96. Cited in J. J. Goldberg, *Jewish Power: Inside the American Jewish Establishment* (Reading, MA: Addison-Wesley, 1996), 210. Sherer was grateful to Schindler for disagreeing with some influential Reform Jews who wanted the UAHC to come out against kosher slaughter as being cruel to animals. See Nosson Scherman, "Remembering Rabbi Moshe Sherer," *Jewish Observer*, May 2008, 12.
97. Eran Kaplan, *The Jewish Radical Right: Revisionist Zionism and Its Ideological Legacy* (Madison, WI: University of Wisconsin Press, 2005), 163.
98. "Report of the Conference of Presidents of Major American Jewish Organizations for the Year Ending March 31, 1978" (New York, 1978), 3.

99. Alexander Schindler, "The Odd Couple: Begin and I," *Moment*, December 1978, 23.
100. *Menachem Begin, the Sixth Prime Minister: Selected Documents (1913–1992)* (Jerusalem: State of Israel State Archives, 2014), 275.
101. Begin to Schindler (telegram), May 20, 1977, MSS 630, 21/7, AJA.
102. Schindler, "The Odd Couple," 23.
103. Schindler, "The Odd Couple."
104. Schindler, "The Odd Couple."
105. Schindler, "The Odd Couple."
106. Edward Tivnan, *The Lobby: Jewish Political Power and American Foreign Policy* (New York: Simon and Schuster, 1987), 112.
107. Arye Naor, *Begin in Power: A Personal Testimony* [Hebrew] (Tel Aviv: Yediot Aharonot, 1993), 113–14.
108. Mentioned in an incompletely preserved manuscript, n.d., 14, MSS 630, 24/2, AJA. As noted earlier in chapter 2, Schindler had used the Yiddish version of the expression in speaking to rabbinical students.
109. "Report of the President of the Union of American Hebrew Congregations to the Board of Trustees," New York, June 9–12, 1977, 2.
110. "Report of the President," 5.
111. Schindler to David Polish, June 6, 1977, MSS 630, 21/7, AJA.
112. Schindler, "The Odd Couple," 22.
113. Schindler, "The Odd Couple," 26.
114. Statement released by Conference of Presidents of Major Jewish Organizations, June 3, 1977, n.d., MSS 630, 21/7, AJA.
115. Charles S. Liebman to Alexander Schindler, June 9, 1977, MSS 630, 21/8, AJA.
116. Alexander Schindler to Charles S. Liebman, June 13, 1977, MSS 630, 21/8, AJA.
117. Schindler to Liebman.
118. "Report of the Conference . . . Ending March 31, 1978," 5.
119. David Gross, "Three-Way Street Rocky for Schindler," *Jewish Exponent*, March 31, 1978, 11.
120. Jimmy Carter, *White House Diary* (New York: Farrar, Straus and Giroux, 2010), 57.
121. Stuart E. Eizenstat, *President Carter: The White House Years* (New York: St. Martin's Press, 2018), 455.
122. *Time*, July 18, 1977.
123. Eizenstat, *President Carter*, 456.
124. Eizenstat, *President Carter*, 456.
125. Cited in Kai Bird, *The Outlier: The Unfinished Presidency of Jimmy Carter* (New York: Crown, 2021), 260.
126. "U.S. Policies Anger Jews," *New York Post*, October 27, 1977, 4.

127. Statement by Rabbi Alexander Schindler, October 5, 1977, MSS 630, 21/7, AJA.
128. Schindler to President Jimmy Carter, December 16, 1977, Carter Library, Atlanta, GA.
129. Carter, *White House Diary*, 171.
130. Carter, *White House Diary*, 171. According to one scholar, Carter had developed a "personal enmity" to Schindler. See Daniel Strieff, *Jimmy Carter and the Middle East: The Politics of Presidential Diplomacy* (New York: Palgrave Macmillan, 2015), 106. I found no indication that the enmity was mutual.
131. Cited in Bird, *The Outlier*, 291. Franklin Delano Roosevelt had been charged with not being responsive to Jewish requests for assistance during the Holocaust.
132. *Menachem Begin, the Sixth Prime Minister*, 339–40.
133. "Begin Praises Schindler," *Reform Judaism*, September 1977, 3.
134. Cited in *Time*, April 3, 1978.
135. "Report of the Conference... Ending March 31, 1978," 9.
136. Gross, "Three-Way Street," 64.
137. Gross, "Three-Way Street," 64.
138. Schindler's successor, Theodore R. Mann, chairman of the National Jewish Community Relations Advisory Council (NJCRAC), did not enjoy the same unanimous support that Schindler received, either when first elected or later when his term was extended. Mann, a liberal civil rights attorney, was elected by a vote of 21 to 6. His opponents were the five Orthodox groups and the Zionist Organization of America. See "Theodore Mann Named to Head Jewish Group," *San Francisco Jewish Bulletin*, January 23, 1978. Begin had wanted Schindler to continue as "spokesman" on Jerusalem issues even beyond his term of office, but Mann regarded agreement with this proposal an abdication of his own responsibilities as chairman and therefore declined to pass that responsibility to Schindler (Theodore R. Mann to Alexander M. Schindler, November 27, 1978, MSS 630, 20/2, AJA). Later Schindler accused Mann of unilaterally strengthening NJCRAC at the expense of the Presidents' Conference by giving undue authority to NJCRAC's Israel Task Force (Schindler to Theodore Mann in Philadelphia, August 14, 1979, MSS 630, 22/5, AJA). Schindler also later claimed responsibility for the nomination of B'nai B'rith's Seymour Reich to be Mann's successor (Schindler to Shimon Glick in Beer Sheva, Israel, November 29, 1988, MSS 630, 2/4, AJA). Whereas Schindler had gotten on very well with Yehuda Hellman, executive director of the Presidents' Conference during the first part of his term, he was critical of his successor, Malcolm Hoenlein, whom he accused of neglecting himself and the Union. "As you know, Malcolm," he wrote to him, "I have my own access [to political figures] and will feel free to use it in the future if the UAHC continues to be ignored" (Schindler to Malcolm Hoenlein in New York, November 20, 1989, MSS 630, 20/1, AJA).

139. Tivnan, *The Lobby*, 125.
140. Tivnan, *The Lobby*, 125.
141. "Report of the Conference . . . Ending March 31, 1978," 20.
142. Remarks of Rabbi Alexander Schindler, Community Meeting with Prime Minister Begin, March 23, 1978, New York, MSS 630, 24/2, AJA.
143. Carter sent Schindler and his wife a personal invitation to attend the signing ceremony on the White House Lawn and the preceding festive dinner, even though Schindler was at that point no longer chair of the Presidents' Conference. His expression of thanks to Carter was signed simply "Alexander." Schindler to The President, March 30, 1979, Schindler File, Carter Library, Atlanta, GA.
144. "Schindler in Egypt as Sadat's Guest," *Reform Judaism* 6, no. 5 (February 1978): 1.
145. "Schindler in Egypt," 16–17.
146. "Schindler in Egypt," 1.
147. Schindler to Anwar Sadat in Cairo, January 27, 1978, Alfred Gottschalk Papers, uncat., AJA.
148. "Schindler in Egypt," 17–18. Yet, despite Schindler's consistent opposition to American Jewish leaders becoming surrogates for Israel, that is precisely what they were accused of being at this stage, according to an article by Sol Stern, "Menachem Begin vs. the Jewish Lobby," *New York Magazine*, April 24, 1978, 63.
149. "Schindler in Egypt," 18.
150. "Report of the Conference of Presidents of Major Jewish Organizations for the Year Ending March 31, 1979."
151. *Jerusalem Post*, April 21, 1978, 6. It was also claimed that the term was extended as a vote of confidence in Schindler at a time when he was under pressure from the White House, instigated by Brzezinski (*American Israelite*, March 30, 1978).
152. Manuscript of Schindler's speech, July 3, 1978, MSS 630, 24/2, AJA.
153. Manuscript of Schindler's speech.
154. "Solomon Bublick Award," Wikipedia: The Free Encyclopedia, https://en.wikipedia.org/wiki/Solomon_Bublick_Award.
155. Thank you to Elisa Frankel, Schindler's eldest daughter, for providing me with a copy of the citation, signed by Avraham Harman, president of the Hebrew University.
156. Alexander M. Schindler to "Dear Fellow Board Member," August 2, 1978, MSS 20, J86-20, AJA.
157. Schindler to "Dear Fellow Board Member."
158. Schindler to "Dear Fellow Board Member."
159. Schindler to UAHC Board Members, August 2, 1978, MSS 20, J86-20, AJA; *Reform Judaism*, September 1978, 2.
160. Schindler to "Dear Fellow Board Member."

Chapter 5: Reaching Out

1. "Introduction" to *Initial Findings of National Jewish Population Study* (New York: Council of Jewish Federations and Welfare Funds, 1972), 15.
2. Mark L. Winer, Sanford Seltzer, and Steven J. Schwager, *Leaders of Reform Judaism: A Study of Jewish Identity, Religious Practices and Beliefs, and Marriage Patterns* (New York: UAHC, 1987), 60–61, 71; Jonathan D. Sarna, "Reform Jewish Leaders, Intermarriage, and Conversion," *CCAR Journal* 37 (Winter 1990): 1–9.
3. Lydia Kukoff, ed., *Reform Jewish Outreach: A Program Guide* (New York: UAHC, 1981), 24.
4. Fred Massarik, "A Report on Intermarriage," in *Intermarriage Facts for Planning* (New York: Council of Jewish Federations and Welfare Funds, 1972), 1.
5. As noted earlier, the *Look* magazine article "The Vanishing American Jew" had brought the issue to wider attention as early as 1964. By the 1970s, the crisis was perceived as becoming yet more severe. Elihu Bergman, "The American Jewish Population Erosion," *Midstream*, October 1977, 9–19; Egon Mayer and Carl Sheingold, *Intermarriage and the Jewish Future* (New York: American Jewish Committee, 1979).
6. Sanford Seltzer, *Jews and Non-Jews Getting Married* (New York: UAHC, 1984), 1.
7. "Report of the Special Committee on Mixed Marriages," *CCAR Yearbook* 72 (1962): 88.
8. "Address of Rabbi Alexander M. Schindler, President of the Union of American Hebrew Congregations, to the Board of Trustees, Houston, Texas, December 2, 1978," in *Reform Jewish Outreach: A Program Guide*, ed. Lydia Kukoff (New York: UAHC, 1981), 2–10.
9. "Address of Rabbi Alexander M. Schindler."
10. "Address of Rabbi Alexander M. Schindler."
11. Central Conference of American Rabbis, *Rabbi's Manual*, rev. ed. (New York, 1961), 112.
12. Rabbi Gunther Plaut thought that the rabbis were all agreed that if Schindler had not raised the question of patrilineal descent, they would have been content with the statement in the *Rabbi's Manual*. In his view, "The more we attempt to say, the more we will divide the Conference" (Plaut to Committee on Patrilineal Descent, August 16, 1982, MSS 729, 31/2, AJA).
13. "Address of Rabbi Alexander M. Schindler."
14. "Address of Rabbi Alexander M. Schindler."
15. Resolution of the Board of Trustees, December 2, 1978, in Lydia Kukoff, ed., *Reform Jewish Outreach: A Program Guide* (New York: UAHC, 1981), 10.
16. Schindler to Donald S. Day, December 18, 1978, MSS 72, A-4-2, AJA.
17. Donald S. Day to Rabbi Alexander Schindler, December 7, 1978, MSS 72, A-4-2, AJA.

18. "On the Bright Side," *Reform Judaism*, Fall 1984, inside cover.
19. Cited in Dana Evan Kaplan, *The New Reform Judaism: Challenges and Reflections* (Philadelphia: Jewish Publication Society, 2013), 237–38.
20. Kaplan, *The New Reform Judaism*, 237–38.
21. Schindler to Barbara Solomon in Ormond Beach, Florida, November 17, 1983, MSS 72 A-4-2, AJA.
22. Cited in Ellen Jaffe-Gill, "Patrilineality," *Moment*, December 1998, 71.
23. Moses Cyrus Weiler to Herman Schaalman, May 31, 1982, MSS 215, AJA.
24. This was clearly stated with reference to Schindler in Orthodox circles; see Nisson Wolpin, "The Case of the Non-Conservative Conservatives," *Jewish Observer*, February 1983, 6.
25. "Remarks of Rabbi Alexander Schindler at the CCAR Conference, June 29, 1982, in Support of Patrilineal Descent," *CCAR Yearbook* 92 (1982): 71. See also the brief summary of his views in *CCAR Yearbook* 93 (1983): 148–49. Schindler used the expression "tinsel imitation of Orthodoxy" on more than one occasion.
26. This is the language of the resolution. It can be found in Michael A. Meyer and W. Gunther Plaut, eds., *The Reform Judaism Reader: North American Documents* (New York: UAHC Press, 2001), 172.
27. Neal Barsky, "Rabbi Schindler Defends Reform Rabbis' Vote Stating That the Identity of a Jewish Child Can Be Determined by Either Mother or Father," Union of American Hebrew Congregations News Release, May 20, 1983, MSS 72, A-4-2, AJA.
28. "Patrilineal and Matrilineal Descent," in *Contemporary American Reform Responsa*, ed. Walter Jacob (New York: Central Conference of American Rabbis, 1987), 61–68. The responsum is dated October 1983.
29. David Polish, "A Dissent on Patrilineal Descent," in *Toward the Twenty-first Century: Judaism and the Jewish People in Israel and America*, ed. Ronald Kronish (New York: KTAV Publishing House, 1988), 228.
30. Ben Halpern, "Those Entitled to Be Jews," *Judaism*, Winter 1985, 45.
31. "Outreach Has Helped Heal Interfaith Couples' Wounds," *Jewish Bulletin of Northern California*, June 4, 1999.
32. "Outreach Has Helped Heal."
33. Shaye J. D. Cohen, *From Maccabees to the Mishnah* (John Knox Press, 1987).
34. Alexander M. Schindler, "Facing the Realities of Intermarriage," *Judaism*, Winter 1985, 85–88. Schindler's statement was one of twenty-four contributions to a forum on the subject of patrilineal descent, convened by *Judaism*. The participants included Orthodox, Conservative, Reconstructionist, Reform, and secular writers.
35. Robert Gordis, "To Move Forward, Take One Step Back: A Plea to the Reform Movement," *Moment*, May 1986, 58–61.
36. Irving Greenberg, "Should a Child of a Jewish Father Be Presumed to Be

Jewish By Birth?," National Jewish Resource Center Memorandum, June 13, 1983, MSS 72, A-4-2, AJA. Unmitigatedly condemnatory was the full-page advertisement in *The New York Times* of June 21, 1983, inserted by the United Orthodox Rabbinate, which called a patrilineal Jew a fake (*ersatz*) Jew and claimed that the CCAR resolution would serve only to advance assimilation.

37. Simcha Abeles Friedman to Alexander Schindler, May 8, 1991, MSS 630, 12/4, AJA, cited in Lynne Goldsmith, "Bridge to the Future: Alexander Schindler and His Influence on the Development of Reform Judaism's Outreach Program," (HUC-JIR rabbinical thesis, Cincinnati, 2007), 119.
38. Cited in Jonathan S. Tobin, "Reform Rabbi Alexander Schindler Leads His Movement into the Future Amid Controversy," *Stamford Jewish Ledger*, December 3, 1993, 16; Schindler to Gabriel Cohen, Publisher of *The Jewish Post and Opinion*, July 17, 1989, MSS 630, 12/4, AJA.
39. Cited in Jaffe-Gill, "Patrilineality," 97.
40. See the correspondence over whether there was any basis for right-wing Orthodox rabbis accepting patrilineal descent in the uncatalogued Alfred Gottschalk Papers and the Moses Weiler papers, MSS 215, AJA.
41. An undated copy of the resolution by the United Synagogue is appended to Alexander M. Schindler to Alan J. Tichnor, President, United Synagogue of America, December 6, 1991, MSS 630, 12/4, AJA.
42. "Schindler Rejects Proposal," *American Israelite*, December 26, 1991, 9.
43. Schindler to Alan J. Tichnor, President, United Synagogue of America, in New York, December 6, 1991, MSS 630, 12/4, AJA; "Schindler Rejects Proposal," 9.
44. After Schindler's death, patrilineal descent received endorsement from a prominent leftwing Israeli politician, Yossi Belin, writing in *Haaretz*, December 3, 2006 (cited in Goldsmith, "Bridge to the Future," 136).
45. "Presidential Keynote Address by Alexander M. Schindler," November 4, 1989, 7, available in Klau Library, HUC-JIR, Cincinnati, OH. Of course, Schindler must have realized there were other traditional texts that expressed wariness with regard to converts. But, of course, he did not cite those texts.
46. Cited in Michael A. Meyer, *Rabbi Leo Baeck: Living a Religious Imperative in Troubled Times* (Philadelphia: University of Pennsylvania Press, 2021), 199, 244 note 125. After the Holocaust, Baeck went so far as to ask rhetorically, "Should we not send out missionaries to Asia, to East Africa and to other places to the people there waiting for us?" Cited in Albert Friedlander et al., *Leo Baeck Werke* (Gütersloh: Gütersloher Verlagshaus, 2003), 6: 528. Schindler never spoke or wrote anything that radical.
47. *CCAR Yearbook* 64 (1954): 115–18. Schindler's most complete documentation for his advocacy of Jewish proselytism is his "Introduction" to Walter Homolka et al., eds., *Not by Birth Alone: Conversion to Judaism* (London and

Washington: Cassell, 1997), 1–8.
48. Robert Gordis, *Judaism for the Modern Age* (New York: Farrar, Straus, and Cudahy, 1955), 345; cf. also his "Has the Time Arrived for Jewish Missionaries? The Pros and the Cons," *National Jewish Monthly*, March 1958, 6–7, 24.
49. "UAHC Approval Requested for Proselytizing," *American Israelite*, November 18, 1965, 1, 4. Eisendrath's proposal came in the wake of the "The Vanishing American Jew" article in *Look* magazine. His suggestion may have originated with Schindler, who was in charge of Jewish education for the Union at that time.
50. Dean Kelley, *Why Churches Are Growing* (1972), cited in Dean R. Hoge, "A Test of Theories of Denominational Growth and Decline," in *Understanding Church Growth and Decline: 1950–1978*, ed. Hoge and David A. Roozen (New York: Pilgrim Press, 1979), 179–80.
51. "Conversion of the Jews Rejected by the Church," *News Briefs of the New York Federation of Reform Synagogues*, May 1977, MSS 776, 25/4, AJA.
52. "Conversion of the Jews Rejected."
53. David P. Kasakove, "UAHC Video Exposes Missionizing Threat," *Reform Judaism*, Winter 1988–89, 23; Schindler to Richard England in Landover, MD, August 23, 1989, MSS 630, 3/11, AJA.
54. Peter L. Berger, "Converting the Gentiles?," *Commentary* 67, no. 5 (May 1979): 35–39.
55. Berger, "Converting the Gentiles?"
56. However, Stendahl privately suggested that Schindler's speech had presented a stereotyped and distorted view of Christianity, somewhat akin to prejudiced Christian understandings of Judaism. Marc Saperstein (then assistant professor of Jewish studies at the Harvard Divinity School) to Rabbi Alexander Schindler, April 6, 1982, MSS 630, 11/6, AJA.
57. Kenneth A. Briggs, "Jews Say Christians Back Proselytizing: Church Leaders Reportedly Favor New Effort in Reform Judaism, Despite Some Misgivings," *New York Times*, May 20, 1979, 25–26.
58. Aron Hirt-Manheimer, compiler, "Why Jews Should Seek Converts," *Reform Judaism*, Spring 1994, 11ff.
59. "Schindler Mission to 'Unchurched' Draws Fire from Opposing Groups," *Jewish Week-American Examiner*, December 10, 1978, 3.
60. "Schindler Mission to 'Unchurched.'"
61. "Comment by Wolfe Kelman," *Moment*, March 1979, 25.
62. Harold M. Schulweis to Alexander Schindler, January 15, 1980, MSS 630, 10/1, AJA.
63. Kenneth A. Briggs, "Rabbis Meeting Focuses on Proselytizing," *New York Times*, March 30, 1979, 17.
64. David Polish, "Jewish Proselyting—Another Opinion," *Journal of Reform Judaism* (Summer 1979): 1–9. See also Robert P. Jacobs, "Rabbi Schindler's

Call to Convert: Are We Ready?," *Journal of Reform Judaism*, Spring 1980, 31–39.
65. Trude Weiss-Rosmarin, "Conviction and Conversion," *Jewish Spectator*, Spring 1979, 6–8.
66. "Comment by Harold Schulweis," *Moment*, March 1979, 27.
67. Milton Himmelfarb, "A Time for Jewish Activism," *Congress Monthly*, November 1979, 12–14.
68. Irving Greenberg, "Hopefully, We Will Soon All Become Jews by Choice," *Jewish Exponent*, October 15, 1982, 21, 28.
69. The interview originally appeared in *Ha-Do'ar*, August 1985. Excerpts are contained in "Conciliatory Views of the Rav on the Problem of Intermarriage," *National Jewish Post and Opinion* 55, no. 15 (January 4, 1989): 1.
70. Alexander Schindler to "Dear Friend," December 7, 1993, MSS Proselytism '93, AJA.
71. "Conciliatory Views of the Rav on the Problem of Intermarriage," 1.
72. Haim Shapiro, "Reform Leader: Most of Us Don't Support Proselytizing," *Jerusalem Post*, October 28, 1993; Schindler to Rabbi Richard Hirsch in Jerusalem, November 9, 1993, MSS Proselytism '93, AJA. However, actually bringing in the pledged money was not a success.
73. Sue Fishkoff, "US Orthodox, Conservatives Rap Reform Proselytization Plan," *Jerusalem Post*, October 27, 1993.
74. Jack Wertheimer, "Should Judaism Become a Missionary Religion?," *New Haven Jewish Ledger*, November 12, 1993, 17.
75. "Should Judaism Become a Missionary Religion?," 17.
76. Dru Greenwood to Alexander Schindler, April 21, 1993, MSS 72, D-11, AJA.
77. Richard G. Hirsch to Alexander Schindler, November 11, 1993, MSS 16, E3/13, AJA.
78. Alexander Schindler to Richard Hirsch, November 9, 1993, MSS Proselytism '93, AJA.
79. Raquel H. Newman to Alexander Schindler, November 15, 1993, MSS 630, 15/2, AJA.
80. Alexander Schindler to Raquel H. Newman, November 23, 1993, MSS 630, 15/2, AJA.
81. Schindler to Newman.
82. Schindler to Newman.
83. Daniel Schiff to Alexander Schindler, November 29, 1993, MSS 630, 11/3, AJA.
84. Alexander Schindler to Daniel Schiff in Pittsburgh, December 8, 1993, MSS 630, 11/3, AJA.
85. Schindler to Schiff.
86. Schindler to Schiff.
87. Schindler to Schiff.

88. Belin authored two short volumes favoring the cause: *Why Choose Judaism: New Dimensions of Jewish Outreach* (New York: UAHC, 1985) and *What Judaism Offers for You: A Reform Perspective* (New York: UAHC, 1993). He thought that Schindler gave too much attention to social action issues and too little to outreach and Jewish spirituality. As a political conservative, he objected to the Union's opposition to Clarence Thomas's elevation to the United States Supreme Court. David W. Belin to Allan B. Goldman in Los Angeles, September 30, 1991, MSS 630, 10/6, AJA.
89. "A Summary of the Report of the Joint UAHC/CCAR Task Force on Reform Jewish Outreach," August 1981, 11, ScBox, A883, Klau Library, HUC-JIR, Cincinnati.
90. "A Summary of the Report."
91. "A Summary of the Report."
92. Schindler to Rabbi Stephen Listfield in Washington, D.C., May 17, 1982, MSS 630, 11/1, AJA.
93. Schindler to Rabbi Steven L. Jacobs in Mobile, Alabama, MSS 630, 12/1, AJA.
94. Schindler to Listfield, 1982.
95. Sanford Seltzer, "Who Enrolls in the Introduction to Judaism Program? A Report from Four American Cities, An Horizon Institute Report," October 1984, SCBox A-84, 878, Klau Library, HUC-JIR, Cincinnati.
96. Schindler to Sarah Grossman in Cincinnati, Ohio, March 14, 1984, MSS 630, 11/2, AJA.
97. Lydia Kukoff, *Choosing Judaism* (New York: UAHC, 1981).
98. According to Kukoff, she had spoken to Schindler before he gave his 1978 address, urging him to deliver it. She took over the job of making Schindler's proposals happen via an extensive structure and through the program that she put together and ran. At one point, she was able to persuade the philanthropist Charles Schusterman to give her the first million dollars for outreach. She left the Union in 1993, when she was not given broader responsibilities. Interview with Lydia Kukoff, May 5, 2023.
99. "Report of Rabbi Alexander M. Schindler to the Board of Trustees," December 5, 1986, 3, 6.
100. "Report of Rabbi Alexander M. Schindler to the Board of Trustees," December 5, 1986, 3, 6. Lydia Kukoff put it even more strongly. Despite her devotion to outreach, she did not want Reform Judaism to become known as "the Movement of Outreach." Lydia Kukoff, "Outreach: The First Decade," *Reform Judaism*, Winter 1988–89, 22.
101. Alexander Schindler, "Outreach Address, CCAR Philadelphia, March 27, 1996," MSS 630, 26/3, 4, AJA.
102. E.g., Schindler to William M. Daniel in Santa Barbara, California, October 18, 1995, MSS 630, 10/3, AJA; "Dear Reader," *Reform Judaism*, Spring 1996, 4.

Chapter 6: Issues and Actions

1. "Union of American Hebrew Congregations News," June 1975, MSS 72, D-6, AJA.
2. Alexander M. Schindler, "Remarks by the President of the Union of American Hebrew Congregations," *CCAR Yearbook* 92 (1982): 62–63. After Reform rabbi Dow Marmur was quoted in *The Canadian Jewish News* as claiming that Jews were seeking Orthodoxy rather than Reform in response to growing disillusionment with liberalism, Schindler responded by insisting that from his United States perspective, and according to independent studies, there was, on the contrary, "a virtual crumbling of Orthodoxy from its once high state" while Reform "has grown dramatically" (Schindler to Rabbi Dow Marmur in Toronto, May 30, 1985, Personal and Confidential, MSS 72, A4-1, AJA). Late in Schindler's term, the Union's Task Force on the Unaffiliated instituted a UAHC Privilege Card for unaffiliated Jews in their twenties, providing the holders with time-limited free or significantly reduced congregational memberships; see Schindler to Robert Geskin in Los Angeles, February 11, 1992, MSS 630, 15/2, AJA.
3. "Report of the President to Board of Trustees," May 30–June 1, 1975.
4. Schindler argued that it was passion born of denominational loyalty, whether to Orthodox, Conservative, or Reform Judaism, that alone had "the capacity of making Judaism come to life in the hearts of our children." "Speech to Union Board of Trustees," May 15–17, 1992 (privately published).
5. Rabbi Lennard Thal [director of the Union's Pacific Southwest Council] to Schindler, July 25, 1994, and Schindler's reply, August 2, 1994, MSS-72, A4-1, AJA.
6. Alexander Schindler, "Presidential Address to the Mid-Atlantic Council Biennial," Williamsburg, Virginia, November 24, 1994, MSS 630, 26/1, AJA.
7. For the organizational history of the Union, written by a former member of the Board of Trustees, see Russell Silverman, "The Union for Reform Judaism, 1873–2009: A History According to the Minutes of the Organization," 2011 (unpublished), available from the author.
8. When Schindler rebuked Saperstein for sending out letters in his boss's name that he had himself written in Washington, Saperstein replied with a frank statement of loyalty: "For fourteen years I have worked for you. I have tried mightily to involve you in positive situations, to nourish your image and visibility, and to protect you with good advice." Saperstein to Schindler, March 31, 1988, David Saperstein Papers, Correspondence, AJA.
9. "The Report of the Independent Investigation," Union of Reform Judaism, https://urj.org/sites/default/files/2022-02/URJ_Investigation_Report.pdf, 15–16.
10. Jonathan [sic] to Rabbi Schindler, February 9, 1993, MSS 630, 12/6, AJA.

11. Schindler to Jonathan Pollard in Marion, IL, April 20, 1992; Pollard to Schindler, May 2, 1992; Eric H. Yoffie to Arthur Susswein in Great Neck, NY, November 25, 1992; Pollard to Schindler, February 9, 1993; Schindler to Herbert M. Levetown in Englewood, NJ, April 23, 1993; Schindler to The President, September 28, 1993; Schindler Memo to Seymour Reich in New York, September 28, 1993; Schindler to President William J. Clinton, August 19, 1994; Clinton to Schindler, September 13, 1994. All of the above at MSS 630, 12/6 AJA.
12. "Aide Is Appointed to Rabbi Schindler," *American Israelite*, July 1, 1976, 11.
13. For example, see his memo to Saperstein, Yoffie, and Vorspan, August 23, 1995, Saperstein Papers, Correspondence, AJA.
14. That is, Maurice N. Eisendrath's.
15. Alexander to David, no date, David Saperstein Papers, Correspondence, AJA.
16. Bush's reply to author's questions, December 11, 2022.
17. Bush's reply to author's questions. In 2007, he published *Waiting for God: The Spiritual Explorations of a Reluctant Atheist* (Teaneck, NJ: Ben Yehuda Press, 2007).
18. "Kol-Ischa [sic]," lecture delivered at Leo Baeck Temple in Los Angeles, June 8, 1993, 3, MSS 630, 25/5, AJA.
19. Remarks by Rabbi Alexander M. Schindler, "Freedom of Choice in Abortion," Religious Coalition for Abortion Rights, Washington, DC, January 22, 1981, MSS 630, 13/5, AJA.
20. "Statement of Rabbi Alexander M. Schindler, President Union of American Hebrew Congregations to the United States Senate Judiciary Subcommittee on the Separation of Powers," May 15, 1981, MSS 630, 13/5, AJA.
21. For thoroughly documented histories of the history of this issue in the American Reform Movement, see Margaret Moers Wenig, "Truly Welcoming Lesbian and Gay Jews," in *The Jewish Condition: Essays in Contemporary Judaism Honoring Rabbi Alexander M. Schindler*, ed. Aron Hirt-Manheimer (New York: UAHC Press, 1995), 327–48; and Dana Evan Kaplan, *American Reform Judaism: An Introduction* (New Brunswick, NJ: Rutgers University Press, 2003), 209–32.
22. Schindler to Rabbi Robert Blinder in St. Louis, MO, February 8, 1973, MSS 72, A4-2, AJA.
23. Schindler to twenty-three rabbis, confidential, February 9, 1973, MSS 72, A4-2, AJA.
24. Eugene B. Borowitz, "Response to a Letter from Alexander Schindler," MSS 630, 4/8, AJA. The accompanying letter to Schindler is dated May 9, 1973.
25. Solomon Freehof reply to Schindler confidential letter, undated, MSS 72, A-42, AJA.
26. Schindler to Dr. Solomon B. Freehof in Pittsburgh, PA, May 25, 1973, MS 72, A4-2, AJA.

27. Schindler to Zifre Lurie in Brookline, MA, April 1, 1975. Schindler had by then abandoned the word "homosexual" and begun to use "gay" instead.
28. David W. Belin to Charles W. Rothschild, Jr. [chairman of the Union Board] in Teaneck, NJ, MSS 630, 4/8, AJA. Copies of the letter were sent to two other board members, but not to Schindler.
29. Jakob J. Petuchowski, "The Impact of Beth Geneva Chadasha," *CCAR Journal*, Summer 1985, 125–27, where "Geneva" refers not to the city but to the Hebrew word for theft.
30. Schindler, "Communication," *CCAR Journal*, Winter 1986, 92–93. Lawrence Bush, in his letter to the author, claimed that he had weaned Schindler from thinking that gays "can't help themselves, they are who they are. Judaism bids us to be compassionate." He advised Schindler to avoid pity or condescension and substitute respect and love.
31. "Address by Rabbi Alexander M. Schindler at Jewish Community Service in Support of People with AIDS," Los Angeles, CA, March 12, 1989, Nearprint File, AJA.
32. "Address ... at Jewish Community Service."
33. "Address ... at Jewish Community Service."
34. "Address ... at Jewish Community Service."
35. Schindler to "Dear Colleague," November 26, 1986, MSS 72, A4-2, AJA. Rhea Schindler, who seldom wrote for publication, published an article titled "AIDS Outreach" in *Reform Judaism*, Summer 1989, 17, in which she praised joint participation by sisterhood members of New York's Central Synagogue with a local Catholic project to serve weekly dinners and provide family counseling to local AIDS patients.
36. Rabbi Alexander M. Schindler, "Centennial Sermon," Cincinnati, Ohio, June 23, 1989, 7, available at the Klau Library, HUC-JIR, Cincinnati.
37. Schindler to Howard Metzger in Washington, DC, September 30, 1992; Gustav Niebuhr, "Push on Gay Ban Roils Religious Community: Clinton Move Seen as a 'Godsend' for Foes," *Washington Post*, January 29, 1993. When the Jewish National Fund chose to honor Peter McPherson, the president of Michigan State University, who opposed domestic partner benefits for gay and lesbian faculty and staff, Schindler sought to prevent it from happening, but to no avail. Lev Raphael and Gershen [*sic*] Kaufman to Schindler, December 9, 1995; Schindler to Edward Rosenthal of the Jewish National Fund in Southfield, MI, December 20, 1995, MSS 630, 6/8, AJA.
38. Solomon H. Friend to Alexander M. Schindler, September 14, 1990, MSS 630, 4/8, AJA.
39. Schindler to Rabbi Samuel Silver in Delray, FL, August 1, 1990, MSS 630, 4/8, AJA.
40. Rabbi Alexander M. Schindler, "Reaching Out to Gay and Lesbian Jews," Elul, 1992, MSS 630, 4/9, AJA.

41. "Report of the President of the Union of American Hebrew Congregations to the Board of Trustees," November 21, 1980, MSS 630, 7/4, AJA.
42. David W. Belin in Des Moines, IA, to Melvin Merians in New York, November 15, 1993, MSS 630, 3/10, AJA.
43. Belin to Merians, 1993.
44. David W. Belin in Des Moines, IA, to Melvin Merians in New York, November 15, 1993, MSS 630, 3/10, AJA.
45. "Social Justice and Judaism," sermon by Alexander M. Schindler at Washington Hebrew Congregation, June 10, 1994, MSS 630, 26/1, AJA.
46. Schindler to The President, March 21, 1977, Carter Library, File: Schindler. If there was a Carter reply, it is not extant.
47. Annette Lawrence to Rabbi Alexander Schindler, March 16, 1994, MSS 630, 4/6, AJA.
48. For an early example of concern regarding Jewish withdrawal from the "Negro revolution," see Albert Vorspan, "The Negro Victory and the Jewish Failure," *American Judaism*, Fall 1963, 7, 50–54. For a historical examination of the problems inherent in the Black-Jewish alliance, see Carol Lynn Greenberg, *Troubling the Waters: Black-Jewish Relations in the American Century* (Princeton: Princeton University Press, 2006). The author, on page 94, cites Schindler on how the split between Blacks and Jews could only serve to delight their common enemies.
49. For background, see among other works, Jonathan Kaufman, *Broken Alliance: The Turbulent Times Between Blacks and Jews in America* (New York: Scribner's, 1988).
50. Alexander M. Schindler, "The Andrew Young Affair," *NATA Journal*, Winter 1980, 11.
51. David Frum, *How We Got Here: The 70's* (New York: Basic Books, 2000), 272–73.
52. Rabbi Ira S. Youdovin, "The Young Controversy and the PLO," August 21, 1979, MSS 99, 13/5, AJA.
53. "Statement By Rabbi Alexander M. Schindler, President, Union of American Hebrew Congregations," August 16, 1979, MSS 630, 2/9, AJA.
54. "Statement By Rabbi Alexander M. Schindler," 1979. See also the anonymous and undated "Ten Questions and Comments about the Andy Young Affair and the Black-Jewish Fallout," MSS 630, 2/9, AJA.
55. Schindler, "The Andrew Young Affair," 12.
56. Schindler to Jerome A. Cooper in Birmingham, AL, September 13, 1979, MSS 630, 2/9, AJA.
57. Schindler to Rev. Jesse L. Jackson in Chicago, IL, August 24, 1979, MSS 630, 2/9, AJA.
58. Schindler to Bertram W. Korn, Jr., January 22, 1980, MSS 530, 2/9, AJA.
59. "Introduction of the Rev. Jesse Jackson to the Conference on Racism,

Antisemitism, Xenophobia, and Other Forms of Intolerance," Brussels, Belgium, July 7, 1992, in *New Perspectives in American Jewish History: A Documentary Tribute to Jonathan D. Sarna*, ed. Mark A. Raider and Gary Phillip Zola (Waltham, MA: Brandeis University Press, 2021), 380–84.

60. "Rabbi Alexander M. Schindler's Introduction of Jesse Jackson," UAHC Board Meeting, Palm Beach, Florida, December 12, 1992," MSS 630, 25/4, AJA.
61. Schindler to Morton P. Meisner in Massapequa, NY, July 21, 1983, MSS 630, 3/3, AJA.
62. Schindler to Meisner, 1983, MSS 630, 3/3, AJA. By the beginning of August, if not earlier, Schindler's name was listed on the stationery of the Twentieth Anniversary Mobilization for Jobs, Peace and Freedom among the conveners of the march, along with Jesse Jackson and Senator James Abourezk of the American-Arab Anti-Discrimination Committee. The only other recognizable Jew among the conveners was the feminist Bella Abzug. MSS 630, 3/3, AJA.
63. "Statement by Rabbi Alexander M. Schindler," August 12, 1983, MSS 630, 3/3, AJA.
64. Schindler to Sidney J. Brown in Greenbelt, MD, August 22, 1983, MSS 630, 3/3, AJA.
65. Schindler to Bernice S. Tannenbaum, Chairman World Zionist Organization, American Section, August 23, 1983, MSS 630, 3/3, AJA.
66. Schindler to Meir Rosenne, Embassy of Israel in Washington, DC, August 30, 1983, MSS 630, 3/3, AJA.
67. Union of American Hebrew Congregations, "News Release," August 12, 1983, "Why We're Marching," August 18, 1983; Mary Lynn Kotz in Washington, DC to Rabbi Alexander Schindler, September 1, 1983, MSS 630, 3/3, AJA.
68. Closing Prayer, 20th Anniversary March on Washington, August 27, 1983, MSS 630, 3/3. AJA. Coretta King and members of her family had attended the preceding Friday evening Sabbath service at Sinai Temple in Washington. Schindler to Herman Bistrin in Eureka, CA, August 29, 1983, MSS 630, 3/3, AJA.
69. George E. Curry, "Apartheid Protest Revives Bond between Jews, Blacks," *Chicago Tribune*, December 16, 1984.
70. [Resolution on] South Africa, Adopted by the General Assembly of the Union of American Hebrew Congregations, October 31 to November 5, 1985, MSS 630, 2/6, AJA.
71. Schindler to President F. W. De Klerk in Cape Town, South Africa, June 5, 1990, MSS 630, 2/6, AJA.
72. Albert Vorspan to Nelson Mandela in Soweta, Johannesburg, South Africa, March 1, 1990, MSS 630, 2/6, AJA.

73. Vorspan to Mandela, 1990.
74. "SBC President Who Said God Hears Only Christian Prayers Dead at 79," *Baptist Global News*, January 15, 2019, https://baptistnews.com/article/sbc-president-who-said-god-hears-only-christian-prayers-dead-at-79/.
75. Helen Parmley, "'Chosen People' Hit by Rev. Smith Again," *Dallas Morning News*, November 14, 1980.
76. "Head of Reform Judaism Sees a Link between Rise of Radical Right and Anti-Semitic Acts," UAHC News Release, November 22, 1980, MSS 630, 7/4, AJA.
77. "Head of Reform Judaism," 1980.
78. Schindler did realize, however, that the Christian Right's support of Israel was based on Christian theological expectations.
79. Alexander M. Schindler, "Anti-Semitism Reborn," *Reform Judaism*, February 1981, 1, 15.
80. "Rabbi Schindler's Charges Refuted by Falwell," *American Israelite*, December 11, 1980, 14.
81. "Rabbi Schindler's Charges Refuted by Falwell."
82. "Rabbi Schindler's Charges Refuted by Falwell"
83. Joshua O. Haberman to Rabbi Alexander Schindler, April 10, 1981, MSS 915, 26/2. Five years later, Haberman continued to criticize UAHC publications for claiming that Jews like himself, who favored a cooperative dialogue with Evangelicals, were willing to "crawl into bed" with unacceptable partners just for the sake of getting their support for Israel. Haberman to Schindler, March 26, 1986, MSS 915, 88/10, AJA.
84. Schindler to Yehiel Kadishai in Jerusalem, January 26, 1981, MSS 630, 7/4, AJA.
85. Schindler to Donald S. Day, February 26, 1981, MSS 630, 7/4, AJA.
86. Jerry Falwell to "Dear Rabbi," February 26, 1985. It is not clear whether this letter was written to multiple rabbis, to Schindler, or to Rabbi Haberman. It is to be found in the Haberman papers, MSS 915, 26/2, AJA.
87. William F. Buckley, Jr., "Have We Survived Falwell?," *New York Daily News*, February 21, 1985; Schindler to William F. Buckley, Jr., at the *National Review* in New York, March 13, 1985, MSS 630, 7/4, AJA.
88. Rabbi Alexander M. Schindler, "Consultation on Conscience," Washington Hebrew Congregation, Washington, D.C., April 14, 1985, MSS 630, 7/4, AJA.
89. Schindler, "Consultation on Conscience."
90. Schindler, "Consultation on Conscience."
91. Schindler, "Consultation on Conscience."
92. Alexander M. Schindler, "The Separation of Church and State," in Milton S. Eisenhower Symposium on Religion and Politics, Johns Hopkins University, October 1986, MSS 630, 24/6. AJA.

93. Schindler, "The Separation of Church and State," 1986.
94. Schindler, "The Separation of Church and State," 1986.
95. Schindler, "The Separation of Church and State," 1986.
96. Schindler, "The Separation of Church and State," 1986.
97. Rabbi Alexander M. Schindler to Board of Trustees, UAHC, "Report on Rome Mission," September 8, 1987, MSS 16 G-11, Folder 39, AJA.
98. Schindler to Lucy Dawidowicz in New York, December 5, 1977, MSS 630, 7/1, AJA.
99. Alexander M. Schindler, Memorandum to Members, Commission on the Holocaust Re: *Pinkasei HaK'hilot*, February 2, 1977, MSS 630, 7/1, AJA.
100. Julius Berman, Memorandum, March 25, 1996, MSS 630, 6/12, AJA. In 1986 Schindler also agreed to be on the Executive Committee, and then the secretary, of the Joint Distribution Committee, promising at the start to "do what I can" for the organization. Schindler to Theodore Comet, Associate Executive Vice President, Joint Distribution Committee, Inc., in New York, October 8, 1991, MSS 630, 1/4, AJA. Schindler's position inside the JDC enabled him to argue for allocations directed to the Israel Movement for Progressive Judaism. See Schindler to Barbara Epstein in Jerusalem, August 7, 1990, MSS 630, 6/4, AJA. As early as 1974, he had also agreed to be a co-chairperson of the U.S. Interreligious Committee on Peace of the United Methodist Church. Schindler to Herman Will in Washington, D.C., November 12, 1974, MSS 630, 16/4, AJA. By 1986 he was, as well, a vice president of the World Jewish Congress. Toward the end of his career he was also a member of the board of the Conference on Jewish Material Claims Against Germany. The multiple offices that he held attest to Schindler's unflagging willingness to take on new responsibilities.
101. Alexander M. Schindler, "Ensuring Jewish Continuity," May 1995, MSS 630, 6/12, AJA; "Group to Inventory Judaica in Eastern Europe," *Jewish Bulletin of Northern California*, October 17, 1997.
102. Schindler to Jerry Hochbaum, Memorial Foundation for Jewish Culture in New York, September 9, 1994, MSS 630, 6/12, AJA.
103. Schindler, "Ensuring Jewish Continuity" and "Group to Inventory Judaica in Eastern Europe." By contrast, there is no evidence that Schindler was concerned with establishing continuity for the postwar Jewish community in Germany with its German Jewish cultural heritage. This may have been, at least in part, on account of Schindler's contempt for its leading figure, Heinz Galinski, whom Schindler had met and whom he considered "a ruthless and tyrannical person" who deprecated Eastern European Jews and anyone who was poor. Schindler to Gerard Daniel in Rye, NY, September 30, 1980, MSS 630, 17/7, AJA.
104. Schindler to Richard Cohen, Albert Vorspan, and Betty Golomb, July 25, 1979, MSS 630, 14/2, AJA.

105. He was also able to meet more briefly with Anatoly Dobrynin, a member of the Party Secretariat, who had recently returned to the Soviet Union after serving as its ambassador to the United States. Schindler to Jeffrey Glassman at the American Embassy in Moscow, June 9, 1987, MSS 630, 14/3, AJA.
106. Schindler to Dr. Bernard Lown, June 9, 1987; Lown to Schindler, June 18, 1987, MSS 630, 9/10, AJA. The seedlings were later nurtured by Rabbi Richard Hirsch and his Russian-born wife, Bella.
107. Alexander Schindler, "Address to UAHC General Assembly," December 4, 1981, MSS 630, 24/4, AJA.
108. Elliott Abrams to Rabbi Alexander M. Schindler, December 22, 1981, Uncatalogued Alfred Gottschalk Papers, AJA. If Schindler replied to Abrams, the letter seems not to be extant.
109. Rabbi Alexander M. Schindler, *East-West Relations: A Jewish Perspective*, World Jewish Congress, Vienna, Austria (privately published, January, 1985), 8.
110. "Presidential Keynote Address by Rabbi Alexander M. Schindler," November 4, 1989, available in Klau Library, HUC-JIR, Cincinnati, OH.
111. Shlomo Ben-Israel to Rabbi Alexander Schindler, January 2, 1976, MSS 630, 17/5, AJA. Ben-Israel promised to limit demands on Schindler's time. Apparently, it was more the name of the man who was about to become chair of the Presidents' Conference that was sought, rather than the time he would devote the cause.
112. Samuel Silver, "Rabbi Schindler Can Be Trusted," *Jewish Post and Opinion*, July 20, 1979.
113. "Rabbi Schindler Helps Win Release of Polish Prisoner," *Reform Judaism*, March 1982, 5.
114. Menachem Begin to Armand Hammer, August 23, 1982, MSS 72, D-41, AJA.
115. Schindler to Mrs. G. Seifer in Long Beach, CA, January 24, 1983, MSS 72, D-41, AJA.
116. Neil Barsky, "Despite 'Agonizing' Experience, Schindler Satisfied," *Intermountain Jewish News*, May 27, 1983; Alexander M. Schindler, "Why We Went to Warsaw," *Jewish Week*, May 27, 1983.
117. Barsky, "Despite 'Agonizing' Experience, Schindler Satisfied," 1983; See also, Alexander M. Schindler, "Why We Went to Warsaw," *Jewish Week*, May 27, 1983.
118. "Statement By Rabbi Alexander Schindler . . . Before the Senate Committee on Finance," September 8, 1976, MSS 630, 22/11, AJA.
119. "Summary of a Conversation Between the Prime Minister and Rabbi Alexander Schindler in the Office of the Prime Minister in Jerusalem" (secret), Diary of the Prime Minister, November 21, 1976 [Hebrew], Israel State Archives. See also Schindler to Zalman Abramov in Toronto, Ontario, September 7, 1976, MSS 630, 22/11, AJA.

120. "Statement by Rabbi Alexander M. Schindler . . . on President Reagan's Decision to Visit a German War Cemetery," April 12, 1985; "Statement by Rabbi Alexander M. Schindler . . . On President Reagan's Decision to Include a Visit to a Nazi Concentration Camp During His Trip to Germany," April 17, 1985; "Comment by Rabbi Alexander M. Schindler . . . On President Reagan's Statement of April 18 on Visiting Bitburg Cemetery"; all at MSS 630, 2/8, AJA.
121. Konrad Adenauer, the first chancellor of the Federal Republic of Germany, negotiated a reparations agreement for Jewish victims of the Holocaust.
122. Schindler to Thomas C. Gordon in McCloud, CA, May 24, 1985, MSS 630, 2/8, AJA.
123. Schindler to the President, February 11, 1983; and News Release: "Reform Jewish Leader Calls for Inquiry into U.S. Government Links with Nazis," Daniel Patrick Moynihan to Schindler, July 13, 1983; both at MSS 630, 9/6, AJA.
124. "Rosh Hashanah Sermon 5750," Union Temple, Brooklyn, Fall 1990, MSS 630, 26/4, AJA. See also "Lecture at the College of the Holy Cross," Worcester, MA, April 7, 1992, in Hirt-Manheimer, ed., *The Jewish Condition*, 166–67.
125. Elliot L. Richardson to Rabbi Alexander Schindler, May 9, 1988; and Schindler to Richardson, May 11, 1988; both in MSS 630, 16/7, AJA. Schindler was first elected to the position in 1978.
126. Kurt Waldheim to Rabbi Schindler, December 1, 1977, Schindler File, Carter Library, Atlanta, GA.
127. Schindler to the Honorable Edwin Meese in Washington, April 4, 1986, MSS 630, 17/1, AJA.
128. Jimmy Carter to Rabbi Alexander Schindler, June 12, 1979, Carter Library, File: Schindler.
129. "A World in Transition—Reform Judaism in Action," Presidential Address, 59th General Assembly, Union of American Hebrew Congregations, October 29–November 3, 1987, 7, available in the Klau Library, HUC-JIR, Cincinnati, OH.
130. "A World in Transition," 7.
131. "Address by Rabbi Alexander M. Schindler at the Center for Defense Information Forum on National Security and Defense," February 10, 1982, MS 630, 24/4, AJA. Printed in the *NATA Journal*, October 1983, 5.
132. The resolutions can be accessed at https://urj.org/what-we-believe/resolutions/control-nuclear-arms and https://urj.org/what-we-believe/resolutions/preventing-nuclear-holocaust.
133. Nuclear Freeze Foundation, "Joint Statement by Religious Leaders on Senate Vote on the Kennedy-Hatfield Amendment," October 31, 1983. Senator Kennedy responded in a personal letter to Schindler expressing appreciation for the statement, November 1, 1983, MSS 630, 9/10, AJA.

134. Rabbi Alexander Schindler, "The Nuclear Debate: Some Jewish Perspectives," IPPNW World Congress, Moscow, May 1987, Schindler Nearprint, AJA.
135. Arthur Waskow to Rabbi Alexander Schindler, November 18, 1988, MSS 630, 14/1, AJA.
136. Alexander Schindler, "The Shalom Center Brit HaDorot Peace Award," New York, NY, May 31, 1989, MSS 630, 25/1, AJA.
137. Rochelle Saidel Wolk, "Reform Rabbi Says Carter Exploits Jews for Political Reasons," *Intermountain Jewish News*, November 23, 1979, 7.
138. *Al Ha-Mishmar*, February 26, 1980; *Haaretz*, February 26, 1980.
139. "World: New Signs of Flexibility," *Time*, April 14, 1980.
140. "Key U.S. Jews Revolt Against Begin Policies, *San Francisco Jewish Bulletin*, July 4, 1980.
141. "Melbourne and Sydney Reject Zionist Federation Speaker," *Australian Jewish Times*, October 30, 1980, 5.
142. "Report to Board of Trustees," December 3, 1982, SC Box A-98/140, Klau Library, HUC-JIR, Cincinnati.
143. Schindler to Bernard Lown in Boston, December 23, 1982, MSS 72, D-6, AJA.
144. Schindler to Leo Nevas in Westport, CT, October 31, 1984, MSS 630, 16/1, AJA.
145. Schindler, cable to His Excellency Chaim Herzog, January 23, 1988, Chaim Herzog to Rabbi Alexander M. Schindler, January 25, 1988, MSS 72, D-40, AJA.
146. Schindler to Herzog, February 8, 1988, MSS 72, D-40, AJA.
147. *New York Times*, February 21, 1988.
148. Ruben Schindler to Alexander Schindler, January 31, 1988, MSS 72, D-23, AJA.
149. Alexander M. Schindler to Ruben Schindler in Ramat-Gan, Israel, February 23, 1988.
150. Alexander M. Schindler, "Reflections on the Life of Menachem Begin," Presidents' Conference Hazkarah [sic], March 11, 1992, MSS 630 23/9, AJA.
151. Schindler, "Reflections on the Life of Menachem Begin."
152. In 1981 Schindler interviewed Begin during one of his trips to the United States. When Schindler asked him about his view of "God and Torah," Begin replied simply that he believed in divine providence because Hitler had not succeeded in fully destroying the Jewish people.
153. It should be noted also that within the Labor Party Schindler felt closer to the Belarus-born Shimon Peres than to the Palestine-born Yitzhak Rabin.
154. Alexander Schindler, "Address to the 59th General Assembly of the Union of American Hebrew Congregations," October 29–November 3, 1987, 9.
155. Schindler, "Address to the 59th General Assembly."

156. Alexander Schindler, "Chamberlain Lecture at Lewis and Clark College," Portland, OR, May 18, 1988, 7.
157. Schindler, "Chamberlain Lecture."
158. Schindler, "Chamberlain Lecture."
159. "A Missed Opportunity on a Mission of Peace [Hebrew]," *Haaretz*, April 30, 1993,
160. Shulamit Aloni to Rabbi Alex Schindler, August 18, 1992, Schindler to Aloni, September 3, 1992, MSS 72, A4-3, AJA.
161. Schindler to UAHC Officers (Personal and Confidential), July 14, 1992, 2.
162. Alexander Schindler, "Sermon at Rosh Hashana Morning Service," Union Temple, Brooklyn, NY, September 25, 1995, 6.
163. Alexander Schindler, "President's Address: Reform Judaism, A Tradition of Continuity and Growth," 63rd General Assembly of the Union of American Congregations, November 29-December 3, 1995, 10.
164. Schindler, "President's Address," 1995.
165. Schindler to Honorable Menachem Begin (night letter), July 8, 1981, MSS 72, D-40, AJA.
166. Rabbi Eric H. Yoffie, "The Law of Return," Union of American Hebrew Congregations, September 1983, SC Box P-84, HUC-JIR Library, Los Angeles.
167. Schindler to the Honorable Yitzhak Shamir, September 9, 1983. A copy consists of pages 21–22 of the document listed in note 131.
168. *Jewish Telegraphic Agency Daily News Bulletin*, February 6, 1986.
169. Schindler et al. to H. E. Yitzhak Shamir, July 15, 1987, MSS 72, D-40, AJA.
170. UAHC Board of Trustees, "Ethiopia Relief," December 2, 1984, MSS 630, 9/9, AJA.
171. "Light One Candle, Save One Life: A Jewish Response to the Famine in Ethiopia," *New York Times*, December 16, 1984.
172. "Rabbi Schindler Assails Orthodox Rabbis' Demand That Ethiopian Jews Undergo Conversion in Israel," News Release, January 10, 1985, MSS 630, 9/9, AJA.
173. The photo can be found in Michael A. Meyer, *Response to Modernity: A History of the Reform Movement* (New York: Oxford University Press, 1988), 351.
174. Schindler to Aron Chilewich in New York, February 22, 1984, MSS 630, 13/2, AJA.
175. Schindler to Samuel Hollender, Esq., Legal Adviser to the Prime Minister, October 5, 1994, MSS 630, 5/8, AJA.
176. Schindler to Hollender, 1994.
177. Hirsch to Schindler, October 9, 1986, Richard Hirsch Papers, SC 15544, AJA.
178. Hirsch to Schindler, personal and confidential, May 30, 1982, MSS 630, 18/3, AJA.

179. Schindler to Gerard Daniel in New Rochelle, NY, February 1, 1982, MSS 630, 19/4, AJA.
180. Richard G. Hirsch, *For the Sake of Zion: Reform Zionism, A Personal Mission* (New York: URJ Press, 2011), 229.
181. Alfred Gottschalk, "Memo to Self," April 25, 1985, Alfred Gottschalk Papers, uncatalogued, AJA.
182. Schindler to Mrs. Joshua Chesnie in Toronto, Canada, December 30, 1986, MS-16, G-11/39, AJA. Hirsch's second major project after Beit Shmuel, a magnificent building that housed an auditorium overlooking the Old City as well as World Union and Israeli movement offices and became known as Mercaz Shimshon, was not completed until 2001, a year after Schindler's death. In 1995 it was estimated to cost $12.5 million. Hirsch to Ambassador and Mrs. Mel Sembler in St. Petersburg, FL, September 14, 1995, MSS 16, E3/13, AJA.
183. Richard Hirsch Papers, n.d., SC 15544, AJA; Schindler memo to Charles J. Rothschild, July 17, 1986, MS 72, D-43, AJA.
184. Hirsch, *For the Sake of Zion*, 253.
185. Schindler tribute to Rabbi Richard G. Hirsch, June 16, 1992, MSS 630, 18/1, AJA.
186. Schindler tribute to Hirsch, 1992.

Chapter 7: Reaching In
1. Together with his son Joshua, Schindler attended a *ferbrengen* (community gathering with the rabbi) on July 12, 1984. Joshua recalls that the rebbe pointed to father and son, whereupon they raised their cups of wine. The video can be accessed at https://www.youtube.com/watch?v=K3QfaebSBwE.
2. Schindler to Irving Greenberg in New York, June 13, 1985, MSS 630 13/3, AJA.
3. Ari L. Goldman, "Rabbinical Dialogue: 3 Branches of U.S. Judaism Talk of Differences," *New York Times*, July 2, 1985.
4. Goldman, "Rabbinical Dialogue." At its conference the following spring, the Conservative Rabbinical Assembly did begin to manifest internal differences of opinion regarding patrilineal descent when nearly a third of voting rabbis objected to its Committee on Jewish Law and Standards peremptorily applying sanctions to Conservative rabbis who accepted Jews of solely patrilineal descent as Jews; they believed the matter required "more reasoned debate and reconsideration." "Freedom of Conscience in the Rabbinical Assembly, Concord Hotel," May 19, 1986; Wolfe Kelman to Schindler, June 26, 1986, both at MSS 72, A4-2, AJA.
5. Greenberg to Schindler, October 3, 1985, MSS 630, 13/3, AJA.
6. Greenberg to Schindler, 1985.
7. Yehuda Lev, "Schindler's War on Militant Orthodoxy," *Palm Beach Jewish World*, November 8–14, 1985.

8. Lev, "Schindler's War on Militant Orthodoxy."
9. Alexander M. Schindler, "Centennial Shabbat Sermon," *CCAR Yearbook* 99 (1989): 106.
10. This is the first line of a two-verse song sung by Zionist farmers and stonecutters in Poland during the 1930s. It is accessible at https://yiddishfarkinder.files.wordpress.com/2013/01/d795d795d790d6b8d7a1-d79ed-799d7a8-d796d7b2d6b7d7a0d7a2d79f.pdf.
11. Speech at a conference titled "Will There Be One Jewish People by the Year 2000?," Princeton, New Jersey, March 16, 1986, unpaginated, MSS 630, 3/2, AJA; "Calling for a Truce in the War of Incivility," *Baltimore Jewish Times*, March 1986. Properly speaking, the event was not a dialogue since there was no in-person interchange among the speakers. Schindler had initially been reluctant to accept Greenberg's invitation to participate and did so only after Gerson Cohen of the Jewish Theological Seminary, likewise reluctant at first, agreed. He could not allow himself to be regarded as "the sole refuser." Schindler to Rabbi Jack Stern in Scarsdale, NY, December 30, 1985, MSS 630, 3/2, AJA.
12. "'I love Orthodoxy'—Rabbi Alexander Schindler," *Jewish Post and Opinion*, December 13, 1989, 8.
13. My thanks to Rabbi Joan Friedman, PhD, for informing me regarding Jewish law on issues arising from non-Jews within a Jewish religious context.
14. Within Reform Judaism today there is an effort to find a new designation for the Jewish coming-of-age ceremony that is inclusive of all children, whether male, female, trans, or non-binary; the CCAR has recently adopted the term "bet mitzvah." To avoid anachronism, the designation of the ceremony used in the text is as it was in Schindler's time.
15. Schindler to Cantor Jill Spasser at HUC-JIR in New York, November 16, 1994, MSS 630, 10/2, AJA.
16. In order to provide guidance to congregational leaders, the Union published *Defining the Role of the Non-Jew in the Synagogue: A Resource for Congregations* (New York, 1990). The volume contained discussion exercises, pro and con Reform responsa on the subject, and reflective essays.
17. Joe Glaser to Colleagues, RE: "The Gathering Crisis of Intermarriage," May 19, 1993, MSS 72, D-11, AJA.
18. Glaser, "The Gathering Crisis of Intermarriage."
19. Glaser, "The Gathering Crisis of Intermarriage."
20. "The Reform Jew: Values, Practices, Visions," Presidential Address to 61st General Assembly of the Union of American Hebrew Congregations, October 31–November 4, 1991, 10, Nearprint File, AJA.
21. "The Reform Jew," 11. The effort to achieve conversion set the Reform Movement apart from Jewish community centers that were content to accept interfaith couples in their existing status with no thought of conver-

sion. See Na'ama Batya Lewin, "Does Outreach Threaten the Fabric of Jewish Life?," *Washington Jewish Week*, March 17, 1994.
22. Schindler to Rabbi Stephen Forstein in Sioux Falls, SD, November 18, 1993, MSS 72, D-13, AJA.
23. Nina Mizrahi, "Non-Jews in the Synagogue," *Reform Judaism*, Summer 1992, 5-8, 34.
24. See Myron E. Schoen, "Membership Status of Non-Jews," August 1984, 2. Available in Klau Library, HUC-JIR, Cincinnati.
25. Rabbi Herman E. Snyder to Schindler, May 9, 1990, MSS 630, 10/1, AJA. According to a survey of Reform congregations, by the last decade of the century at least 88 percent of UAHC congregations extended membership to non-Jews as part of a family unit, 62 percent allowed them to vote within that unit, but only 32 percent allowed non-Jews to vote "in their own right." Excerpt from 1991 UAHC Outreach Census, MSS 630, 11/10, AJA.
26. Words spoken by Schindler at a meeting of the UAHC Executive Committee, February 8, 1993, attached to Joe Glaser to Colleagues, 151.
27. "Presidential Address at 62nd UAHC General Assembly," October 21-25, 1993, 15, MSS 630, 25/5, AJA.
28. Alexander Schindler to UAHC Executive Committee, February 8, 1993, MSS 72, D-11, AJA.
29. Cited in attachment to Joe Glaser to Colleagues, 150-152.
30. Alexander M. Schindler, "Outreach Address," *CCAR Yearbook* 105 (1995): 296.
31. *American Jewish Year Book*, 1997, 200. A survey of intermarried Reform Jewish leaders shockingly indicated that 80 percent of their children were receiving at least some instruction in a faith other than Judaism. Mark L. Winer, et al., *Leaders of Reform Judaism: A Study of Jewish Identity, Religious Practices and Beliefs, and Marriage Patterns* (New York: UAHC, 1987), 41. For statistics on continuing attachment to Christian symbols, see Peter Y. Medding, et al., *Jewish Identity in Conversionary and Mixed Marriages* (New York: American Jewish Committee, 1992), 32.
32. Michael A. Meyer, "On the Slope Toward Syncretism and Sectarianism," *CCAR Journal*, Summer 1993,: 41-44.
33. Meyer, "On the Slope Toward Syncretism and Sectarianism."
34. "Presidential Address at 62nd UAHC General Assembly," 16.
35. Schindler to Rabbi Jack D. Spiro in Richmond, VA, April 9, 1979, MSS 72, E-6, AJA.
36. Alexander M. Schindler, "The Role of the Non-Jew in the Synagogue," January 16, 1995, Holy Blossom Temple, Toronto, MSS 630, 26/2, AJA. See also, Schindler to "Dear Colleague", December 7, 1993, "Proselytism '93," AJA.
37. Cited in Jack Wertheimer, *A People Divided: Judaism in Contemporary America* (New York: Basic Books, 1993), 109.

38. Cited in Aron Hirt-Manheimer, ed., *The Jewish Condition: Essays on Contemporary Judaism Honoring Rabbi Alexander M. Schindler* (New York: UAHC Press, 1995), 349.
39. Schindler to Rabbi James Simon, personal and confidential, February 5, 1990, MSS 630, 5/5, AJA. Seven contrasting views on Beth Adam are contained in a section of *Reform Judaism*, Winter 1994, titled "The God Debate," 25–40.
40. Solomon B. Freehof to Schindler, February 21, 1990, MSS 72, D-47, AJA.
41. David Polish to Schindler, n.d., MSS 630, 5/5, AJA.
42. Eugene Mihaly, *Qualifications for Membership in the Union of American Hebrew Congregations: A Responsum* (Cincinnati: privately published, December 7, 1990). The pamphlet was paid for, printed in close to two thousand copies, and distributed by Beth Adam.
43. Schindler to Robert Chaiken in Cincinnati, March 26, 1990, MSS 72, D-47, AJA.
44. Schindler to Chaiken, 1990.
45. James L. Simon to Schindler, February 6, 1991, MSS 630, 5/5, AJA; Asher Gottesfeld Knight, "Drawing Boundaries and Limiting Elasticity: What Did the Reform Movement Learn from Beth Adam's Membership Application to the UAHC?" (ordination thesis, HUC-JIR Cincinnati, 2007), 91–93.
46. Rabbi Lewis H. Kamrass (and four others) to Robert Chaiken, President Midwest Council, UAHC, May 29, 1991, MSS 72, D-47, AJA.
47. "Notes for Beth Adam Debate," 1994, 1, MSS 630, 26/1, AJA.
48. Schindler to James A. Salinger in Cincinnati, November 25, 1992, MSS 630, 5/5, AJA.
49. Schindler to Joseph Lane in Cincinnati, August 3, 1994, MSS 630, 5/5, AJA.
50. "Notes for Beth Adam Debate," 3.
51. "Notes for Beth Adam Debate," 4.
52. "Notes for Beth Adam Debate," 4.
53. "Greetings from the President of the Union of American Hebrew Congregations," *CCAR Yearbook* 104 (1994): 109.
54. Elyse D. Frishman, ed., *Mishkan T'filah: A Reform Siddur* (New York: CCAR Press, 2007), 337, 475.
55. Alexander M. Schindler, "A Salute to the CCAR Journal," *CCAR Journal*, Spring 1978, 8.
56. Presidential Sermon, "Celebrating Our Faith, Creating Our Future," Toronto, 1979, MSS 630, 24/3, AJA.
57. "Presidential Address," 57th General Assembly, Union of American Hebrew Congregations, November 10–15, 1983, 2, MSS 630, 24/4, AJA.
58. "Presidential Address," 58th General Assembly, Union of American Hebrew Congregations, October 31–November 5, 1985, 5, Klau Library, HUC-JIR, Cincinnati.

59. Presidential Address, 59th General Assembly, Union of American Hebrew Congregations, October 29–November 3, 1987, 14. Klau Library, HUC-JIR, Cincinnati.
60. "Outreach Address," *CCAR Yearbook* 105 (1995): 298.
61. Joseph Kleiman and Rabbi Samuel E. Karff to Schindler, March 5, 1984, MSS 630, 15/1, AJA.
62. Even as late as 1983, Schindler continued, albeit inconsistently, to use the Ashkenazic pronunciation of Hebrew. Here, in the Hasidic context, it seemed especially appropriate.
63. Untitled speech at Centennial Dinner Dance, Temple Emanuel, Wichita, KS, December 7, 1985, 8, MSS 630, 24/5, AJA.
64. Untitled speech at Centennial Dinner Dance, 1985.
65. Alexander M. Schindler, "Two Truths to Live By," *Reader's Digest*, March 1988.
66. One example of Schindler citing Baeck is Schindler's "Byron T. Rubenstein Memorial Lecture," Temple Israel, Westport, CT, March 26, 1993, 5, MSS 630, 25/5, AJA.
67. "Yom Kippur Sermon" at Union Temple Brooklyn, 1987, MSS 630, 24/7, AJA.
68. "Yom Kippur Sermon."
69. "Here and Hereafter," in Rifat Sonsino and Daniel B. Syme, eds., *What Happens After I Die? Jewish Views of Life After Death* (New York: UAHC Press, 1990), 73. Schindler's theology was largely analogous to "Golden Rule Christianity" in American Liberal Protestantism, which locates God in moments of transcendence and in the "everyday virtues of doing good." See Nancy T. Ammerman, "Golden Rule Christianity: Lived Religion in the American Mainstream," in *Lived Religion in America: Toward a History of Practice*, ed. David D. Hall (Princeton, NJ: Princeton University Press, 1997), 196–216.
70. Byron T. Rubenstein Memorial Lecture, 5.
71. *Shaarei Mitzvah, Gates of Mitzvah: A Guide to the Jewish Life Cycle* (New York: CCAR, 1979). Much later the Union issued a brief guide of its own with a foreword by Schindler, in which he once again stressed that religious autonomy in Reform Judaism did not mean that nothing is required of the Reform Jew and nothing forbidden. Simeon J. Maslin, *What We Believe . . . What We Do . . . A Pocket Guide for Reform Jews* (New York: UAHC Press, 1993).
72. Schindler to Rabbi Eugene Mihaly in Cincinnati, December 7, 1993; Schindler to Rabbi Herbert Bronstein in Glencoe, IL, December 15, 1993, MSS 72, D-43, AJA.
73. Schindler, "Dear Reader," *Reform Judaism*, Spring 1994, 2.
74. Candidates (as of July 28, 1994), MSS 72, D-47, AJA. Later the name of Rabbi Peter Knobel, a Chicago Reform rabbi and Movement liturgist, was brought into serious consideration. See A. Engler Anderson, "New Chief on

Tap for UAHC," *Philadelphia Jewish Exponent*, February 17, 1995. Politically conservative Board member David Belin had attempted to derail the nomination of Eric Yoffie on account of his prominent leadership in the area of social justice. See Debra Nussbaum Cohen, "New UAHC Leader Calls for New Focus on Spirituality," *Jewish Bulletin of Northern California*, May 26, 1995.

75. "Yoffie Nominated UAHC President," *American Israelite*, March 2, 1995. Yoffie had been a student of Schindler when he served as the rabbi of Temple Emanuel in Worcester, Massachusetts.

76. "Yoffie Nominated UAHC President."

77. For an overview of the Union's multiple activities during the Schindler years, see Suzanne Griffel and Eric Polokoff, *The Guide: A Directory to the Programs, Services, and Resources of the Union of American Hebrew Congregations and the Reform Movement* (New York: UAHC, 1988–89).

78. However, Conservative Judaism still had more affiliated households. Barry A. Kosmin et al., *Highlights of the CJF National Jewish Population Survey* (New York: Council of Jewish Federations, 1991), 32, 37.

79. 1991 Biennial Assembly, MSS VT-83, AJA.

80. Albert Vorspan, "Introduction: Ohev Yisrael, Alexander Schindler A Profile," in Hirt-Manheimer, ed., *The Jewish Condition*, 3–4; Union of American Hebrew Congregations, *Directory of Member Congregations* (New York, 1995). Schindler himself claimed "some 1.3 million men, women, and young people." "Presidential Address," 58th General Assembly, 4.

81. The following citations are from "President's Address, Reform Judaism: A Tradition of Continuity and Growth," 63rd General Assembly of the Union of American Hebrew Congregations, November 29–December 3, 1995, Atlanta, GA; available in Klau Library, HUC-JIR, Cincinnati, SC Box A98/140.

82. Samuel I. Cohen [executive vice president of the Jewish National Fund] to Schindler, July 15, 1987, MSS 630, 6/8, AJA. In its time, it was the most successful drive for a forest in the history of the Jewish National Fund. The English and Hebrew marker reads: "UAHC Rabbi Alexander M. Schindler Forest: *Alexander Moshe Schindler, nesi ichud l'yahadut mitkademet ba-Amerikah* [President of the Union for Progressive Judaism in America]. Schindler was pleased that it did not include "Dr.," an honorific that had been applied to Reform rabbis in America in earlier times whether or not they possessed a doctorate, and which would have contradicted Schindler's principal self-designation as a rabbi.

83. Shabbat Service, November 10, 2000, Baltimore Hebrew Congregation, Tape C-5782, AJA.

84. In a letter to the author, Rabbi Orkand related that Weiss, being a *kohen*, could not enter the synagogue for the funeral, where the coffin was present,

and therefore had to stand at its outer door. Yet he felt obligated to express his love for Schindler by being present at least in that fashion.
85. The text of Vorspan's words was received from Schindler's daughter Elisa Frankel.
86. The source is *B'reishit Rabbah* 82:10, "Rabbi Simeon ben Gamaliel taught: 'One does not erect tombstones for the righteous; their words are their memorials.'"

Chapter 8: The Private Life
1. This chapter relies heavily on family recollections and information from Schindler associates.
2. "Rabbi Alexander Schindler Remarks Concerning the Los Angeles Riots," UAHC Board Meeting, Minneapolis, MN, May 1992, MSS 630, 25/4, AJA.
3. According to Rabbi Clifford Kulwin in an email to the author.
4. Schindler to Rabbi Amos Schauss in Cincinnati, August 9, 1968, MSS 630, 21/6, AJA.
5. Another version, with thanks to Lennard Thal, who claims that it is the genuine one, gives the seatmate the last word: "So, tell me, how do you keep the apples from turning brown?"
6. Schindler to Judith K. Rowland in New York, December 27, 1995, MSS 630, 1/2, AJA.
7. "Presidential Address," 58th General Assembly, Union of American Hebrew Congregations, October 31–November 5, 1985, 8, Klau Library, HUC-JIR, Cincinnati, OH.
8. Schindler to Rabbi Harold H. Gordon in New York, April 20, 1977, MSS 630, 9/7, AJA.
9. Samuel Silver, "Digest of the Yiddish Press," *Jewish Post and Opinion*, July 18, 1984.
10. "Ordination Address," Congregation Emanu-El, New York, May 28, 1995, 4, MSS 630, 26/2, AJA.
11. Schindler recited the story, in slightly different formulations, as early as his Consecration Address for the UAHC presidency in 1973; again, as we have seen, at the banquet Menachem Begin tendered for him in Jerusalem in 1978; and yet again not long before his retirement in "Dear Reader," *Reform Judaism*, Winter 1992, 2.

Index

Page numbers in italics refer to photographs.

"A & S Schindler," 3
Abba Hillel Silver (Raphael), ix
abortion rights, 124–25
Abourezk, James, 134, 226n62
Abramov, Zalman, 71, 87
Abrams, Elliott, 143
Abzug, Bella, 226n62
Adenauer, Konrad, 230n121
Adler, Hugo Chaim, 19, 197n2
AIDS, 127–28, 190, 224
Alexander Schindler Forest (Israel), 179, 238n82
Aloni, Shulamit, 154
American Israel Public Affairs Committee (AIPAC), 80
Amichai, Yehuda, 151–52
Amitay, Morris J., 80
antisemitism, 1, 6, 9, 59, 94, 129, 136–37, 141, 144, 206nn95–96
apartheid (South Africa), 135–36
Arafat, Yasser, 66, 89, 136, 147
Arbatov, Georgi, 142
Armstrong, James, 148
Association for a Progressive Reform Judaism, 45, 203n32
Association of Reform Zionists of America (ARZA), 121, 159, 176
Atlas, Samuel, 199n37

Baeck, Leo, 12, 109, 173, 195n29, 198n26, 218n46
Baerwald, Leo, 6, 195n19
Bais Yaakov movement, 4–5
Bamberger, Bernard, 34
Barbie, Klaus, 146
Barr, Robert, 170
"Bearers of Light" (Adler), 197n2

Begin, Aliza, 89
Begin, Menachem: and American Jews, 85; basic facts about, 84–85; Camp David Accords, 94; and Carter, 89, 90, 93; death of, 152; and Falwell, 138; on Holocaust, 231n152; and Israeli invasion of Lebanon, 150; Jesse Jackson on, 133; Reform Movement's opinion of, 88
Begin, Menachem, Schindler and, *86*; admiration for, 152, 153; as advocate for, with Carter government, 88–90, 91–92; criticism of Israeli policies, 151; first meeting, 54, 85–86; first meeting after election, 86–88; personal relationship, 87, 88, 91–92, 95–96, 97, 191; and Sadat, 94; similarities with, 152–53
Belin, David W., 115, 127, 129–30, 221n88, 238n74
Belin, Yossi, 218n44
Benamozegh, Elijah, 14
Ben-Israel, Shlomo, 229n111
Berger, Peter L., 111
Bernadotte, Folke, 22
Beth Adam (congregation), 169–71, 236n42
Beth Chayim Chadashim (Los Angeles), 125, 126
Bettan, Israel, 16, 197n50
Biden, Joseph R., 69, 209n30
Birnbaum, Nathan, 3–4, 194n14
Blanshard, Paul, 25
B'nai B'rith, 16, 41, 58, 61
Borowitz, Eugene: American Jewish dissent on Israeli policies, 72; and "covenant theology," 30; and "Reform Judaism: A Centenary Perspective," 47; and Reform religious school curriculum,

199n36; and rights of homosexuals, 126; and Union presidency, 51
Breira, 73–74
B'reishit, 9, 20
Brickner, Balfour: and Breira, 73; and civil rights, 121; at HUC, 16; as Schindler's best man, 26; and Union, 205n64; and Vatican's Commission for Religious Relations with the Jews, 110
Brown, George S., 59, 206nn95–96
Brzezinski, Zbigniew, 80, 83–84, 89, 93
Buber, Martin, 30
Burg, Yosef, 141
Bush, Lawrence, 123–24, 224n30

Camp David Accords, 94, 215n143
Canadian Reform rabbis and patrilineal descent, 105
Carter, Jimmy, 81; appointments made by, 82–83; and Begin, 89, 90, 93; Camp David Accords, 94, 215n143; Middle East solution, 83–84; and nuclear arms limitation, 147; and PLO, 90–91, 94; as religious Christian, 80, 82; and Schindler, 149; and Schindler and election of 1976, 80–82; Schindler as advocate for Begin with government of, 88–90, 91–92; Schindler's trip to Israel after Begin's election, 86; and Vietnam War, 82; and Young, 131, 132
Catholic Church, 110
Ceausescu, Nicolae, 145
Central Conference of American Rabbis (CCAR): and patrilineal descent, 105–6, 216n12; and proselytizing non-Jews, 109; rabbis' participation in interfaith marriages, 44–45, 100; "Reform Judaism: A Centenary Perspective," 47; role of non-Jews in congregations, 164; on "situation ethics" and individual responsibility, 204n57; Task Force on Religious Commitment with Union, 173; and Wise, 39

Central Conference of American Rabbis Journal, 19, 127, 172
Chicago Tribune, 135
Choosing Judaism (Kukoff), 117
Christianity: Evangelical, 136–41, 227n78, 227n83; proselytizing Jews, 25, 109–10; response to Schindler's proposal to proselytize non-Jews, 111, 219n56
Church, Frank, 138
City College (CCNY), 9, 12–15, 24, 196n32
civil rights: and Brickner, 121; relations between Jews and African Americans, 130–36, 225n48, 226n62, 226n68; Schindler's connections with leaders of, xiv; in Soviet Union, 142
Coalition on the Environment and Jewish Life, 130
Cohen, Gerson, 234n10
Cohen, Shaye J. D., 107
Cohon, Beryl, 197n2
Coleman, Alvin E., 207n4
Commentary, 111
Conference of Presidents of Major American Jewish Organizations (Presidents' Conference), 61–67, 93, 94, 207n1, 208n11, 214n138. see also as Presidents' Conference president under Schindler, Alexander Moshe
Conference on Jewish Material Claims Against Germany, 228n100
Conservative Movement: growth of, 43; and Orthodox Judaism, 107–8; and patrilineal descent, 104, 107, 108, 162, 233n4; response to Schindler's proposal to proselytize non-Jews, 111, 112, 113–14; and Schindler's Jewish philosophy, 30
"covenant theology," 29–30
Cox, Harvey, 111

Dachau, 12, 195n28
Day, Donald, 103
Dinitz, Simcha, 86, 159

Dobrynin, Anatoly, 229n105
Dreyfus, Marianne, 185
Dreyfus, Stanley, 185
Dulles, John Foster, 61

Eban, Abba, 68
Eckhardt, A. Roy, 111
Edelman, Marek, 144
education, 2, 4, 31. *see also* education *under* Reform Movement
Egypt, 69–70, 84, 91, 94–95
Einstein, Albert, 6
Eisendrath, Maurice, 50; characteristics of, 40, 181; death and final Union speech of, 51–53; and Glueck, 40; on Lenn and Fein Reports, 50; and Presidents' Conference, 61–62, 63, 207n1; and proselytizing non-Jews, 109, 219n49; and rabbis' participation in interfaith marriages, 45; and Reform Jewish day schools, 34, 200n63; and Schindler as Union's national director of education, 29; and Schindler as Union's president, 50, 51; social justice commitment of, 129; as Union president, 39–41; and Vietnam War, 135; views of, 40, 202n4; and Vorspan, 57
Eizenstat, Stuart, 81, 86, 90
Elon, Amos, 151–52
environmental issues, 130
Ethiopian Jews, 155, 194n14
ethnicism, 26, 29, 32–33
Evangelical Christianity, 110, 136–41, 227n78, 227n83
Evans, Rowland, 71–72

Falwell, Jerry, 136–39, 227n86
Fauntroy, Walter, 134
Fein, Leonard, 101
"Fein Report," 47–48, 50, 204n47
Fensterwald, Henry J., 207n4
Fisher, Eugene, 111
Fisher, Max, 69
Ford, Gerald, 59, 64, 69–70, 79–80

Freehof, Solomon, 126, 128, 169
Friedman, Herbert, 55–56, 206nn82–83
Friedman, Israel, 185
"From Discrimination to Extermination: The Evolution of the Nazi Government's Anti-Jewish Policy 1933–1945" (A. Schindler), 13
"From Rome to Israel: The Life-Story of Aimé Pallière" (A. Schindler), 14

Galinski, Heinz, 228n103
Gamoran, Emanuel, 29, 33
Gamoran, Mamie, 29
gay and lesbian rights, xiv, 125–29, 224n30, 224n37
Germany, Nazi, 5–8, 146
Germany, postwar: Jews in, 228n103; Reagan visit to, 145–46; reparations from, 12, 195n30, 228n100, 230n121; reunification of, 146–47; Schindler's attitude toward, 12, 145–46, 186
Gittelsohn, Roland B., 29, 44, 52
Glaser, Joseph, 114, 164, 165
Glueck, Nelson, 16, 39, 40, 57
Goldmann, Nahum, 61–62, 96, 141, 207n5
Golomb, Betty, 142
Gordis, Robert, 107, 198n26
Gottschalk, Alfred, 57
Green, Arthur, 210n50
Greenberg, Irving (Yitz), 107, 108, 112–13, 161–62, 234n10
Gruenewald, Max, 197n2
Gumbleton, Thomas J., 148
gun control, 129

Ha'am, Ahad, 178
Haaretz, 70, 153
Haberman, Joshua O., 137, 227n83
Hadassah, 76
Halpern, Ben, 106
Hammer, Armand, 144
Hasidim, 1, 2, 65, 96, 142, 186
Hasidism, xiv, 1, 186

Ha-Tzofeh, 53, 205n72
Hebrew Union College-Jewish Institute of Religion (HUC), 15–17, 19, 31, 39, 57, 196n39
Hecht, Abraham, 137
Hellman, Yehuda, 94, 144, 208n11, 214n138
Herman, Erwin, 50, 100, 125, 205n64
Hertzberg, Arthur, 72
Herzog, Chaim, 151
Heschel, Abraham Joshua, 30, 179
Heshel, Avraham Yehoshua, Rabbi of Apt (Opatów), xi
Hiat, Philip, 144
Himmelfarb, Milton, 112
Hirsch, Bella, 229n106
Hirsch, Richard: and Russian Jewry, 229n106; and Schindler as Union president, 55, 56, 157–59; and Schindler's language as president of Presidents' Conference, 77, 91, 209n40; and Union millions to proselytize non-Jews, 114; and World Union for Progressive Judaism, 55, 56, 71, 157–59, 205n64, 233n182
Hirschberg, Gunter, 36
Hochbaum, Jerry, 141
Hoenlein, Malcolm, 214n138
Hoffman, Abbie, 33
Hoffman, Lawrence, 176
Holocaust: Begin on, 231n152; and Memorial Foundation for Jewish Culture, 141; and proselytizing non-Jews, 102, 109, 218n46; reparations from, 12, 195n30, 228n100, 230n121; Schindler family deaths, 2; Schindler's curriculum about, 30–31; E. Schindler's songs during, 5; silence of world during, 22. *see also* specific concentration and death camps
homosexuals, rights of, 125–29, 224n37, 224n39
Horowitz, David, 14, 196n35
Hoyda, Sali (mother). *see* Schindler, Sali (mother)

interfaith marriages: children raised as Jewish in, 99, 235n31; importance of, to "Fein Report," 47, 204n47; and Jacobs, 190; number of, 44, 99, 216n5; and patrilineal descent, xiii, 101, 104–8, 216n12, 217n34, 218n36; Reform rabbis' participation in, 44–46, 100, 203n32, 203n40; and role of non-Jews in congregations, 163–68, 234n16, 235n25; Union and outreach to families in, 100–105, 113, 115–18, *117*, 216n12, 221n100
Israel: Alexander Schindler Forest, 179, 238n82; American Jews' criticism of, 72–73, 74–76, 150–52, 191; Arab refugees, 22; Arabs and peace process, 74, 78; as best vehicle for the nurturing Jewish identity, 42; Brown on military aid to, 59, 206nn95–96; Christian Right's support, 137, 138, 227n78; Diaspora and future of, xiv; and Entebbe skyjacking, 77–78; and Ethiopian Jews, 155; invasion of Lebanon by, 150; Jewish responsibility for Jewish terrorists, 22; Law of Return, 154–55; Orthodox Judaism in, 97, 105; and patrilineal descent, 104–5, 218n44; and Presidents' Conference, 64; and Reform Movement, 55, 66, 97, 104, 154–55, 156–59, 228n100; and Schindler's proposal of proselytizing non-Jews, 114; Schindler's support for, as "prophetic" Zionism, 178; and South Africa, 135; and Soviet Jews, 68; as "surrogate synagogue" for American Jews, 66; and threats against Schindler's life, 186; treaty with Jordan, 154; UN and right to exist of, 78–79; US role in peace, 94; West Bank expansion by, 71–72, 84, 91, 149, 150–51; women's rights at Kotel, 157; and World Union for Progressive Judaism, 55, 56, 71, 157, 205n64, 205n76, 233n182; Yom Kippur War, 54; Young's characterization of, 131–32. *see also* Begin, Menachem; Israel and *under* Schindler, Alexander Moshe;

INDEX   245

Rabin, Yitzhak
Israel Movement for Progressive Judaism. *see* Reform Movement *under* Israel

Jabotinsky, Ze'ev, 84
Jackson, Henry, 138
Jackson, Jesse, 131, 133, 134, 226n52
Jacobs, Rick, 189–92
Janowsky, Oscar, 13, 15
Jerry Falwell and the Jews (Simon), 138
Jerusalem Post, The, 53, 94
Jews: current identification with Reform Movement, 189; Ethiopian, 155; in Poland, 143–45, 229n111; in postwar Germany, 228n103; in Romania, 68, 145, 208n28; Schindler on criticism of, 22; in Soviet Union, 67–68, 142–43, 229nn105–6. *see also* interfaith marriages
Jews, American: acceptance of patrilineal descent by, 108; and Begin's election, 85; Christianity's proselytization of, 25; of Color, 190; criticism of Israel by, 72–77, 150–52; cults and "Jews for Jesus," 110–11; and election of 1976, 79–80; increase in unaffiliated, 119; isolation of leadership of, ix; Israel as "surrogate synagogue" for, 66; Israeli criticism of, 75; and Jewish terrorists in Israel, 22; meaning of fulfillment of Zionism for, 32; and need to support Israel, 93; and problem of Arab refugees, 22; and relations with African Americans, 130–36, 225n48, 226n62, 226n68; social justice as expression of Jewish identity for, 190; solidarity with Israel, 70–71; as surrogates for Israel, 61, 95, 215n148
John Paul II (pope), 140–41
Joint Distribution Committee, 228n100
Jordan, 154
Judaism: ability of, to tolerate internal Jewish pluralism, 108; absence of substitute, for in Jewish life, x; basis for political advocacy by, 26; as disappearing in America, 43; divorce in, 108; Einstein on, 6; importance of religious community, 24; linkage of belief in God and belief in immortality, 24; and passion of denominational loyalty, 222n4; and patrilineal descent, xiii, 101, 104–8, 216n12, 217n34, 218n36, 218n44; Schindler and assertive, 6; unity among branches of, 161–62, 163, 234n11; without basic theological concepts as folkway, 172
Jung, Leo, 9

Kahn, Robert I., 198n26
Kaplan, Kivie, 130–31
Kaplan, Mordecai, 30, 199n37
Katz, Robert L., 196n39
Kaufman, Jay, 33, 41, 58, 63
Kelman, Wolfe, 63, 112
Kennedy, Edward, 122
King, Coretta, 134, 226n68
Kissinger, Henry: basic facts about, 209n31; and Presidents' Conference, 67; and Schindler, xiii, 66, 69–70, 80, 209n31, 211n78
Klein, Joseph, 19–20, 27, 44
Kleinbaum, Sharon, 129
Klutznick, Philip, 61–62, 207n5
Knobel, Peter, 238n74
Kohler, Kaufmann, 39
Kukoff, Lydia, 117, *117*, 118, 221n98, 221n100
Kulwin, Clifford, 205n64

Lamm, Norman, 199n37
Landau, David, 64, 65
Lebanon, 150
Lenn Report, 44, 46–47, 50
Leo Baeck Institute, 12
Levitt, Norma, 123
LGBTQ rights, xiv, 125–29, 224n30, 224n37
Lichtmann, Sarah, 194n4
Liebman, Charles S., 88

Look magazine, 219n49
Loth, Moritz, 39

Maariv, 76–77
Machzikei Hadas, 1
Madoff, Bernard, 184
Mandela, Nelson, 135–36
Mann, Louis, 39
Mann, Theodore R., 214n138
Margalit, Dan, 67
Marmur, Dow, 222n2
Marranos, Christian descendants of, 194n14
Maslin, Simeon, 45
Matzkin, Rose, 76
McPherson, Peter, 224n37
Meir, Golda, 54, 75, 76–77
Memorial Foundation for Jewish Culture, 141, 142
messira, 75, 210n56
Metzenbaum, Howard, 138, 166
Mihaly, Eugene, 45, 169
Miller, Edith (Edie), 58, 58–59, 123
Miller, Israel, 65, 67
Moral Majority, 16, 137–40
Morgenstern, Julian, 39
Moynihan, Daniel Patrick, 71, 146
music: Schindler's love of, 3, 183–84, 197n2; Yiddish songs by father, 20, 52–53
mysticism, 17, 49, 52

National Association of Temple Educators, 32
National Federation of Temple Youth, 20
National Jewish Community Relations Advisory Council (NJCRAC), 214n138
Netanyahu, Benjamin, 151, 191
Netzach Lied (E. Schindler), 52–53
Neues Realgymnasium, 6
New York Jewish Week, The, 103
New York Times, The, xii, 78–79, 93, 211n69, 218n36
New Yorker, The, 48–49

Niebuhr, Reinhold, 25, 110
Nixon, Richard, 64
Novak, Robert, 71–72
nuclear arms, 11, 147–49, 230n133

Olan, Levi, 19, 29, 44
Or P'nei Moshe (Sofer), 1
Orkand, Robert, 179, 182
Orthodox Movement: common ground with Reform Movement, 161, 233n1; and Conservative Movement, 107–8; education of girls, 2, 4; in Israel, 97, 105, 154–55; and patrilineal descent, 107, 108; and Plessner, 16–17; and Presidents' Conference, 63; Reform as more "authentically Jewish" than, 178; and Reform legitimacy, 107, 144, 218n36; response to Schindler's proposal to proselytize non-Jews, 111, 112–13; and Schindler's education, 6; and Schindler's family, 6, 9; Schindler's treatment of, xiv, 162, 163
outreach: acceptance by non-Reform rabbis of all Reform Jews, 104; and decline in conversion, 103–4; as diluting Jewishness, 164; importance of, to Schindler, 177–78; as ingathering to Schindler, 178; inreach as in symbiotic relationship with, 173; and Jacobs, 190; patrilineal descent as obstacle to conversion, 106; Union institutional structure for, 115–18, 117, 221n100. *see also* proselytization; proselytization of non-Jews, Schindler's proposal for
Oylim (Spiritual Ascenders) Society, 3–4
Oz, Amos, 151–52

Palestine Liberation Organization (PLO), 73, 83, 90–91, 94, 131, 132, 149
Palestinians, 149, 151, 153
Pallière, Aimé, 14
patrilineal descent: and Canadian Reform rabbis, 105; and CCAR, 105–6, 216n12; and Conservative Movement, 104, 107,

108, 162, 233n4; and interfaith marriages, xiii, 101, 104–8, 216n12, 217n34, 218n36; and Israel, 104–5, 218n44; and Orthodox Movement, 107, 108; Schindler's speeches on, 105, 162
Pawlikowski, John, 111
Peres, Shimon, 85, 231n152, 231n153
Petuchowski, Jakob J., 104, 127
Pinkasei HaK'hilot, Encyclopedia of Jewish Communities from Their Foundation till after the Holocaust, 141
Plaut, W. Gunther: and criteria for individual being Jewish, 216n12; and rabbinical officiation at interfaith weddings, 45–46; and Reform Jewish Torah commentary, 37, 38, 200n82
Plessner, Solomon, 16–17
Poland, 143–45, 229n111
Polish, David, 44, 106, 112, 169
Pollard, Carol, 122
Pollard, Jonathan, 121–23
Prinz, Joachim, 62, 64, 207n4
proselytization: of Jews, 25–26, 109–10, 198n27; of non-Jews, 5, 194n14, 198n26, 219n49
proselytization of non-Jews, Schindler's proposal for, 102; Christian responses to, 111, 219n56; competition among religions as productive, 111, 112–13; Conservative Movement responses to, 111, 112, 113–14; Holocaust and, 109, 218n46; married to Jews, 113, 164–65; Orthodox Movement responses to, 111, 112–13; Reform Movement responses to, 109, 112, 114–15; Talmudic text in favor of, 218n45
"Proselytizing Is Bad for the Jews" (Wertheimer), 113–14

Quandt, William B., 84

Rabin, Yitzhak: assassination of, 154, 178; and Breira, 73; and Carter, 83; overview of government of, 153–54; and Schindler as Presidents' Conference president, 85; and Schindler as Union president, 55, 70, 151, 231n153
race relations, 131–36, 225n48, 226n62, 226n68
Raisin, Max, 15
Raphael, Marc Lee, ix
Reagan, Ronald, 129, 137, 143, 145–46, 230
Reb Avrom Yitzchak, 1–2
Reconstructionist Movement, 30, 108, 172
Reform Jewish Appeal (RJA), 56, 120
"Reform Judaism: A Centenary Perspective," 47
Reform Movement: Begin and, 88; "big brother" system, 28–29; criteria for individual being Jewish, 101; current identification with, 189; essence of, according to Schindler, 178; growth of, under Schindler, 177; influence of, xiii; influence of laity in, 29, 34–35, 39–40, 41, 43, 50–51; and Israel, 55, 66, 97, 104, 154–55, 156–59, 228n100; *kavonoh* leading to *devekus* in, 30, 42, 173; and kosher slaughter of animals, 212n96; laity's view of role of rabbi, 47; Lenn Report, 44, 46–47, 50; liturgical links to Jewish past as necessary for, 171; and Orthodox Movement, 161, 178, 233n1; performance of *mitzvot,* 172, 174; prayer book (2007), 172; and proselytization of non-Jews prior to Schindler's Union presidency, 109, 219n49; rabbis' participation in interfaith marriages, 44–46, 100, 203n32; as "religion of convenience," 172; Religious Action Center of Reform Judaism established, 40; response to Schindler's proposal to proselytize non-Jews, 109, 112, 114–15; role of non-Jews in congregations, 163–68, 234n16, 234n21, 235n25; role of ritual, 172, 174, 237n71; theology, xiv, 29–30, 42, 168–71, 172, 236n42; Torah

commentary, 29, 37–38, 176, 201n82, 201n84; Union predominance in, 39–40, 124; and youth, 48, 49. *see also* Schindler, Alexander Moshe, as Union president

Reform Movement, education and: under Borowitz, 199n36; under Gamoran, 29, 33; Jewish day schools, 33–37, 200nn63–64; of lay leadership, 35; non-Jews as teachers, 166; under Schindler, 29, 30–35, 37–38, 176, 201n82, 201n84

Reich, Seymour, 214n138

Reichert, Victor, 33

religion: decline of organized, in America, 43, 204n46; growth of liberal streams of, 40; rapid societal change and need for, 42; Schindler's view of elements of, "at its finest," 48; secularism and "death of God," 48–49; separation of church and state, 26; as shaping institutions of American culture, 26; and "situation ethics" and individual responsibility, 49–50, 204n57. *see also* Christianity; Judaism; specific branches of Judaism

Religious Action Center (RAC), 34, 40, 129, 130, 131, 176

Religious Right, 136–41, 227n78, 227n83

Remy Lazarus, Nahida Ruth, 14–15

Rise and Fall of the Third Reich, The (Shirer), 198n28

Robertson, Pat, 137, 139

Romanian Jews, 68, 145, 208n28

Roosevelt, Franklin Delano, 91, 214n131

Rosen, Moses, 145

Rosenblum, Rhea. *see* Schindler, Rhea

Rosensweig, Bernard, 111, 112

Ross, Matt, 54

Russian Jewry, 142–43, 229nn105–6

Sadat, Anwar, 69, 84, 91, 94–95

Safire, William, 93

Santayana, George, 173

Saperstein, David, xvi, 73, 120, 121, 122, 123, 129, 223n8

Sarna, Jonathan D., ix–xii

Schacter, Herschel, 63

Schechter, Solomon, 30, 31

Schiff, Daniel, 115

Schindler, Abraham (grandfather), 1–2

Schindler, Alexander (uncle), 2, 3

Schindler, Alexander Moshe, 7, *50*, *122*; on America as home, 8; in Army, 9–12, *10*, 24, 196n31; bar mitzvah, 8–9; belief in life after death, 173–74; and Breira, 74; Brit HaDorot Award, 148–49; and Conference on Jewish Material Claims Against Germany, 228n100; as congregational rabbi, 16, 19, 20–21, *23*, 26, 27; death, funeral, and burial of, 179–80, 184, 239n84, 239n86; effect of Dachau on, 12; ethnicism views of, 26, 29, 32–33; God as "of this world," 179; health of, 183; home life and marriage of, 26, 27, 181–82, 183, *185*; and humanism/naturalism versus "covenant theology," 30, 199n37; and Joint Distribution Committee, 228n100; Judaism's ability to tolerate internal Jewish pluralism, 108; on *kavonoh* leading to *devekus* in Reform Judaism, 30, 42; and Kissinger, xiii, 66, 80, 209n31, 211n78; and kosher slaughter of animals, 212n96; and Memorial Foundation for Jewish Culture, 141, 142, 195n30; and Nixon, 64; and NJCRAC, 214n138; and nuclear arms, 147–48; as opponent of rabbinical officiation at interfaith weddings, 45–46, 203n40; and Orthodox Judaism, xiv, 17, 161, 162, 163, 233n1; personal religious principles of, 170–71; political philosophy, 69; and postwar Germany, 12, 145–46, 186; and Presidents' Conference, 63–67; "Reform Jewish Educator" designation by National Association of Temple Educators, 32; ritual observances of, 185–86; and Shalom Center, 148–49; on Silver as spiritual ancestor of, ix–xi; Solomon H. Bublick Public

Service Award, 96; and United Nations Association of the United States of America, 79, 147; and U.S. Interreligious Committee on Peace of the United Methodist Church, 228n100; Vorspan as friend, 182–83; and Waldheim, 79, 140–41, 147; and Waskow, 210n50; on Wise, ix; and World Jewish Congress, 228n100; and Yiddish language, xi, 163, 177, 186; and Yoffie, 176, 238n75

Schindler, Alexander Moshe, as Presidents' Conference president, 67–73, 74–77, 91; election of Begin, 85; extension of term, 92–93, 94, 215n151; and Hirsch, 77, 91, 209n40; Jews in Romania, 145; political influence of, 141; and Rabin, 85; and United Nations, 78–79; and Young, 131, *132*

Schindler, Alexander Moshe, as Union president, *58*; achievements of, x, xii, 176–78, 189; administrative abilities, 58–59, 120–21, 123, 222n8; and Beth Adam congregation, 169–71, 236n42; Black-Jewish relations, 130, 131–36, 225n48, 226n62; and Carter, 80, *81*, 93, 94, 149, 215n143; connections with civil rights leaders, xiv; consecration speech, 52–53; and Eisendrath, 50, 51; and Ethiopian Jews, 155; and Evangelical Christianity, 136–41, 227n78, 227n83; and financial problems of Union, 56, 120; and Ford, 69; and Friedman, 55–56, 206n82; fundraising by, 120; gay and lesbian rights, xiv, 125–29, 224n37, 224n39; gun control, 129; and Hirsch, 55, 56, 157–59; importance of performing *mitzvot*, 172, 174; influence of, xiv, 153; inreach as in symbiotic relationship with outreach, 173; and institutional structure for outreach, 115–18, *117*, 221n100; interfaith marriage initiative, xiii, 100–106, 115–18, *117*, 221n100; intervention after Brown's remarks, 59, 206n95; and Israel, 54, 70–71, 149, 150–51, 154, 155; and Jackson, 133; and John Paul II, 140–41; location of HUC, 57; and nuclear arms, 147–48, 230n133; opposition to election of, 50–51, 205n64; and Palestinians, 149, 151, 153; and Peres, 154, 231n153; and Polish Jewry, 143–45; and Rabin, 55, 151, 154, 231n152, 231n153; and RAC, 129; and Reform Jewish Appeal, 120; retirement of, 175, *175*; role of non-Jews in congregations, 164–68, 234n21; role of ritual, 172, 174, 237n71; Russian Jewry, 142–43, 229nn105–6; and Sadat, 94; and sense of sacredness in Judaism, 173, 237n69; and Shamir, 153; social justice commitments, 124–31, 189–90, 224n37, 224n39; Union name change proposal, 175; and Vorspan, 57, 120–21; and women's rights, 124–25, 157. *see also* proselytization of non-Jews, Schindler's proposal for; Schindler, Alexander Moshe, Israel and

Schindler, Alexander Moshe, Begin and, 86; admiration for, 152, 153; as advocate with media and Carter government for, 88–90, 91–92; criticism of Israeli policies, 151; election of, 85; first meeting, 54, 85–86; first meeting after election, 86–88; as messenger to Sadat for, 94; personal relationship, 87, 88, 91–92, 95–96, 97, 191; similarities with, 152–53

Schindler, Alexander Moshe, characteristics of: ability to forgive, 121–23; demeanor as *hassidischer yid* (Hasidic Jew), 65; gambling, 184; German accent, 19; hard worker, xi; immaturity, 16; lack of formality, 20; leadership and organizational skills, xiii, 3; love of music, 3, 183–84, 197n2; love of theater, 183; national identification, 1; as *ohev Yisrael* (lover of peopple of Israel), xi, 4; optimism, 96, 187, 239n11; people person, xi, 181; political acuity, 66; and proselytizing to non-Jews, 102; public persona, 181; self-described, 177; sense

250   INDEX

of humor, 183, 239n5; of speeches, xiv–xv, 76, 181; thrill seeker, 184.
Schindler, Alexander Moshe, education of: at CCNY, 9, 12–15, 196n32; in Orthodox day school, 6; rabbinical, 15–17, 19, 196n39; in US, 9
Schindler, Alexander Moshe, family of: background, 1; escape from Nazi Germany and settlement in US, 7–9; friendship with Baeck, 195n29; influence of father, 3, 6; Jewish observance, 6; and Orthodox Judaism, 6, 9; relationship with mother, xi
Schindler, Alexander Moshe, Israel and: American Jewry solidarity with, 70–71; Arabs and peace, 74, 78; and Begin, 54; as best vehicle for the nurturing Jewish identity, 42; and Carter policy, 83–84; criticism of, 72–73, 74–76, 77, 191; dissent on policies of, 66, 92; and Jewish destiny, 54; need for Americans to speak for, 93; Reform presence in, 55, 156–57; rescue of hostages from Entebbe skyjacking, 77–78; settlement with Egypt, 94–95; support for, as prophetic Zionism, 178; and threats against life, 186; US role in peace, 94
Schindler, Alexander Moshe, sermons by: Arab refugees, 22; belief in God, 23–24; criticism of Jews, 22; on effect and role of, 20–21; Jewish responsibility for Jewish terrorists, 22; personal views in early, 21, 22; rabbinical leadership in modern world, 185–86; reunification of Germany, 146–47; Rosh HaShanah and Yom Kippur, at Union Temple, 185
Schindler, Alexander Moshe, speeches by: abortion rights, 125; on action balancing ideology in Reform Movement, 42; Beth Adam admission to Union, 170–71; characteristics of, xiv–xv, 76, 181; civil rights, 135; consecration, as Union president, 52–53; denominational loyalty of Jews, 222n4; dissent on Israeli policies, 76; eulogy for Begin, 152; Evangelical Christianity, 138–41; and father, 3; Hebrew used in, 173, 237n62; importance of Jerusalem to Reform Movement, 66; Jews in Soviet Union, 143; last, 179; last to Union General Assembly, 177–78; life after death, 174; limits to flexibility of Reform Judaism, 168–69, 172; nuclear arms, 148–49; patrilineal descent, 105, 162; preparation of, 123–24, 224n30; proselytizing non-Jews, 109, 218n45, 219n56; to Reform "alumni groups" on campuses, 28; Reform day schools, 35, 36–37; Reform Movement growth, 119, 222n2; refugees to US, 143; separation of church and state, 26; shaping effective religious leadership, 31; "situation ethics" and individual responsibility, 49–50; social justice, 129, 130; Soviet Jews, 68; at staff retreat at Union camp, 41–42; unity among branches of Judaism, 163, 234n11; Vietnam War, 33, 64
Schindler, Alexander Moshe, Union and: as director of Division of Religious Education, 29, 30–35, 37–38, 201n82, 201n84; and Eisendrath's final Union speech, 51–52; as executive director of New England Conference, 28–29; Union Camp retreat, 41–42; as vice president, 41–47, 48, 62, 63, 207n4
Schindler, Alexander Moshe, writings by: about father and *United Israel Bulletin*, 196n35; "Dear Reader" column in *Reform Judaism*, 201n88; election of 1976 and American Jews, 79–80; elements of "religion at its finest," 48; "From Discrimination to Extermination: The Evolution of the Nazi Government's Anti-Jewish Policy 1933–1945" (history honors thesis), 13; on honors received, 97; HUC senior thesis, 16–17, 197n50; introduction to *Abba Hillel Silver*, ix; Judaism and secularism, 49; Mandela, 135; music and religion, 197n2; patrilineal

descent, 106–7, 217n34; peace in Middle East, 78; on Presidents' Conference, 63; proselytization of Jews, 25–26, 198n27; rabbinical officiation at interfaith weddings, 45; on Reform Jewish youth, 48, 49; in Reform prayer book (2007), 172; response to Lenn Report, 47; secularism and "death of God," 48; on Union membership in World Jewish Congress, 62, 207n4; *United Israel Bulletin* articles while at CCNY, 14–15

Schindler, Eliezer (father), 4, *10*; Alexander's installation at Temple Emanuel, 20; characteristics, 3–4; death, 5; escape from Nazi Germany, 7; and Ethiopian Jews, 194n14; and HUC, 196n39; and Pallière, 14; personal life, 2–3, 194nn3–4; and proselytization, 5, 194n14; relationship with Alexander, 3, 6; settlement in US, 8–9; and *United Israel Bulletin*, 196n35; as writer, 4, 5; Yiddish songs by, 20, 52–53

Schindler, Eva (sister), 3, 6, 7, 8–9

Schindler, Joshua (son), 233n1

Schindler, Judith (daughter), 4, 124, 181, 182, 184

Schindler, Lazar (or Feser, father), 2–3. *see also* Schindler, Eliezer (father)

Schindler, Nechama (grandmother), 1, 2

Schindler, Pesach (cousin), 2

Schindler, Rhea (wife), 26–27, *27*, 77, 154, 182, 184, *185*, 224n35

Schindler, Ruben (cousin), 2, 152

Schindler, Sali (mother), *10*; as businesswoman, 7–8, 197n20; characteristics of, 3; and HUC, 196n39; marriage, 2–3; relationship with Alexander, xi, 3; settlement in US, 8–9

Schonfeld, Fabian, 72

Schorsch, Ismar, 113

Schulweis, Harold M., 108, 112

Schusterman, Abraham, 198n26

Schusterman, Charles, 221n98

Scowcroft, Brent, 69

Scranton, William, 71, 78, 79

Seltzer, Sanford, 99–100, 115

separation of church and state, xiv, 31, 34

sermons. *see* Schindler, Alexander Moshe, sermons by

"Sermons of Solomon Plessner, The" (A. Schindler), 16–17, 197n50

Shamir, Yitzhak, 151, 153, 155

Shapiro, Alexander, 161–62

Shapiro, Max, 115

Sharon, Ariel, 150

Sherer, Moshe, 84, 212n96

Shirer, William, 198n28

Silver, Abba Hillel, ix–xi

Simon, Merrill, 138

Smith, Bailey, 136

social justice: and Eisendrath, 40, 129, 202n4; and Schindler, 124–31, 189–90, 224n37, 224n39

Sofer, Moshe, 1

Soloveitchik, Joseph (Dov), 113

South Africa, 135–36

Soviet Union, 142–43, 229nn105–6

speeches. *see* Schindler, Alexander Moshe, speeches by

Stendahl, Krister, 111, 219n56

Stern, Sol, 215n148

Sternstein, Joe, 76

Syme, Daniel, 121, 176

Temple Emanuel (Worcester, Massachusetts), 19–21, 26, 27

Teplitz, Saul, 111, 112

Thomas, Clarence, 221n88

Tillich, Paul, 25

Time magazine, 88, 149

Toon, Malcolm, 71

Torah, Reform Jewish commentary, 29, 37–38, 176, 201n82, 201n84

Torczyner, Jacques, 76

Union of American Hebrew Congregations (UAHC, Union): AIDS response, 128; Black-Jewish relations, 134; and

Breira, 74; confirmation requirements, 32; congregants' views on "synagogue worship," 46; congregational membership decline, 43–44, 57; congregational membership growth, 40, 56–57, 119, 222n2; and congregations whose beliefs did not align with Reform Judaism, 168–71, 236n42; *Defining the Role of the Non-Jew in the Synagogue*, 234n16; Eisendrath as president, 39–41, 55; established, 39; and Ethiopian Jews, 155; Falwell at, 138–39; "Fein Report," 47–48, 50, 204n47; financial situation of, 43, 56, 102, 119–20; headquarters moved, 40; and interfaith marriages, 100–105, 216n12; lay influence in, 19; lay versus rabbinic leadership of, 50–51; membership growth under Schindler, 176–77; Miller in, 58–59; New England Council of, 28–29; Nuclear Handbook, 148; outreach institutional structure, 115–18, *117*, 221n100; outreach to unaffiliated Jews in urban areas, 100; president of, as Reform Movement's unchallenged principal leader, 124; and Presidents' Conference, 62–63; proselytization of non-Jews, 113; and Reform Jewish education, 29–35, 199n36; relationship to HUC, 39; Religious Action Center, 129, 130, 131, 176; role of non-Jews in congregations, 235n25; role of ritual, 237n71; search for Schindler's successor, 176, 237n74; social justice commitment of, after Schindler, 190; staff issues, 57–58; support of Reform youth movement, 28; Task Force on Religious Commitment with CCAR, 173; as Union for Reform Judaism, 175; and World Zionist Organization, 75. *See also* proselytization; Schindler, Alexander Moshe, as Union president; Schindler, Alexander Moshe, Union and

Union Temple (Brooklyn), 185
United Israel Bulletin, 14–15, 196n35

United Nations, 78–79
United Nations Association of the United States of America, 78–79, 147
United States Supreme Court, 31
United Synagogue of America, 108
U.S. Interreligious Committee on Peace of the United Methodist Church, 228n100

Vance, Cyrus, 83, 84, 90
"Vanishing American Jew, The" (*Look* magazine), 219n49
Vietnam War, 33, 40, 64, 74, 82, 135
Vorspan, Albert: characteristics of Schindler's speeches, 181; and Eisendrath, 57; eulogy for Schindler, 179, 180; and Mandela, 136; and Schindler, 57, 120–21, 182–83; and Schindler's view of Begin, 88

Waldheim, Kurt, 79, 140–41, 147, 211n72
Waskow, Arthur, 148, 210n50
Weiler, Cyrus, 104
Weiss, Avi, 180, 239n84
Weiss-Rosmarin, Trude, 112
Wertheimer, Jack, 113–14
What Judaism Offers for You (Belin, editor), 221n88
Why Choose Judaism (Belin, editor), 221n88
Wise, Isaac Mayer, 39, 62
Wise, Louise Waterman, 14
Wise, Stephen S., ix, 9, 13
Wolf, Jacob, 199n37
women's rights, 124–25, 157
World Jewish Congress, 61, 62
World Union for Progressive Judaism: after Six-Day War, 205n76; and Eisendrath, 53; and Friedman, 55–56, 206nn82–83; and Hirsch, 55, 71, 157–59, 205n64, 233n182
World Zionist Organization (WZO), 61, 75
writings. *see* Schindler, Alexander Moshe, writings by

Yehoshua, A. B., 151–52
Yiddish language: and A. Schindler, xi, 163, 177, 186; and E. Schindler, 4–5, 14, 20, 52–53
Yiddish un hasidish (Yiddish and Hasidic) (E. Schindler), 5
Yoffie, Eric, *175*; basic facts about, 20; Brickner and Union presidency, 205n64; characteristics of Schindler, xiii, 181; chosen as Schindler's successor as Union president, 176, 238n74; as director of Association of Reform Zionists of America, 121; and Law of Return, 155; relationship with Schindler, 176, 238n75
Young, Andrew, 82–83, 131–32, *132*

Zelizer, Gerald, 113
Zionism: ARZA, 121, 159, 176; and Belzer Hasidic tradition, 2; and Goldmann, 61; meaning of fulfillment of, for American Jews, 32; as racism, 78–79; and Raisin, 15; in Reform Judaism's educational program, 29; Schindler's, as "prophetic," 178

About the Author

MICHAEL A. MEYER, PhD, was born in Berlin, Germany and grew up in Los Angeles, where he graduated from UCLA with highest honors. His doctorate in Jewish history is from Hebrew Union College–Jewish Institute of Religion in Cincinnati, where he served as professor of Jewish history for fifty years. He has also been a guest professor at three Israeli universities and has served as president of the Association for Jewish Studies and international president of the Leo Baeck Institute. He is the recipient of three National Jewish Book Awards and has published more than two hundred scholarly articles and longer reviews. His books include *The Origins of the Modern Jew*, *Response to Modernity: A History of the Reform Movement in Judaism*, and *Rabbi Leo Baeck: Living a Religious Imperative in Troubled Times*. He is the recipient of an honorary degree from the Jewish Theological Seminary and the Cross of Merit from the German Federal Republic.

www.ingramcontent.com/pod-product-compliance
Lightning Source LLC
Chambersburg PA
CBHW060604190426

43202CB00032BA/2887